Religion and the Common Good

Catholic Contributions to Building Community in a Liberal Society

Brian Stiltner

ROWMAN & LITTLEFIELD PUBLISHERS, INC.
Lanham • Boulder • New York • Oxford

ROWMAN & LITTLEFIELD PUBLISHERS, INC.

Published in the United States of America
by Rowman & Littlefield Publishers, Inc.
4720 Boston Way, Lanham, Maryland 20706
http://www.rowmanlittlefield.com

12 Hid's Copse Road
Cumnor Hill, Oxford OX2 9JJ, England

British Library Cataloguing in Publication Information Available

Library of Congress Cataloging-in-Publication Data

Stiltner, Brian. 1966–
    Religion and the common good : Catholic contributions to building
community in a liberal society / Brian Stiltner.
        p. cm.
    Includes bibliographical references and index.
    ISBN 0-8476-9435-6 (cloth : alk. paper). —
    ISBN 0-8476-9436-4 (pbk. : alk. paper)
    1. Christianity and politics—Catholic Church. 2. Common good—
Religious aspects—Catholic Church. 3. Liberalism—Religious
aspects—Catholic Church. 4. Communitarianism—Religious aspects—
Catholic Church. I. Title.
    BX1793.S75 1999
    261.8'088'22—dc21   99-19013
                                                          CIP

Printed in the United States of America

♾™ The paper used in this publication meets the minimum requirements of American
National Standard for Information Sciences—Permanence of Paper for Printed Library
Materials, ANSI/NISO Z39.48–1992.

Contents

Acknowledgments   vii

Introduction   1

1 The Enlightenment as Problem and Resource   17

2 The Common Good and Religious Discourse in a Modern
   Liberal Society   45

3 Linking Liberalism and Communitarianism Through Common
   Good Theory   83

4 Religion's Contributions to the Common Good Through the
   Vista of Catholicism   113

5 Creating a Politics of the Common Good: A Case Study of the
   Abortion Debate   143

Conclusion   177

Bibliography   183

Index   193

About the Author   203

Acknowledgments

In writing this book, I have received much support from friends and colleagues, for which I am enormously grateful. Those who offered advice at early stages or who discussed outlines, drafts, and specific topics with me include M. Shawn Copeland, David Hollenbach, S. C. Campbell Lovett, Steven B. Smith, Jeffrey Stiltner, and Todd David Whitmore. Nicholas Wolterstorff, Gene Outka, and Richard Fern read the whole manuscript and provided insightful, critical advice that helped me revise it for publication. In particular, Richard Fern has been a tremendous inspiration to me. He first introduced me to the political thought of Jacques Maritain and to liberal and communitarian philosophers. It was he who suggested and outlined in his class lectures the possibility of a communal liberalism. Professor Fern carefully read this work and greatly improved it through his probing criticisms.

I wish to thank several other colleagues. Barbara Blodgett's comments and questions on several pieces of this book have helped me develop and sharpen my ideas. David Clough has been a patient and careful critic. His input has improved and clarified the work, and conversation with him has influenced my own thinking at several points. Roger Taylor closely read chapter 2 and discussed John Rawls and Michael Sandel with me at length. His comments helped me focus and support my critique of Rawls, even though he does not agree with my criticisms. I have found immensely valuable Paul Lauritzen's feedback on the manuscript and his role as both a mentor and a colleague.

The most significant influence on this work was Margaret Farley. The work simply would not have come together as a fairly coherent argument without her close reading and broad vision. Through her I have begun to learn what it means to articulate and sustain a thesis for a whole book. At the same time, many of my specific ideas and arguments have developed out of her comments and questions. In ways both large and small, her direction has immeasurably benefited the final product.

I thank the reviewer for Rowman & Littlefield, who carefully read the manuscript twice, providing many encouraging comments and helpful suggestions. I am grateful to Jonathan Sisk for first expressing interest in my proposal and encouraging me to submit it to Rowman & Littlefield; I am very glad I did. I thank my editor, Steven Wrinn, and his staff for all their assistance in bringing this book to publication.

I gratefully acknowledge the following publishers who granted permission to use excerpts from their works. Excerpts from *Political Liberalism* by John Rawls © 1993 by Columbia University Press; reprinted with the permission of the publisher. Excerpts from *Jerusalem* by Moses Mendelssohn © 1983 by the Trustees of Brandeis University, Brandeis University Press; reprinted with the permission of the University Press of New England. A portion of chapter 3 first appeared in my article "The Common Good and Liberal Democracy: The Problem of Particularity," published in *The Role of Religion in Fostering a Free and Virtuous Society* © 1992 by the Acton Institute for the Study of Religion and Liberty, Grand Rapids, Michigan; reprinted with the permission of the publisher.

Finally, I tremendously grateful to my family, to my wife's family, and to my close friends who offered so much moral encouragement throughout my graduate studies. I thank my wife, Ann, for putting up with my late nights, my working on weekends, and my generally outrageous work habits. More significantly, I appreciate her faith and support. Among other things, she has been an intellectual partner who helps me keep my abstract thoughts at least partly grounded in reality. Because she shared in all the struggles and joys of this writing process, Ann is one of the two people to whom I dedicate this book. The other is Jean Fritsch, a family friend who passed away shortly after I graduated high school. I promised her I would dedicate my first book to her, and I am honored to keep that pledge.

Introduction

The idea of the common good has recently received renewed attention in American public life and in religious discourse. A document released in 1993 by the general secretaries of three national religious organizations—the United States Catholic Conference, the National Council of Churches, and the Synagogue Council of America—called the common good "an old idea with a new urgency." Their statement acknowledged the challenges facing the common good in the United States, and trumpeted the promise of a revived commitment to the common good. These religious leaders identified several social deficits that undermine many citizens' opportunities for living full and rich lives and for contributing their talents to society. These problems include social and political indifference, poverty, lack of jobs, irresponsible sexual behavior, violence, racism, and sexism.

In the face of these forces that rend our social fabric, the common good is "an imperative to put the welfare of the whole ahead of our own narrow interests, . . . an imperative for a national embrace of responsibility and sacrifice, of compassion and caring as building blocks for meaningful lives and for a healthy society."[1] The general secretaries firmly believe that Jews and Christians, along with other believers and all people of goodwill, want to see these social deficits eradicated and our society drawn closer together in civic friendship. Of that there can be little doubt. But we know that contemporary democratic societies—and not only democracies—are rife with disagreements about these negative social forces. How do we even begin to talk about the common good, let alone pursue it?

From the outset, the civic discussion about the common good faces the challenge of multiple voices and perspectives. This pluralism is a crucial feature of modern societies, one that elicits both celebration and worry in citizens. Most of us celebrate pluralism as a by-product of the freedom that lies at the center of a democratic society. A good number of us celebrate pluralism as a great social good in its own right, for it lets people live by their own lights; it lets them lead a life that is interesting and meaningful to them. In addition, the existence of many groups and subcultures within society presents to citizens a wide range of opportunities for aesthetic, intellectual, and spiritual enrichment. Yet citizens also worry about pluralism because of the tensions it can create among people with different views of the world. Political debates about such issues as multicultural education, a national language, religious displays on public property, affirmative action, and so on, are all, at bottom, debates about how much pluralism and what kind of pluralism a country can accept.

One particular kind of pluralism has always presented special challenges for the United States and other democracies—religious pluralism. Again we find the same tension: citizens generally celebrate religious freedom, which of itself encourages a diversity of religious groups to take hold in society, yet at the same time many worry about how religious believers should act in the public and political arenas. Given the history of the United States, we have reason to valorize the role that religions can play in public life. I think of examples such as the desire for religious freedom that has inspired many different religious peoples to come to America throughout its history; the model of religious tolerance set by the colony of Pennsylvania under William Penn; the role that churches served as centers of democratic politics in colonial New England; the courage of those religious leaders and citizens who worked for the abolition of slavery and the power of religious conviction among African Americans during that long time of trial; and the same religious leadership and inspiration evident in the civil rights movement of the 1960s.

But despite the valuable role played by religious citizens and institutions in U.S. public life, Americans are often skittish about religion's engagement with politics. We have always expected religion to affect positively our public life—particularly through the morals that people take from their religious education and worship into their day-to-day activities—while trying to keep churches out of politics. Perhaps in part because we have seen how religious groups and individuals can undermine the common good and divide citizens against one another—after all, one can find counterexamples to match each of my positive examples of religion's influence—we want to mollify religion's potential to do harm.

The difficulty with any such plan is that we cannot sharply separate public life and politics. I understand *public life* to encompass the whole range of institutions—including cultural, economic, educational, political, and religious institutions—through which the members of a society maintain their bonds with one another and pursue cooperative activities. *Politics* is the arena of public life wherein governance and policy making occur, including all the formal and informal ways that citizens decide the rules they live by; this in turn must be distinguished from *governance* itself, which is the way citizens exercise authority over themselves and one another.

If I am correct in asserting that politics and governance are subsets of public life, then it would be very difficult to allow religious believers and churches to influence the broad arena while preventing them from influencing the subsets. In fact, I do not think it is possible. If we look again at the positive examples of religion in American public life, in each case religious groups had some effect on politics and governance. In the case of abolition and civil rights, activists were seeking to change fundamental laws governing the nation. This is not to deny that there are some boundaries that can and should be drawn to prevent improper incursions by the state into the church and vice versa. Some of these matters of religion and governance will be mentioned in the course of this book. Yet my main focus will be what role religion can play in the broad arena of public life to promote the common good for the public at large. That is, I will inquire as to the proper role of religion in a pluralist, liberal society, including its general role in politics. Is religion beneficial to such democracies? Is it dangerous? Can we say, as a matter of principle, that religion is important to the life of pluralist, liberal democracies; and can we go so far as to say that religion is essential to them?

I argue that there can be a fit between liberal and religious accounts of what makes for a good society, even though that fittingness has come under attack in the modern era. From early liberalism's rather clear reliance on religious ideas, we have come to a point where most liberal polities are officially neutral to religion and where many critics consider liberal political philosophy to be hostile to religious belief or practice. Stephen Carter's 1993 book *The Culture of Disbelief* gained national attention for its argument that the liberalism practiced in the United States encourages religious belief to become a private, even trivial, affair. Concerning our political culture, Carter writes:

> We are trying, here in America, to strike an awkward but necessary balance, one that seems more and more difficult with each passing year. On the one hand, a magnificent respect for freedom of conscience, including freedom of religious belief, runs deep in our political ideology. On the other hand, our understandable fear of religious domination of politics presses us, in our public personas, to be wary of those who take their religion too seriously.[2]

We Americans have inherited this tension in liberal thought, and it is reflected in our jurisprudence (as various courts have set the Establishment and Free Exercise Clauses of the First Amendment against each other and deferred to the Establishment Clause), our politics (witness our acceptance of religious rhetoric from a president during moments of national crisis yet our concern about politicians who use such rhetoric to justify proposed policies), and in our culture. Carter thinks the cultural effect has been the most insidious: "Our public culture more and more prefers religion as something without political significance, less an independent moral force than a quietly irrelevant moralizer, never heard, rarely seen."[3] In spite of these problems, Carter wants to retain many of the political and constitutional policies made possible in a liberal political framework, as well as much of the progressive public culture promoted by liberal philosophy. So his work could be understood as an effort to pull liberalism back from the extremes of secularism and religious indifference.

I fully share that desire. Whereas Carter's analysis largely focuses on the current legal and political manifestations of the underlying problem, I focus directly on the philosophy of liberalism and the correctives offered by a Catholic philosophy of the common good with a threefold task. First, I investigate what the common good, a good life for the public, looks like in a pluralist, liberal democracy such as that of the United States today. To do that, I explore contested accounts of the common good among theorists who try to describe the basic nature and purpose of a liberal society. This exploration takes us into the works of political philosophers of both today and the Enlightenment. Second, I aim to show how a way can be made through opposed positions in those debates, a way lighted by the common good theory that has been developed in Roman Catholic circles. Third, I discuss how religion might help us understand and pursue the common good in a liberal society. I believe that liberal theory can not only tolerate a strong role for religious believers and institutions, but can affirm this as beneficial to the very good of liberal society. These arguments are now explained in more detail.

THE COMMON GOOD IN THE
LIBERAL-COMMUNITARIAN DEBATE

Before embarking on this exploration, we must first get a good handle on the terms under consideration. Politicians, theologians, and ethicists frequently invoke the *common good* without defining what they mean by it. At its most basic level, the common good clearly denotes society's overall well-being; it refers to conditions that will benefit every member of society in some way. Like *justice,* the common good is an evocative term: its use aims to justify the importance of a particular issue or policy for all members of society, and so it is meant to garner support for the issue or policy at hand by motivating people to act for the benefit of others. But, also like justice, the common good has been subject to diverse interpretations over the five thousand years since Plato and Aristotle first theorized on the nature of political community.

Different interpretations perdure, so different people can mean quite different things in appealing to the common good. It matters greatly to know whether an appeal to the common good is an appeal to the good of every member of society, including oneself, or to a social good that transcends and supersedes individuals' goods. It matters whether each subcommunity within a society has its own common good and whether these can conflict with the common good of the whole society—and, if so, how the conflicts are to be settled. It matters whether a democratic society can have a common good only in the procedural sense, by making the political process open to all on an equal basis, or whether it can share a substantive common good wherein citizens experience unity around shared moral, or even religious, values. When one tries to answers these complex questions, the common good seems increasingly abstract and vague. It might be well to let it serve only as a term of rhetoric and to abolish it as a concrete political principle.

But this would be a mistake, for the common good is a useful and important principle for a democratic polity. The concept of the common good can be fruitfully employed in contemporary political thought, both to resolve tensions in the theory of liberal democracy and to direct institutional arrangements that preserve freedom while promoting social cooperation and civic friendship. A pluralistic, democratic society can have a common good in both its procedural and substantive senses; I hope to contribute to the renaissance of common good thinking by demonstrating the principle's theoretical and practical fecundity. To make the task manageable, the discussion must be focused in several ways.

First, my investigation begins with the Enlightenment, not only because it is the genesis of liberal political practices that shape Western societies to this day, but also because Enlightenment philosophy is often accused—wrongly, I think—of eroding the ideal of the common good. Second, three political traditions within Western post-Enlightenment thought will serve as the conversation partners for the book: liberalism, communitarianism, and Roman Catholic social thought. The conversation among twentieth-century representatives of these traditions constitutes a large part of the book. My third limitation is that when I consider concrete political and institutional issues, as I do in the last chapter, the context will be the United States.

Each of the conversation partners presents concepts and ideals of the common good. Not only do these differ among the three traditions, but all three traditions contain subsidiary strands, each one with its own interpretation of the common good. The following categories and brief definitions of liberal and communitarian views, which will be expanded upon at the appropriate places, will help us place some of the authors and arguments to be considered.

The *liberal* tradition generally locates the common good in citizens' agreement to live in a society structured by respect for rights and by common pursuit of liberty and individual opportunity. While in some respects it is presaged by political and philosophical trends during the Reformation and the Renaissance, the liberal tradition of political thought formally began with Enlightenment philosophers such as John Locke and Moses Mendelssohn, both encountered in chapter 1.

Three strands of liberalism highlight particular aspects of the tradition's general conception of the common good:

1. *Classical liberalism* values a minimal, constitutional state and a free market as the proper means to achieve the common good in politics and the economy. Liberals of this strand see an important role for shared moral and religious values in the culture, the responsibility for which falls mainly on private institutions and only minimally and indirectly on the state. Classical liberalism has itself split into several subsets: *libertarians* endorse an extremely minimal state and maximally free society and culture; *welfare liberals* stress the importance of social and economic equality and, therefore, of the state's role in redistributing wealth to provide a basic subsistence level for all; and more traditional liberal ideas endure under terms like *conservatism, neoconservatism,* and *neoliberalism.*

2. *Philosophical liberalism* locates the common good in a common morality founded on respect for universal human rights. The social role for particular moral and religious views is minimal; indeed, it is essential that a conception of justice regulate and take priority over individual conceptions of the good life. That is to say, principles of justice and rights, not tradition-bound views of the good life, must be the determinative bases for making decisions about the structures of society, especially its forms of governance.

3. *Political liberalism* is a contemporary variant more aligned to philosophical than to classical liberalism. Proponents of this ideology locate the common good in the process by which citizens agree to a form of society that will be fair for all. John Rawls, a representative of this subset encountered in chapter 2, argues that a just society should set up certain ground rules to ensure that fundamental political decisions are isolated from the distorting effects of the particular religious and moral worldviews that citizens hold. Classical liberals and political liberals will especially concern us in this study.

Communitarianism is in one sense a recent phenomenon. It comprises a loosely associated group of philosophers who join in faulting liberalism for its individualistic excesses. These thinkers agree more in their criticisms of liberalism than in promoting a substantive alternative to it. Here, too, we can identify at least three strands:

1. *Narrative communitarianism* highlights the pervasive role a community and its stories play in the formation of its members' characters, values, and beliefs. Such communitarians deny that it is possible to engage others in general conversation about values, virtues, and good forms of life—or for short, "the good"—as if we all belong to a universal audience. Rather, cultural and religious traditions rely upon distinctive, particular ways of thinking and talking; these particular rationalities and narratives can be properly understood from within the community itself. Therefore, the common good in its fullness is found only within a fairly homogenous community.

2. *Discourse communitarianism* locates the common good in a form of society that allows all members to discuss and articulate their conceptions of the good. This strand sees community as held together through conversation. It differs from the prior strand both in its greater hope that citizens in a pluralist society can pursue the common good and in its preference for a procedural common good focused more on the form of the civic conversation than its content.

3. *Egalitarian communitarianism* focuses less on communal narratives and more on communal relationships. It highlights how people are fulfilled as individuals only by being connected to one another in community. It stresses that people should be free and empowered to participate in community, and it wants to break down social and economic divisions so that wider community can be created. This strand is similar to the prior one, though it identifies equality as the primary social good.

In the course of the argument, we will encounter ideas representative of all three of these strands, for many communitarians draw on the conceptual frame of more than one of them. It is worth noting, too, that many contemporary communitarians consider their work a correction of liberalism, rather than a wholesale rejection of it.

A central political problem in the contemporary debate between liberalism and communitarianism is to determine what role particular communities play in a society that favors individual rights and protections. How should we settle conflicts between the rights of an individual and the needs of society, as well as clashes between the interests of a minority community and those of the majority? Should the state accommodate, protect, or remain neutral toward the interests, practices, and mores of various religious and ethnic subcommunities? Some have framed this debate as a stark choice: modern societies can strive to protect primarily either rights and freedom or values and mores. It is often assumed that this is a zero-sum game; for instance, to ensure more political freedom means further to privatize and stigmatize citizens' religious beliefs, while a political accommodation of some citizens' beliefs entails a greater burden on those citizens who do not participate in the favored religion(s). While such trade-offs do exist, to focus on them is not the best way to characterize the role that religious and other communities can and should play in public life. By contrast, my investigation proposes that various communities and persons within a pluralistic society have something to contribute to the common social good from the wealth of their particular worldviews. Political society, and even the state, has a stake in their contributions.

Underlying the political problems just described is a many-sided debate involving contested views of society, government, human nature, religion, history, and the nature of morality. Philosophical views on these matters shape one's response to the political problems. Some propose that a liberal polity should separate political debate and policy making from debates about these issues, because there is simply no way for citizens to come to general agreement upon them. Yet these foundational issues erupt into policy debates concerning such pertinent topics as religious symbols in public spaces, public funding for private schools, abortion laws, state recognition of gay and lesbian marriages, the right to refuse medical treatment, and many others. A pluralist society is not likely to move toward resolution of such issues without a further probing of the philosophical foundations of democracy and liberalism. It is important, I think, that such exploration and debate involve people not only as citizens, but as members of particular communities and traditions. The third conversation partner, the Roman Catholic tradition, can make a significant contribution to the discussion.

CATHOLIC COMMON GOOD THEORY AS A COMMUNAL LIBERALISM

The possibility of substantive agreement in the debate I have outlined seems remote unless there emerge both a philosophical mediation of liberalism and communitarianism, and a better way to mediate the political interests of the bureaucratic, liberal state and those of small, voluntary communities. The challenge is to show that each "side" has a stake in the other. This challenge is very difficult, of course, because there are more than two sides to the debate: there is a variety of philosophical schools of thought and an even wider variety of particular communities in any society. Yet in the academic and political debates, many people are interested in some kind of mediating option. This general interest bodes well for such a project.

I argue that the theory of communal liberalism in Catholic thought successfully mediates liberal and communitarian views. This variety of liberalism is not easy to articulate; on some issues it is simply a combination of liberal and communitarian views, while on others it offers a distinctive idea that differs from, and even transcends, both sides. I have chosen the name *communal liberalism* because it suggests a political theory that justifies policies of freedom, tolerance, and pluralism by reference to the good of the political community and its subcommunities, not only by reference to the rights of individuals.[4] No doubt the shape of such a liberalism would vary with each society. More specifically, then, I want to describe a communal liberal approach to the challenge of pursuing the common good that would be applicable to a Western democratic society such as the United States.

Throughout the study, I pay particular attention to the role of religious belief and religious communities in the theory and practice of communal liberalism. One reason for this focus is that I have a special interest in the role of religion in public life, arising out of my conviction that religious traditions are an important resource for understanding and pursuing the common good. Moreover, because religious doctrines often inform "thick" views of the good life, views not shared or readily grasped by those outside the tradition, some people think religious belief presents a problem, or at least a challenge, to the functioning of a pluralistic society. While there is certainly historical and current testimony to support this concern, the charge must be carefully investigated. Finally, since religion involves both belief and practice, as well as both cultural and institutional expressions, a focus on religion helps us investigate the variety of pluralism—cultural, institutional, religious, and ideological—in modern society.

Catholic thought enters the debate not to provide a deus ex machina answer to the debate between liberals and communitarians, but because Catholicism has been one important part of Western culture's ongoing struggle to identify and pursue the common good. Though Catholic common good theory historically precedes liberalism and communitarianism, it has been significantly influenced by parts of these two traditions in the modern age. Catholicism has been the primary locus of explicit common good theorizing since the Middle Ages, when St. Thomas Aquinas adopted Aristotle's account of the common good and gave it a prominent place in his doctrine of law. Catholicism viewed the rise of liberalism in the sixteenth century with suspicion and often outright hostility. Since the late nineteenth century, liberal ideas have gradually exerted an influence on Catholic political thought, with the result that Catholic ethicists and the institutional Church now embrace human rights, democracy, and liberal economic policies—including both free market and social-welfare institutions. Here I work with this tradition as it appears in the twentieth century.

The modern Catholic social tradition holds that a political society can pursue a substantial common good, defined as "the sum of those conditions of social life which allow social groups and their individual members relatively thorough and ready access to their own fulfillment."[5] The common good in this sense is not the province of any particular religious group, but of the whole political society. Because the definition refers to the aspirations of persons and voluntary associations, it sets limits to what the state or any single sector of society may do in defining or enforcing the common good. In short, the Catholic tradition believes it is possible for a pluralist society to have a substantial common good that is politically legitimate and noncoercive.

My exploration of the conception of the common good is shaped by the Roman Catholic tradition and particularly by the French philosopher Jacques Maritain. Maritain, who spent two decades of his career in the United States, presents a remarkably progressive and dynamic account of the common good. I employ his political thought for my constructive project of developing a theory of communal liberalism through common good theory. The *ideal vision* of the common good in the modern Catholic conception is the mutually beneficent relation of social actors oriented toward protecting and enhancing the dignity of persons and toward supporting the flourishing of diverse and good institutions. What is required to approach this ideal are *procedures* for cooperation and dialogue within a pluralistic, democratic framework and *substantive norms* such as defending human dignity through rights and providing opportunity for participation in society's common life through its public and voluntary institutions. The broad definition of the common good in modern Catholic writings is beneficial because it is flexible enough to accommodate developments in moral sensibilities and to be applied in various sociopolitical contexts. I hope to show that it is also specific enough to guide political and social choices within a pluralistic, liberal society.

Central to the Catholic view are two seemingly contradictory claims: first, that a pluralist society can share a common good without doing violence to the personal rights and dignity of its individual members and, second, that religion is an essential component of the common good, even though citizens are divided in their religious views and even though such divisions can cause social conflict. In its affirmation of both claims, the Catholic tradition attempts to retain and join liberal and communitarian views of the common good. But can the mediation succeed?

RELIGION'S CONTRIBUTIONS TO THE COMMON GOOD

My third area of inquiry concerns a pointed question: Can religion make significant and vital contributions to the common good of a liberal society?

The tension beneath this question arises in trying to identify whether religion can play a proper role in politics as a public enterprise. Is religion unifying or divisive in this regard? My aim is to see if citizens and churches acting on religious beliefs contribute resources to the common good in the following three areas. Do they contribute intellectual resources that assist our reflection on public and political matters? Do they help establish conditions for social harmony among citizens of various worldviews and among the subcommunities of a pluralistic society? Do they make arguments that draw the public's attention to goods of persons and communities not otherwise made prominent in public discourse and political decision making? My view is that religion can make these vital contributions.

Two questions are sure to be asked about this claim. First, in what sense am I using the term *religion*? By *religion,* I mean simply those commonly recognized communities that are organized around a belief in a divine being (or some transcendent reality or experience of the holy), that express their beliefs through rituals, and whose members are guided in their personal and social actions at least in part by the ideas and values held by the community.[6] To consider the impact of religion on society and the common good, we will attend to these aspects of religion: institutions, believers, and ideas and values.

Religious institutions are the organized structures by which the community orders its life, perpetuates itself over time, and facilitates interactions among its members and between the community itself and other institutions in society. Religions can be arranged very differently, of course, but all established religions have some discernable pattern of organization and typically have official bodies and representatives or leaders. These institutions can have a powerful influence not only in their members' lives, but on other cultural, social, and political institutions. Common religious institutions that can shape public life are local churches, denominational bodies, para-church organizations, religious social-service organizations, and religious schools.

Religious believers are the adherents of a given religion, the members of a religious community. Religious believers influence public life in their dual capacity as believers and citizens, insofar as they allow their religious beliefs and codes to shape how they comport themselves in the public and political arenas. Liberals and others are concerned to identify to what extent citizens may properly rely upon their religious beliefs when acting politically: What does it means to be a virtuous citizen in this regard?[7]

Finally, *religious ideas and values* can contribute intellectual, spiritual, and moral content to the culture and mores of a society. Ideas and values are not freestanding, but exert their influence through the communications and actions of religious believers, often acting through their institutions.

Much of my analysis in this book occurs at the theoretical level of ideas and values, but I intend not to lose sight of the fact that, to have any salience, these ideas and values must motivate people to act upon them in their society. So these three aspects of religion—institutions, believers, and ideas and values—interlock and together can significantly shape other parts of a pluralist society. (Nor should we forget that other institutions and manifestations of culture can promote change in each of these aspects of religion.) My focus on religious communities as the venues for injecting religious ideas and values into society corresponds to the value that communal liberalism places on voluntary communities, or mediating institutions, for their role in empowering people to pursue the common good.

A second question is this: What is the status of my claim about the benefits of religion? If I say that religion is important to the common good, does that mean that religion has only good effects? Does it mean a society cannot be good without religion? I certainly do not mean that religion has only good effects, for religious institutions and believers, acting upon certain of their ideas and values, can cause great pain and harm to others and to the common good. We have seen this in human history, in U.S. history, and in current world events. I think that most of the deleterious beliefs and actions we think of in this regard, such as the promotion of violence or the oppression of women, are not essential to the major world religions, but usually represent perversions of these religions' true characters. Unfortunately, I cannot argue such a broad claim here. When I am looking at religion, and particularly Catholicism, I mean to show what these institutions can contribute when they put their best foot forward, as it were. Therefore, it is up to religious traditions to make the case, in both their theologies and their practices, that they do have good effects for their members and society at large. For my part, I want to make the pragmatic argument that religious institutions, believers, ideas, and values *can* contribute to the common good, not that they always do. Indeed, it is helpful to put forth an argument like this so that religious groups may reflect on their practices and beliefs and then accentuate what is beneficial in these for the common good. As for whether society can be good without religion, that is another broad and difficult question.

It is natural for a religious tradition to promote itself as the best route for people to take on life's journey. If a religion is enlightening and liberating, why should we not submit ourselves to its discipline? Certainly the conviction on the part of religious groups that their way is best has led to much distress through the ages whenever these groups have tried to force others to accept their message. Such practices violate the spirit of liberalism and of any religious tradition that upholds the inviolability of conscience, the freedom of religious belief, and human dignity in general. Since I am arguing the compatibility of Catholic common good theory with a political theory that values pluralism, there is no room in this theory for asserting the dominance of Catholicism or any religion over others. That religion can make significant, vital contributions to the common good does not amount to the claim that a society must have religion or else be evil; rather, it claims that society can better approximate its authentic good with the help of religious institutions, believers, ideas, and values.

It is important to consider religion's role in public life in dialogue with contemporary political philosophy because there is little agreement as to the role religious belief would play in a well-ordered society. Contemporary liberalism is accused of relativizing religion, yet most classical liberals claim that a Judeo-Christian vision undergirds liberalism. Communitarians criticize modern liberalism for neglecting the vital role of communities, but most communitarians do not address religion substantially. At least in their stronger forms, liberalism and communitarianism agree in denying that a pluralist society can have a substantive common good that includes virtues and religious values. Many liberals think this state of affairs is impossible unless the state enforces a particular view of the good life upon all members of society, while some communitarians argue that liberal democracies, no longer informed by a common narrative, cannot sustain a society-wide common good.

Catholic theory proposes an alternative option. I test liberal and communitarian arguments about the role of religion in promoting the common good against a Roman Catholic articulation of the common good and the Catholic Church's role in advancing it. Catholic thought is particularly useful in this regard, because a Catholic method of reasoning about the common good relies in part on a natural law theory that claims to apply to all persons. Catholic thought also includes a theological approach to the common good. The theological and philosophical articulations of the common good in Catholic thought are potentially in tension with each other, though I intend to show how they can be coherently joined.

By this method of testing liberal and communitarian arguments against a Catholic argument, I defend the thesis that religion contributes substantially and significantly to the common good, as well as the correlative claim that liberal institutions can respect a vital role for religion in civil society without violating liberal rights. This investigation bears directly on political debates over contentious social issues. One test of the value of my investigation will be whether my account of the common good helps us think through such issues with greater clarity.

The arguments outlined above proceed in five chapters. The first chapter shows how the political philosophies of early European liberals include conceptions of the common good. In these conceptions, religion serves to unify society and to specify citizens' rights and responsibilities. John Locke focuses on Christianity's role in defining the social compact as based on trust and in setting limits to political authority. Moses Mendelssohn emphasizes the role of Judaism in promoting benevolence, tolerance, and the motivation to act for the common good. This chapter aims to draw resources from these early liberals for a contemporary theory of communal liberalism.

From early liberalism's clear reliance on religious ideas, modern liberalism has come to consider it the state's duty to be officially neutral, if not indifferent, toward religion. In chapter 2, I hold that John Rawls's version of liberalism—political liberalism—constrains religious argument and practice by placing unjustified conditions on religious speech in the political arena. In his recent writings, Rawls can be considered communitarian in a limited sense, but not to the extent that he accommodates religious or other communal traditions in his conception of a just and well-ordered society. Michael Sandel, a communitarian who draws substantially on the discourse and narrative strands, criticizes Rawls for not providing a substantial basis for social unity. Sandel points the way toward bridging liberal and communitarian concerns, but his specific political proposals need to be fleshed out further: his politics of the common good is subject to divergent interpretations about the extent to which it repudiates liberal politics, and it does not substantially address religion's role in a pluralist society.

The third chapter demonstrates what the Catholic tradition contributes to the common good. I employ the thought of Jacques Maritain because his account of the common good proceeds as both a natural law argument and a theological argument. The former, universal mode has affinities to the liberal approach, while the latter is congenial to communitarianism. These approaches are in some tension, yet I show how Maritain unites them, thus strengthening his theory of the common good. His theory mediates methodological questions in the liberal-communitarian debate by presenting nuanced versions of moral universalism and moral objectivism.

Maritain's substantive theory of the common good is treated in chapter 4. This theory sees religion—Catholic Christianity in particular—contributing to the common good in three areas: (1) the intellectual resources include a moral anthropology that specifies the components of human flourishing, a communal orientation of human rights, and principles for revitalizing society through intermediate institutions; (2) the conditions for social harmony include the church's and each Christian's expressions of neighbor-love and actions for justice; and (3) important human goods are given voice through prophetic critique of society from the perspective of the Kingdom of God and in fidelity to Jesus' preferential option for the poor. I compare Maritain's substantive approach to Rawls and Sandel on the matters of society's role in constituting individual identity and the state's attitude toward particular conceptions of the good.

Taken together with Maritain's positions on the methodological questions, this comparison shows that he successfully articulates a theory of communal liberalism.

Moving finally to applied issues, chapter 5 demonstrates how Catholic common good theory can contribute to political debate by promoting greater civility and possibility for consensus and by holding up important public goods that are not otherwise given their due. I apply the communal liberal framework to the moral and political problem of abortion in order to show how common good principles can guide a pluralistic society to points of consensus in this often contentious debate. Returning then to the role of religion, I present maxims to guide the churches' speech and actions regarding abortion. By modeling community in their own lives and by seeking to provide resources so that all persons can participate in public life, churches make their most significant contributions to the common good of liberal societies.

NOTES

1. United States Catholic Conference, National Council of Churches, and Synagogue Council of America, "The Common Good: Old Idea, New Urgency," *Origins* 23, no. 6 (24 June 1993): 82–86, quote at 82.

2. Stephen L. Carter, *The Culture of Disbelief* (New York: Basic Books, 1993), 8.

3. Carter, *Culture of Disbelief*, 9.

4. The term *communal liberalism* was introduced to me by Richard Fern.

5. Second Vatican Council, *Gaudium et Spes: Pastoral Constitution on the Church in the Modern World* (7 December 1965), in *Catholic Social Thought: The Documentary Heritage*, ed. David J. O'Brien and Thomas A. Shannon (Maryknoll, N.Y.: Orbis, 1992), par. 26.

6. It is notoriously difficult to give a satisfactory definition of religion, partly because the world's religions are complex and vary greatly in their content and partly because people approach religion through so many interpretive lenses. A sociological definition that I consider helpful is this: "Religion is a human phenomenon that unites cultural, social, and personality systems into a meaningful whole. Its components generally include (1) *a community of believers* who share (2) a common *myth* that interprets the abstractions of cultural values into historic reality through (3) *ritual behavior,* which makes possible personal participation in (4) a dimension of experience recognized as encompassing something more than everyday reality—*the holy.* These elements are united into recognizable *structures* that undergo *processes* of change, development, and deterioration" (Barbara Hargrove, *The Sociology of Religion: Classical and Contemporary Approaches,* 2nd ed. [Arlington Heights, Ill.: Harlan Davidson, 1989], 29–30).

7. For an instructive debate about the virtues of a liberal citizen with regard to religious convictions, see Robert Audi and Nicholas Wolterstorff, *Religion in the Public Square: The Place of Religious Convictions in Political Debate* (Lanham, Md.: Rowman & Littlefield, 1997).

Chapter 1

The Enlightenment as Problem and Resource

This study is by no means the first to try to locate the place of religion in a liberal society. Two attempts from the times when modern liberal societies began to emerge illustrate some of the main issues involved and provide background for a discussion of what we might best strive for today. It is especially enlightening to identify communitarian elements present from the beginnings of liberal political thought. So I begin this inquiry by exploring what resources for a contemporary theory of communal liberalism can be distilled from liberal philosophers during the Enlightenment. It makes sense to begin with the Enlightenment because the problems at hand received sustained philosophical examination during that period and because the variety of responses proposed continue to shape the philosophy and institutions of Western democracies.

In this chapter, I focus on two Enlightenment philosophers and their contributions to the theory and practice of the common good. John Locke (1632–1704) is justly considered the founding philosopher of Western constitutional liberalism and, for that reason, is lauded by some for liberalism's successes in securing liberty and prosperity and criticized by others for sowing the seeds of individualism and laissez-faire government. Many communitarian writers today take this latter tack. For instance, Robert Bellah and his coauthors write:

> One way of summing up the difficulty Americans have in understanding the fundamental roots of their problems is to say that they still have a Lockean political culture, emphasizing individual freedom and affluence (the American dream) in a society with a most un-Lockean economy and government. We have the illusion that we can control our fate because individual economic opportunity is indeed considerable, especially if one starts with middle-class advantages; and our political life is formally free. Yet powerful forces affecting the lives of us all are not operating under the norm of democratic consent.[1]

It is true that Locke's thought has had a profound influence on U.S. political culture. Yet it is a mistake to equate his doctrines with popular notions of "the American dream." I argue that Locke's political thought is committed to a substantial common good, based on the notion of trust as the foundation of civil society. Locke's liberalism has both strong communal and strong egalitarian aspects, which makes it a useful resource for a contemporary theory of communal liberalism. On the other hand, there are time-bound and problematic parts of Lockean liberalism that require correction and supplementation.

To begin that work, I turn in the second half of the chapter to Moses Mendelssohn (1729–1786). Mendelssohn's arrangement of the relationship among state, church, and civil society constitutes, in my view, a significant mediation of communitarianism and liberalism. Mendelssohn's ideas are an important yet largely overlooked resource for moving this project forward. Mendelssohn's contribution is especially important because he spoke from a minority position. He endeavored to show his Christian contemporaries that the Jewish community could not only coexist with the larger society, but even had something distinctive to contribute to it. Usually thinkers who argue for a robust role for religion in civil society represent the dominant religion of that society—in the West, Christianity. Talk of "civil religion" rightly worries non-Christians and even those belonging to minority denominations within Christianity. Communal liberalism, on the other hand, aims to justify an important role for religionists and churches in securing the common good of civil society, while protecting freedom *of* religion and freedom *from* religion. As a Jewish believer living in Christian Europe, Mendelssohn was well aware of the difficulty of achieving such a balance; nonetheless, he neither renounced his religion as a means to pursuing the common good, nor did he think a common good impossible and thus retreat into his particular community. His genius was to see that a social common good is compatible with, and in fact requires, religious pluralism. The limitations evident in Locke's liberalism need not derail the liberal project as a whole but may be better handled by a communal liberal such as Mendelssohn.

LOCKE'S LIBERALISM AND THE COMMON GOOD

Locke is the thinker who has probably had the most profound effect on Western political thought and practice: his ideas of social contract, limited government, property rights, and religious tolerance provided a philosophical foundation for the institutions of the American and British constitutional orders. The American revolutionaries, such as Thomas Paine, frequently appealed to his arguments against absolute monarchy and in defense of the right of revolution. Locke's liberalism has also unquestionably influenced the popular political culture of Western democracies. But for all that, many scholars have failed to provide a clear and persuasive account of Locke's political thought in the context of his moral and religious beliefs and his political activities and commitments.[2] In recent years, however, ahistorical and overly philosophical interpretations have been corrected by authors who ground Locke's political thought in his Calvinist religious beliefs[3] and in his commitment to the radical political movement associated with the first Earl of Shaftesbury.[4] Surprisingly enough, the picture of a secular, politically conservative Locke has given way to a Locke who is religiously traditional yet politically "revolutionary" and "radical."[5] The proper historical interpretation of Locke is useful but adjunct to my purpose here, which is to consider what resources and challenges Locke raises for a theory of communal liberalism. This constructive task will govern my use of Locke's ideas. Nevertheless, it is hardly useful to employ Locke without sensitivity to the meaning that he wanted his texts to convey. Overlooking Locke's intentions leads not only to misunderstandings of his arguments, but also to overestimations and underestimations of what we can learn from him today.

Trust as the Foundation of Civil Society

Locke neatly summarizes his conception of the nature and purpose of a civil society, or commonwealth, as follows:

> The Commonwealth seems to me to be a Society of Men constituted only for the procuring, preserving, and advancing of their own *Civil Interests*.
>
> *Civil Interests* I call Life, Health, and Indolency of Body; and the Possession of outward things, such as Money, Lands, Houses, Furniture, and the like.
>
> It is the Duty of the Civil Magistrate, by the impartial Execution of equal Laws, to secure unto all People in general, and to every one of his subjects in particular, the just Possession of these things belonging to this Life.[6]

In this model of society, the authority of government is established by a contract among the citizens. In the *Second Treatise of Government* (1690), Locke describes a "state of nature" in which persons existed before they agreed to enter civil society. Early in the treatise, the state of nature is described as a state of peace, perfect freedom, and even equality.[7] The distinguishing characteristic of this state is that, in it, people have to defend their own person and property by themselves. There is no appeal to a common authority under a rule of law. People agree to enter together into civil society in order to avoid a state of war wherein they have to defend themselves. In doing so, they surrender and transfer to an authority two powers: to do whatever is necessary to preserve their life and property, and to punish crimes.[8]

Locke attaches a political, historical meaning to the social contract. He first gets at this meaning by contrasting the state of nature with political society in three characteristics. First, the state of nature "wants [i.e., lacks] an *established,* settled, known *law* . . . and the common measure to decide all controversies"; second, "in the state of nature there wants *a known and indifferent judge,* with authority to determine all differences according to the established law"; and third, "in the state of nature there often wants *power* to back and support the sentence when right, and to *give it* due *execution.*"[9] Essentially, then, people are in a state of nature when they lack a written law, the judicial power to decide cases, and the executive power to enforce laws. Setting up these institutions puts people into political society.

> And this *puts men* out of a state of nature *into* that of a *common-wealth,* by setting up a judge on earth, with authority to determine all the controversies, and redress the injuries that may happen to any member of the commonwealth; which judge is the legislative, or magistrates appointed by it. And where-ever there are any number of men, however associated, that have no such decisive power to appeal to, there they are still in *the state of nature.*[10]

While it would seem that a majority of individuals could agree to place power in the hands of an absolute monarch, Locke employs an argument against this possibility, which simply reduces to the principle that where citizens have a controversy with the executive power, that executive cannot be an impartial judge in his own case.[11] Though he did not distinguish the making of law from judging by the law, Locke did build a separation of the legislative and executive powers into the meaning of political society, such that "in order for political society to exist these two forms of power must be divided and allocated to different persons."[12]

To this denial of a monarch's right to absolute rule, Locke affirms a corresponding right of citizens to resist—and in the last resort, to revolt against—an unjust authority. This reading is persuasive in light of Locke's radical political commitments. The last four chapters of the *Second Treatise* employ Locke's conception of the social contract to describe those instances in which an authority breaks trust with the citizens, allowing them to defend themselves. "Whosoever uses *force without right,* as every one does in society, who does it without law, puts himself into a *state of war* with those against whom he so uses it; and in that state all former ties are canceled, all other rights cease, and every one has a right to defend himself, and *to resist the aggressor.*"[13] John Dunn claims that the *Two Treatises,* as we have it today, is primarily designed to assert this right to resist.[14]

Underlying this reading is the centrality of *trust* in Locke's conception of government and civil society.[15] Trust is crucial to human existence, for it is the "bond" that makes society possible.[16] Locke, argues Dunn, sees trust as a duty that derives from our dependence on God the Creator. "For human beings who are still aware of this dependence, the attempt to trust in one another, in rulers as much as in fellow subjects, is a duty under the law of nature."[17] The right of citizens to resist and rebel becomes operative when the ruler breaks the trust of the social compact by seriously harming the lives or the civil interests of the people.

Here Locke was no doubt influenced by his religious forebear, John Calvin. Though Calvin promoted a strong duty of obedience to political rulers, even corrupt ones, because their power is dispensed by God,[18] he also allowed for exceptions justifying resistance and rebellion.[19] Yet in his view of trust as the basis of society, Locke comes closer to the philosophy of Thomas Aquinas than to that of Calvin.[20] Aquinas approaches the meaning of government primarily through the category of *law* rather than obedience. A ruler is one who has "care of the community" and promulgates and enforces law for the sake of the common good.[21] Although Calvin and Aquinas are similar in seeing a broadly positive role for civil government—including providing for material needs, helping people live in harmony, and in certain ways protecting virtue and piety—Aquinas, unlike Calvin, allows for a political definition of just and unjust rule, which in turn allows citizens to take a greater critical perspective on their government. Only a government that administers for the common good is "just and fitting to free persons."[22] I draw attention to these connections between Locke and the two theologians to indicate that Locke's political thought cannot be understood without reference to its religious sources and sensibilities. Locke's moral and religious vision shaped his account of civil society as based on trust; this notion of society in turn informed his conception of personal rights and social duties.

Property Rights and the Duties of Institutions

In leaving the state of nature for civil society, people are able to acquire certain rights against the society, the preeminent right being that to private property. The social right to private property derives from the natural right of property we have in our own persons and in our labor, which we extend to common goods by mixing our labor with them. These goods then become our property, to which we have as much right as we can use before spoilage. Before the creation of money, Locke argues, the right of property was inherently limited by the condition of use before spoilage; yet with the creation of money, goods could be converted into nonperishable form, and the right to property became essentially unlimited.[23] However, Locke does not contemplate that this development justifies a monopoly on goods by some at the expense of the poverty of others.

> He who appropriates land to himself by his labour, does not lessen, but increase the common stock of mankind: for the provisions serving to the support of human life, procured by one acre of inclosed and cultivated land, are (to speak with much compass) ten times more than those which are yielded by an acre of land of an equal richness lying waste in common.[24]

In short, the institution of money along with trade benefits the whole society. Disparities of possession are justified by the supposition that all will be better off, though some will have more than others. (Locke saw the wealth of the American colonies as an empirical confirmation of his argument.)

For Locke, then, power of government is limited by the political principle that it must protect and secure those interests for which people constituted and entered the civil society and by the natural principle that each human being has rights to life, liberty, and property. As I read Locke, only the first of these three natural rights is unqualified. The other two have a qualifying social component that emerges when persons enter in society. For instance, Locke distinguishes *natural* liberty ("to be free from any superior power on earth, and not to be under the will or legislative authority of man") from liberty *in society* ("to be under no other legislative power, but that established by consent, in the common-wealth; nor under the dominion of any will but what that legislature shall enact, according to the trust put in it").[25] There are two points here. First, persons do have a natural right to liberty, but it is qualified by their entrance into civil society. Second, the relation of the right to liberty to the right to life is that the former is bound up with the latter and protects it:

> This *freedom* from absolute, arbitrary power, is so necessary to, and closely joined with a man's preservation, that he cannot part with it, but by what forfeits his preservation and life together: for a man, not having the power of his own life, *cannot*, by compact, or his own consent, *enslave himself* to any one, nor put himself under the absolute, arbitrary power of another, to take away his life, when he pleases.[26]

For Locke, the same relation obtains with property rights. The natural right of property is to be able to take from the land whatever one needs to survive, for this is obviously essential to preservation of life. When persons enter civil society, this natural right is retained, but it is also changed through the institutions of money and trade. As a social right, the right to property becomes, for Locke, an essential limitation on the power of the state, as well as a means for multiplying the fruits of nature for the benefit of society.

This analysis of natural and social rights has two implications for our discussion. First, private rights (in this case, to property) are justified both as respecting the nature of the human person as a bearer of natural rights and as institutions for the public good, which, for Locke, is the sum of those social conditions necessary to secure and protect opportunity for all. Second, the particularities of instituting private property rights in a political economy are not fully settled by natural law. Locke cannot be interpreted as holding that there is a legitimate natural right to possess as much as one is able. Throughout his argument about property rights, his underlying assumption is that money "may be hoarded up without injury to any one" because it does not cause natural goods to spoil.[27] Should this assumption prove invalid, then the right to possess money cannot be absolute. Even if there is inequality of income, Locke presumes that everyone should be able to meet his or her basic needs (without clarifying exactly what these would be). On principle, then, Locke would be open to empirical discussion about whether any given free market system is securing the basic civil interests of each person. Thus, in his economic as well as his political thought, Locke's arguments have a significantly egalitarian import.[28]

Having considered the foundation of civil society and the role of political institutions, we are in a position to propose a working definition of the common good in Locke. *The common good consists in a social consensus in favor of a democratic form of government, constitutional protection of individual liberties, and social norms such as toleration and honesty.* Although this conception is secular in form, religion influences its content, as the next section will demonstrate.

The Role of Religion: Toleration and Duty

We can specify Locke's conception of the common good by considering how his political theory shapes his view of religious toleration and how his view of faith shapes his account of political duty. The topics of toleration and duty will sharpen our understanding of religion's potential for serving as a public good. In what was his most controversial work, *A Letter Concerning Toleration* (1689), Locke brings his conception of political society to bear on the issues of religious toleration and church-state relations.[29] Quite simply, the power of magistrates extends only to matters of civil interest. Matters of religion are placed solely in the realm of opinion, which government cannot touch, unless these opinions lead to acts injurious to others. The argument for placing religious opinions in a totally private realm is analogous to Locke's argument that persons cannot cede their natural liberty to a despot: "For no man can, if he would, conform his Faith to the Dictates of another. All the Life and Power of true Religion consists in the inward and full perswasion of the mind; and Faith is not Faith without believing."[30] As political liberty is grounded in natural law, so is religious liberty.

> With respect to toleration . . . Locke's political thinking . . . was committed to a natural rights defense of liberty of conscience against the claims of all forms of political authority, including representative government. This defense necessitated an absolute separation between the sphere of religion (which was defined by its concernment for the eternal salvation of the individual's soul) and the sphere of politics (whose province extended only to men's estates and civil interests).[31]

Locke's defense of religious toleration was remarkably foresighted for his time, though not complete. The social norm of toleration is not only a natural right of individuals, but one of the practices necessary for social harmony. These necessary practices set the limits of religious toleration for Locke: "No Opinions contrary to human Society, or to those moral Rules which are necessary to the preservation of Civil Society, are to be tolerated by the Magistrate."[32] As Western societies have become acclimated to pluralism, the scope of opinions considered contrary to the good of society has narrowed considerably. For instance, Locke placed atheism, Catholicism, and Islam under this rubric; whereas few citizens of liberals societies would say this today.[33] Locke placed these belief systems beyond the scope of toleration because he considered them intolerant of others and thus a threat to social order. The case in point was Catholicism. The basic problem for Protestants in Restoration England was the possible succession of the Catholic James II to the throne, which heightened their fear of religious persecution. Locke's view of toleration was formed in a political crucible, namely, "in the context of an attack upon popery and the view that Catholics, but especially a popish prince, existed in a state of war with Protestants and could thus claim no benefits—including, of course, toleration—of natural law, which the practices of popery, ipso facto, violated." Furthermore, Locke's exploration of the possible use of popular force against a magistrate "was raised as a response to the persecution of Dissenters by the Anglican church and the prospects of England's being ruled by a popish king."[34] Locke does not dispassionately aver freedom of religion simply as an abstract right or simply as a way to privatize religion. Rather, he found it crucially important to protect his own religious beliefs and practices, as well as to protect a vital space in public life for religious belief. On balance, it seems appropriate to say that Locke was as tolerant as he was able to be, given his context. His legacy was to help establish a political justification for an expansive policy of religious toleration.

This account of toleration implies that a view of the common good can affect a political view of the limits of acceptable religious behavior. By the same token, religious ideas can shape a society's understanding of citizens' duties to the common good. In Locke's view, revelation completes the moral life and enables all persons to know their duties. "It was only by means of the Christian revelation that [Locke] retained the confidence that men's moral duties were effectively 'made known to all mankind.' "[35] Revelation about one's duties is disclosed through a unique call from God. The Calvinist concept of a calling, the "key to Locke's moral vision," gives to every person a critical standpoint "outside the realm of human contingency from which the rational individual could judge the world and act upon it."[36] The calling defines each person's contribution to the common good. Locke presumed consistently through his mature writings that the calling was sufficient to define "the terrestrial components of human duty."[37] The concept of a calling underscores the egalitarian thrust of Locke's political thought: all persons have gifts to contribute to the common good, and all will benefit from it. The role for religion in the common good is to remind persons of their duties and, in so doing, to facilitate their participation in society.

Though religion serves the common good in these ways, Locke does not draw the conclusion that religious denominations deserve special privileges from the state. The striking exception is the toleration that Jews, Deists, and Protestant Christians enjoy. If there is a positive idea we can retrieve from this now-inconsistent stance, it is that we can justify religious toleration in part on the social contribution made by religious believers. If, for Locke, atheists were not to be tolerated because of their supposed lack of morality, and if Catholics and Muslims were denied toleration because of their purported allegiance to rival political entities, then other believers enjoy toleration because their religious affiliations build up the common good or at least do not detract from it. So the freedom that most believers enjoy is not based simply on the right to free speech or to group autonomy; still less is it based on a principle of state neutrality. Rather, this freedom is based on Locke's conviction that religion can serve the common good. To be sure, any particular content for common good theory that Locke derives from religious views bears the stamp of his Calvinist faith, but the common good he articulates is open to the contributions of any faith—as long as the members of that faith practice toleration toward others.

Assessing Locke's Contribution

Locke has powerful contributions to make to the concept of the common good in a liberal society. Primary among these are the claims (1) that trust is the foundation of both civil society and government, (2) that institutions must be established for the benefit of individuals and their basic needs, which implies an obligation of the community to meet such needs, and (3) that persons as individuals and as members of groups have a contribution to make to the common good. In short, trust flows both ways between the individual and the community, and neither must break its obligations. The obligations of individuals include productive work according to their talents, respect of others' rights, tolerance, prudence, development of their intellects at least minimally through study, and development of their religious knowledge. This latter duty, really the most important for Locke, indicates one's obligation toward, not political society, but the community of the Kingdom of God.[38] The obligation of society toward persons is to provide the educational, economic, and political institutions that make it possible for persons to fulfill their obligations. Examples of such institutions are limited constitutional government, separation of powers, free markets and sound fiscal policies,[39] and freedom of thought, speech, and religion.

What is most important to our discussion here is that all these classically "liberal" institutions are defended by reference to the needs of persons with God-given dignity who live in political communities. Locke's account of the human person (his anthropology) certainly involves individual liberty and claims based on merit, but it does not privilege these as much as some have claimed.[40] His anthropology also includes a moral and religious equality of persons that grounds political equality, a natural equality of needs that justifies a basic level of support for all, and a conception of the individual in a communal context that defines reciprocal duties to the community.

In some areas, though, Locke's account of the common good remains incomplete or problematic. First, the actual role that religious institutions can play in promoting the common good is underdeveloped. Second, over time, Locke's principle of religious toleration came to require broader extension. Third, there is need for more attention to the difficulty of forging the common good out of cultural, moral, and religious pluralism. Finally, in our contemporary understanding of the role of government and public institutions, we stand at a distance from Locke: the state now is much larger than he ever contemplated. Is there a justification for this larger role of government in the framework of communal liberalism, or should we return to Locke's advocacy of a more limited role? With these questions in mind, we turn to a figure who was influenced by Locke, especially by his defense of religious toleration, but who also provided a stronger communitarian basis for liberal political philosophy.

MENDELSSOHN AS A RESOURCE FOR COMMUNAL LIBERALISM

This section investigates Moses Mendelssohn's political thought and his contribution to a theory of communal liberalism based on a detailed reading of his *Jerusalem*. To set this work in context, a few biographical comments are in order.[41] Mendelssohn was a celebrated philosopher and the best-known Jew in Europe in his day. Throughout his career, he often intervened on behalf of Jewish communities in different cities and countries, both through letters to political authorities regarding specific issues and through general writings. For example, he encouraged and assisted Christian von Dohm in publishing *On the Civil Improvement of the Jews*, and he penned the "Preface" to a translation of Mannaseh ben Israel's *Vindiciae Judaeorum*. These high-profile writings drew Mendelssohn into some literary bouts. First was the so-called Lavater Affair, in which the well-meaning but impetuous Johann Lavater challenged Mendelssohn either to refute the argument of a religious tract or to convert to Christianity. Mendelssohn loathed engaging in a skirmish over religion, but since he was challenged, he wrote a public letter to Lavater defending his beliefs. Mendelssohn was not alone: some prominent Christians rebuffed Lavater for his rudeness. Late in his life, Mendelssohn was involved in a controversy over the alleged Spinozism of his recently deceased friend Gotthold Lessing, whom Mendelssohn defended against the charge.

Another contest followed the publication of Mendelssohn's "Preface," where he had argued that ecclesiastical power and the practice of excommunication go against the spirit of all religions, including Judaism. Of several critical pamphlets written in response to Mendelssohn, one—*The Searching for Light and Right* by journalist August Cranz, writing anonymously—questioned how Mendelssohn could maintain the faith of his forebears.

> The gist of the pamphlet was two-fold: did not the Biblical commandments of Judaism require sanctions, without which they would have no continued force? And if the commandments had no force, why did Mendelssohn not ignore them and indeed convert to liberal Christianity, which was hardly other than rational and natural religion, of which Mendelssohn himself was an advocate?[42]

"This objection," Mendelssohn said, "cuts me to the heart."[43] He wrote *Jerusalem: Or, On Religious Power and Judaism* (1783) "both to defend his views on excommunication and religious tolerance and to establish the integrity of his commitment to Judaism."[44] To that text I now turn.

The Orientation of *Jerusalem*

Mendelssohn opens *Jerusalem* with the problem of the relation between church and state:

> State and religion—civil and ecclesiastical constitution—secular and churchly authority—how to oppose these pillars of social life to one another

so that they are in balance and do not, instead, become burdens on social life, or weigh down its foundations more than they help to uphold it—this is one of the most difficult tasks of politics.[45]

This framing of the issue indicates from the very outset Mendelssohn's interest in mediations between secular and religious domains and between universal and communal obligations. The aim of politics should not be to disadvantage religion in the public sphere, nor to grant political control to church authorities, nor merely to establish boundary lines between church and state. Rather, the goal should be to balance their influence on the foundations of social life.

Mendelssohn presumes that both institutions properly contribute to the common good of society. But he distances himself from Locke, who drew a distinction between public interests that are the province of the state, such as peace and prosperity, and private interests that fall within the domain of the church and ultimately the individual, such as spiritual welfare. Mendelssohn does not consider satisfactory Locke's narrow definition of the state's domain:

> And indeed, what reason do we have to restrict the purpose of society solely to the *temporal*? If men *can* promote their eternal felicity by public measures, it should be their natural duty to *do* so, their rational obligation to join forces for this purpose and to enter into social relations. If, however, this be the case, and the state as such be preoccupied solely with the temporal, a question arises: To whom are we to entrust care for the eternal? To the church? Now we are, once again, back at our starting point.[46]

Mendelssohn is imagining an argument that goes like this. If people do have an interest in their eternal happiness, they have a right to join together in pursuit of it. If the state relinquishes any role in determining how citizens achieve their interests, the arena is left to churches. But these interests, because they are eternal and of ultimate significance, appear to take precedence over temporal matters. So, then, why should not churches have a say in temporal matters that affect the pursuit of their members' eternal happiness? Thus Mendelssohn thinks that this argument, which he associates with Locke, unwittingly plays into the hands of those who would put temporal power in ecclesiastical hands.

Like Locke, Mendelssohn sees merit in distinguishing the roles of church and state, but he is not as sanguine as Locke that temporal and eternal values can be neatly untangled. Instead of distinguishing religion and government by different *interests* or *ends,* Mendelssohn demarcates them according to their *methods* and the *human relations* for which they are responsible. Mendelssohn compactly outlines his argument in a few paragraphs, which are worth quoting at length:

As soon as man recognizes that outside of society he can fulfill his duties toward himself and toward the author of his existence as poorly as he can fulfill his duties toward his neighbor, and, hence, can no longer remain in his solitary condition without a sense of wretchedness, he is obliged to leave that condition and to enter into society with those in a like situation in order to satisfy their needs through mutual aid and to promote their common good by common measures. Their common good, however, includes the present as well as the future, the spiritual as well as the earthly. One is inseparable from the other. Unless we fulfill our obligations, we can expect neither felicity here nor there, neither on earth nor in heaven. Now two things belong to the true fulfillment of our duties: *action* and *conviction*. Action accomplishes what duty demands, and conviction causes that action to proceed from the proper source, that is, from pure motives.

Hence both actions and convictions belong to the perfection of man, and society should, as far as possible, take care of both by collective efforts, that is, it should direct the actions of its members toward the common good, and cause convictions which lead to these actions. The one is *government*, the other the *education* of societal man. To both man is led by *reasons*; to actions by *reasons that motivate the will,* and to convictions by *reasons that persuade by their truth.* Society should therefore establish both through public institutions in such a way that they will be in accord with the common good.

The reasons which lead men to rational actions and convictions rest partly on the relations of men to each other, partly on the relations of men to their Creator and Keeper. The former are the province of the *state*, the latter that of *religion*. . . . Public institutions for the formation of man that concern his relations with God I call *church*; those that concern his relations with man I call *state*. By the formation of man I understand the effort to arrange both actions and convictions in such a way that they will be in accord with his felicity; that they will *educate* and *govern* men.[47]

The next three sections will elaborate on this passage and analyze features of Mendelssohn's argument that are pertinent to this study, including his views of society, the person, religion, the common good, and pluralism.

The Common Good, the State, and Religion

We must note Mendelssohn's understanding of some key terms. Though Mendelssohn gives no explicit definition of *society*, the meaning behind his use of it suggests the relation of mutual support among persons by means of various institutions. One institution within this network is the *state*, the institution that governs relations among persons. He asks not which institution is responsible for the common good, but by what means any institution bears responsibility for promoting human fulfillment and social harmony. He looks at society as the broad structure of human relations through institutions, among which the state and the church are the primary (though not the only) "pillars." They both aim to uphold the common good of society, but they do so through different methods.

In Mendelssohn's view, the *common good* consists of two elements: the formation and perfection of each human person, and an ordering of society that facilitates this. The formation of the person is the good in question (for which Mendelssohn often uses the term *felicity*). In the long text quoted above, Mendelssohn indicates that this individual good is also common in three senses: first, it is a good that all persons want (though not all may be aware that they do); second, persons cannot pursue and achieve this good without common cooperation; and third, when persons are empowered in this way, society is strengthened in freedom and tolerance. Now we may consider some political implications of these concepts.

The Personal and Social Elements of the Common Good

The first element of Mendelssohn's common good—*the formation and perfection of the person*—includes promotion of one's spiritual interests. Individual perfection consists in happiness, and happiness is contingent upon the fulfillment of our duties: "Unless we fulfill our obligations, we can expect felicity neither here nor there, neither on earth nor in heaven." Fulfillment of these duties requires action, the external component, and conviction, which "causes that action to proceed from the proper source, that is, from pure motives."[48] As I have noted, for Mendelssohn, both action and conviction belong to the perfection of the person, and society is properly concerned to promote these through the institutions of government and the church, inasmuch as some of the sources of action and conviction rely on human relations and some on our relation to God.

Benevolence is a quality of action and conviction necessary both to secure our relations to others and to bring us happiness:

> In social life, man must renounce certain of his rights for the common good or as one may say, he must very often sacrifice his own advantage to benevolence. He will be happy if this sacrifice is made on his own prompting and when he realizes, in each instance, that he acted solely for the sake of benevolence. *Benevolence*, in reality, makes us happier than *selfishness*; but we must, while exercising it, be aware that it springs from ourselves and is the display of our powers.[49]

Therefore, Mendelssohn holds that the person is able to achieve happiness to the extent that he or she has developed a character that is a wellspring of benevolent and charitable actions. In sum, the way Mendelssohn relates his views of person and society is this: The human person has a natural sociability and capacity for benevolence. By acting benevolently, a person's social ties are strengthened; these relations in turn make her benevolence possible and enlarge it by the influence they exert on her character. The common good consists in and results from this mutual reinforcement.

The second element of the common good is *the proper ordering of society*. The influence social relations have upon one's character is both moral and spiritual. Mendelssohn argues that all public institutions are properly concerned with the formation of the individual's character, that is, "the effort to arrange both actions and convictions in such a way that they will be in accord with his felicity"; but, as we have noted, the various institutions employ different means. The state uses political means that should focus on persuasion as much as possible: "Blessed be the state which succeeds in governing the nation by education itself; that is, by infusing it with such morals and convictions as will of themselves tend to produce actions conducive to the common weal, and need not be constantly urged on by the spur of the law." Mendelssohn would measure the excellence of any government by "the degree . . . to which government is by education itself." His reasoning is based on a point of his moral anthropology: "Man is conscious of his own worth when he performs charitable acts . . . when he gives because he *wants* to give. But if he gives because he *must*, he feels only his fetters."[50]

Of course, the state may also employ coercion, when persuasive means have failed and when force is justified by a clear public good, such as peace and order: "If the *inner felicity of society* cannot be entirely preserved, let at least *outward peace and security* be obtained, if need be, through *coercion*."[51] Note that coercion is not justified to attain the inner felicity (i.e., the common good) of society but only to preserve what we might call the *public order*. Force is not justified in the former because it would be ineffective and therefore gratuitous. The common good can be built up only through benevolence, which people must freely give.

But before matters come to this point, religion has a key role to play:

> Knowledge, reasoning, and persuasion alone can bring forth principles which, with the help of *authority* and *example*, can pass into *morals*. And it is here that religion should come to the aid of the state, and the church should become a pillar of civil felicity. It is the business of the church to convince people, in the most emphatic manner, of the truth of noble principles and convictions; to show them that duties toward men are also duties toward God, the violation of which is in itself the greatest misery; that serving the state is true service of God; that charity is his most sacred will; and that true knowledge of the Creator cannot leave behind in the soul any hatred for men.[52]

The idea of a common cause between church and state raises two questions, one regarding the role the church plays in political and civil affairs, and one concerning the degree to which state action can touch morality and religion.

The Church's Role in Political Affairs

Mendelssohn limits the church's role here to moral education and suasion. While the state has recourse to coercive action for the sake of public order, religion may not coerce. There are two interrelated reasons for this. First and most basically, coercion does not belong to the nature of religion: "The state gives orders and coerces, religion teaches and persuades. The state prescribes *laws*, religion *commandments*. The state has *physical power* and uses it when necessary; the power of religion is *love* and *beneficence*."[53] Thus, we might say the church's social duty is to "preach and teach"—to use its moral and spiritual authority to shape the people's character and to educate them about charitable action. People so educated will be more ready to act justly and tolerantly and to cede their own rights when it will benefit those in need. Such character and action conduces to the happiness of the person and of the society.

Wherever the church's teaching and preaching bear on political life, Mendelssohn restricts its influence. At any point where the state must use reward or punishment, religion "withdraws it support," for these cases involve relations among persons, and the question of duty to God does not enter.[54] One upshot is that churches should be neutral regarding the state's police, military, and penal institutions; churches should render no moral support to, and take no active part in, their activities. It is less clear whether churches have any proper role in adjudicating political conflicts. Should they pronounce on specific policies or only on general principles? Should they teach that the state must be obeyed in all its proclamations—as implied by Mendelssohn's phrase "serving the state is true service of God"?[55]

In general, Mendelssohn seems to favor an *indirect* role for religion in these matters. Teaching moral principles is sure to have a political effect, but that concern should be secondary to the church. When it educates on human relations, it should focus more on civil society than government. Mendelssohn certainly supports the freedom of citizens to disagree with laws and to press for peaceful change. It is unclear in *Jerusalem* whether he thinks the church as a teaching body can respectfully dissent as well—and urge citizens to do so—or only support a climate of civil freedom in which this is possible.

The State's Role in Religion and Morality

The obverse issue concerns the state's proper role in the church's domain. Mendelssohn suggests that the state should be interested in citizens' convictions as well as their actions: the state must be concerned with the moral formation of its citizens. For the state cannot support the happiness and perfection of the person without moral education. Further, since the state desires that citizens act in conformity with laws, this is most readily and easily achieved by educating a citizenry that wants to obey the laws. Hence, the state is interested to inculcate the kind of morals that lead persons to pursue their perfection, to respect and tolerate others, and to obey the law. The latter two aspects of morality support the first, for it is in a society marked by tolerance and respect for the rule of law that citizens are most empowered to pursue their moral and spiritual perfection.

For Mendelssohn, it is inevitable that the state express moral values—it does so when it promulgates laws against murder, for religious freedom, and so on. It is appropriate for the public to discuss the values underlying these laws and policies. But he limits the scope of morality in such discussion. First, the values that shape government policy may be only those that bear on relations among persons, not humans' relation to God. Respecting this limit, citizens will recognize that the discussion of values is important to the practical matters of social life. Second, though the state's actions may affect the church at the point where their moral concerns overlap, Mendelssohn limits the state to indirect action in religious matters. Illustrating this principle, he treats the particular matters of atheism and state-appointed religious teachers. These cases demonstrate the extent of the limits placed on state action. The state should restrict the spread of atheism—but only on the ground that atheism is an intolerant doctrine from which society needs to be guarded.[56] And the state should provide and pay for religious teachers—but, again, only on the social-benefit ground that citizens require education in values.[57]

Intolerance of atheism and state payment for religious teachers are two time-bound aspects of Mendelssohn's theory—and they are the points where he most threatens the liberal side of his communal liberalism. But they are neither central nor crucial to his view of the common good, so we may leave them behind as we mine his work for a modern theory of communal liberalism. The part of his argument here that we should retain is the principle of the state's *indirect interest* in religion and morality, mirrored by the church's *indirect interest* in policies and governance. Indeed, the indirect interest principle significantly restrains the state's actions toward unpopular doctrines:

> But it is only from a distance that the state should take notice of [atheism and fanaticism], and only with wise moderation should it favor even those doctrines upon which its true felicity is based. It should not interfere directly in any dispute or wish to decide it through the use of its authority. For it evidently acts contrary to is own purpose when it forbids free inquiry, or allows disputes to be decided in any manner other than by rational arguments.[58]

More generally, this principle guides Mendelssohn's approach to religious pluralism and religious toleration.

The Common Good, Pluralism, and Toleration

Mendelssohn's communal liberalism embraces institutional and religious pluralism as a core feature. Such pluralism is desirable because it guards liberty of conscience (a liberal concern) and fosters the toleration necessary for social cooperation in modern society (a communitarian concern). At the end of *Jerusalem,* he sums up his argument for pluralism and relates it to the quest for tolerance. Pluralism cannot be eliminated for the following reasons: Providence has revealed a plan of diversity, in that no one thinks exactly like anyone else; people follow their own consciences by divine design and natural right; it is exceedingly difficult to capture abstract ideas in words, hence people disagree over the meaning of the same words or think they agree when they really do not.[59] Therefore, any union of faiths "could lie only in the words, in the formula."[60] To draw up such a formula would require the unifiers to squeeze the meaning out of concepts and twist the words until the formula became meaningless. Everyone would still have to make up his or her own mind as to the meaning. Such a union would entail "universal hypocrisy," and Mendelssohn fears it would be the first step toward renewed intolerance. When a society stakes its unity on words and symbols, dissension is inevitable. But those who do dissent will be deemed disturbers of the peace and persecuted. Hence, Mendelssohn urges that "*a union of the faiths is not tolerance*; it is diametrically opposed to true tolerance!"[61]

Mendelssohn identifies a positive and a negative sense of tolerance. The former is what he refers to with the term *true tolerance*; this is the benevolent acceptance of the other as a human being. The negative sense is to put up with the other, to leave him or her in peace if nothing else is possible. Both senses are operative when Mendelssohn implores his Christian fellow citizens to accept the Jewish people in a civil union. He first asks them to accept them as brothers and sisters, as the Jews want to love them in return. Then he remarks,

> Regard us, if not as brothers and fellow citizens, at least as fellow men and fellow inhabitants of the land. Show us ways and provide us with means of becoming better men and better fellow inhabitants, and permit us to be partners in enjoying the rights of humanity as far as time and circumstances permit.[62]

The negative sense of tolerance appeals to the basic humanity of the one petitioned. The positive sense appeals to her benevolence. Toleration, for

Mendelssohn, does not require the tolerant one to pretend there are no differences between herself and another, nor to hide that she has a different point of view, nor to refrain from attempting to persuade the other of her view. Toleration is precisely the acceptance that makes earnest yet peaceful discussion possible. Mendelssohn does not stake his quest for toleration on an abstract notion of the human person; he would not have us wear secular masks. Rather, he is confident that beneath our diverse worldviews lies a basic humanity that makes at least minimal toleration possible. He is further convinced that the main religious views prevalent in his culture—Jewish and Christian—teach moral principles that bolster tolerance.

The state supports tolerance by defending liberty of conscience, free inquiry, and freedom of religion, as well as by educating its citizens to be tolerant. In these ways, the state renders its service to the common good.

The Role of Churches in the Common Good

Mendelssohn obviously sees the church promoting tolerance by educating people in benevolence and charity. He is especially concerned that churches practice toleration themselves, by refusing to excommunicate anyone. His argument against excommunication is partly based on his concepts of rights and contracts and partly on the inherent nature of religion as he sees it. The former involves his complex and controversial claim that the church is not really a social compact, as there can be no contract between humans and God. He thinks, therefore, that churches cannot have a legal status similar to other social institutions.[63] By this logic, they have no right to practice coercion of any sort, including punishment of their members. Since excommunication and minor bans carry the consequences of civil stigmatization, the church may not enact these.[64] This conclusion is bolstered by Mendelssohn's view that religion must use love, not laws, to achieve its aims. To ban a person is to give up on him; he becomes excluded from the possibility of conversion.[65] A church should never do this.

Mendelssohn's arguments against excommunication are well taken as an intrareligious argument; the part of his argument based on the nature of religion is certainly consonant with Jewish (and Christian) principles. To end or severely limit the practice of banning (as has happened in most denominations) contributes to toleration within those faith communities and no doubt can be a good example to the wider society. But the exclusion of churches, however well meaning, from equal legal status under the social contract is problematic. For the denial of certain rights to churches leads to the state taking on too much responsibility for the common good. To have the state directly support ministers and religious teachers is to efface the distinction between state and civil society. In short, Mendelssohn's position on church-state relations, though well meaning and useful within a denomination, cannot be retained in a communal liberalism: the liberal and communitarian sides agree in securing a greater space in political life for the free initiative of voluntary communities.[66] Liberals from the Enlightenment to today are also rightly troubled by having the state take on tasks such as paying ministers and religious teachers. Their concerns about Mendelssohn's theory may be mollified if we keep intact Mendelssohn's own distinction of state and society. This distinction allows church-state cooperation but requires greater autonomy for voluntary groups.

To move from the negative—what churches may not do—to the positive, Mendelssohn holds that religion should be concerned to promote the common good because of its interest in the perfection of the person: the formation of person in temporal virtues and human relations conduces to his or her spiritual happiness. Churches also have a stake in the common good as a structure of institutional and confessional pluralism; this structure secures the freedom to worship and educate as one or one's community pleases. Mendelssohn speaks of this interest not only generally, but he demonstrates to his coreligionists why they have a stake in such a social order. He argues both to Jews and Christians that Judaism is open to civil society. The religious philosophy of Judaism requires its adherents neither to separate themselves into a religious-ethnic enclave nor to submerge themselves into society and dissolve the faith of their forebears. He urges Christian citizens to accept his people as brothers and sisters, but he also warns that the Jews will not make the surrender of their beliefs and laws a condition of civil union.

In a wonderful example of the compatibility Mendelssohn sees, wherever he looks, between adherence to a particular way of life and the good of society, he tells his Christian readers, "We cannot, in good conscience, depart from the law, and what good will it do you to have fellow citizens without conscience?"[67] Instead of a forced homogeneity that breeds hypocrisy and resentment, Mendelssohn values engagement among the members of society's different religious traditions, in which persons, working from particular overlaps and agreements among them, can build a more honest and realistic cooperation. We cannot proclaim ahead of time whether all faiths have a similar stake in the common good thus defined; concord is something we must discover as it arises from dialogue among churches and religious believers. Simply to continue and expand this dialogue among Jews and Christians is a large and urgent task—one that Moses Mendelssohn probably thought would have been much further along by now.

BEYOND THE ENLIGHTENMENT

I have presented Mendelssohn's thought as providing resources for a theory of communal liberalism and have indicated some of his claims and arguments that communal liberalism would have to discard. His two major weaknesses in this regard are his reluctance to extend social toleration to atheism and his argument that churches have no right to ban an offender from their midst. Yet I believe that neither of these undermines the significant contribution Mendelssohn makes to a mediation of liberalism and communitarianism. On some points, his theory is simply a blending of those two sides. For instance, the liberal stresses the negative side of toleration and the need for constitutional protections of individual rights to speech and religion. The communitarian stresses a positive view of tolerance and sees need of civil religion to unite the ethos of a society. Mendelssohn gives weight to both; negative tolerance is necessary in the face of enduring pluralism, but he is confident that a principled commitment to human perfection and a free society will strengthen a positive sense of toleration among citizens.

On other points, his mediation transcends conflicts between the two sides. An example is the way he conceives the role of church and state in civil and moral matters. Whereas liberals tend to make the state responsible only for external actions and the church only for convictions, Mendelssohn sides with the communitarians in holding that both institutions are properly concerned with action and conviction. Yet he ameliorates the danger of state intervention in religious affairs and the danger of church entanglement in political affairs by restricting the state's purview to actions and convictions as they bear on human relations, and the church's to those that bear on the human relation to God. Hence, the state takes an indirect interest in moral and spiritual matters, acting through education; and the church takes an indirect interest in civil affairs, wielding its influence through education and persuasion.

What enables Mendelssohn to effect his mediation throughout is a commitment to the common good. For him, the common good consists in the formation and perfection of the human person and in an ordering of society that facilitates it. Citizens and institutions are most empowered to pursue this good within a framework of institutional and confessional pluralism. As opposed to the liberal quest to stake out a minimal public order, or the communitarian desire to unite the society through a shared set of moral and spiritual values, the communal liberal wants the state to guard the public order while supporting the institutions of civil society. By *support* I mean, first and foremost, providing a legal climate that is conducive to pluralism and free inquiry. Beyond that, the state needs to establish more cooperation with public institutions in the drafting of legislation and the execution of policies.

Is Mendelssohn's approach to the common good superior to Locke's? I think it is clear that there are similarities between the positive characteristics of each. There is no need to review these; let us instead consider the four shortcomings I identified in Locke's approach to see how well they are handled by Mendelssohn. The first was the need for a more developed role for religious institutions. Mendelssohn's argument does identify a direct role for churches in the common good, which generally is to cooperate with the state in the formation of the person through education and which specifically is to focus on spiritual and moral matters. Second, Locke's notion of toleration required extension, and Mendelssohn does broaden toleration significantly—with only a lingering suspicion of atheism. To a greater extent than Locke, Mendelssohn articulates a common good for which all religious believers can cooperate.

The third shortcoming of Locke's approach was the paucity of attention to cultural and ideological pluralism; and the fourth was that his notion of government would be inadequate to take on the range of issues associated with pursuing the common good today. Mendelssohn is more alive to the issue of cultural diversity, but his appeal that we respect the beliefs and traditions of others only raises more questions for us: How do we achieve such toleration in a multireligious society? What means may the government employ to support tolerance and discourage intolerance? To what kinds of moral and political *action* does the principle of toleration extend? Implicated in these questions are questions about the role of the state vis-à-vis voluntary institutions and individual citizens. Exactly how maximal or minimal are its tasks, and what steps may it take to promote the formation and perfection of the person?

Some commentators find that Mendelssohn runs into his greatest difficulty in trying to deal with these interlocking issues. Michael Morgan argues that Mendelssohn has two divergent conceptions of the human self in *Jerusalem*. The first is the universal self, the citizen, "a *thin* self, with just enough content to advocate public institutions aimed at peace and tranquillity but no more."[68] This notion of self correlates to a modus-vivendi liberalism, in which persons seek civic peace by keeping their moral and religious viewpoints out of politics. The second conception is the communal self, a *thick* self defined by communal and traditional attachments. To this conception corresponds an expressive view of politics, in which persons try to exhibit and promote their communal identities through the political process. The question Morgan presses against Mendelssohn is "whether the moral-religious conception of the good life and hence its conception of ideal selfhood is or is not *expressed* at the political level."

> Is the liberal self, to put it differently, pervasive? Does liberalism pervade Mendelssohn's view from top to bottom? If so, then at some level the two conceptions of the ideal self, the universal and the communal, will conflict. They will conflict in the Jew, who is expected to be distinctively Jewish and at the same time univer[s]ally liberal. They will conflict, that is, because the liberal state is expected to be tolerant of the Jew and indeed of all unharmful,

diverse conceptions of the good life, while at the same time expressing and advocating one such conception as superior to the rest.[69]

Morgan interprets Mendelssohn as wanting it both ways yet failing to resolve the inherent tension. Morgan sees this as a problem particularly because it appears to him that an expressive politics undermines toleration: "As the state's tasks become more maximal, advocating one conception of human flourishing, one good, then more conceptions of the good will be ruled out as adversaries, as inferior and inhibiting to conceptions of self."[70]

I agree that Mendelssohn wants it both ways, that liberalism is for him "both a political and a moral-religious theory."[71] Analyzing whether Mendelssohn develops a theoretically successful account of the self is not as important to me as determining whether a theory of communal liberalism can succeed for us today. Therefore, I must move beyond Mendelssohn's own work. My project requires further explication of how communal liberalism can make sense as both a political and a moral-religious theory and of how human flourishing can be the object of the common good without involving the state in enforcing particular views of the good life. With his theory of political liberalism, John Rawls raises the same sorts of challenges to my theory as Morgan raises to Mendelssohn's. So in the next chapter, I dispute the claim, just implied by Morgan, that governmental support for the common good *as defined in communal liberalism* will threaten its toleration of competing views of human flourishing. I will also argue that political liberalism is not as successful as it claims in remaining neutral among diverse worldviews. To endorse a universal conception of the self is to promote a particular conception of the self over others, and so political liberalism is not immune from the danger of discriminating against competing worldviews.

NOTES

1. Robert N. Bellah, Richard Madsen, William M. Sullivan, Ann Swidler, and Steven M. Tipton, *The Good Society* (New York: Alfred A. Knopf, 1991), 79. A stronger, Marxian critique of Locke as a defender of bourgeois capitalist individualism is offered by C. B. Macpherson, *The Political Theory of Possessive Individualism: Hobbes to Locke* (Oxford: Oxford University Press, 1962).

2. For an overview of various interpreters of Locke's political thought and their shortcomings, see "A Critical Note on Locke Scholarship," in Richard Ashcraft, *Locke's Two Treatises of Government* (London: Allen & Unwin, 1987), 298–305.

3. John Dunn, *The Political Thought of John Locke: An Historical Account of the Argument of the "Two Treatises of Government"* (Cambridge: Cambridge Uni-

versity Press, 1969) and John Dunn, *Locke*, Past Masters series (Oxford: Oxford University Press, 1984).

4. Richard Ashcraft, *Revolutionary Politics and Locke's "Two Treatises of Government"* (Princeton, N.J.: Princeton University Press, 1986).

5. Ashcraft, *Locke's Two Treatises*, 1–2.

6. John Locke, *A Letter Concerning Toleration*, ed. James H. Tully (Indianapolis, Ind.: Hackett, 1983), 26.

7. John Locke, *Second Treatise of Government*, ed. C. B. Macpherson (Indianapolis, Ind.: Hackett, 1980), chap. 2.

8. Locke, *Second Treatise*, § 128.

9. Locke, *Second Treatise*, §§ 124, 125, 126, cited in Ashcraft, *Locke's Two Treatises*, 112.

10. Locke, *Second Treatise*, § 89, cited in Ashcraft, *Locke's Two Treatises*, 113–14.

11. Locke, *Second Treatise*, §§ 90–94.

12. Ashcraft, *Locke's Two Treatises*, 114.

13. Locke, *Second Treatise*, § 232.

14. Dunn, *Locke*, 28. Note that Locke probably was at work on the *Two Treatises* during the Exclusion Crisis, when Shaftesbury's party was using political means to prevent the crown from passing from Charles II to his Catholic brother, James II. During this period, Parliament kept passing the Exclusion Bill, which prevented any Catholic from succeeding to the throne and cut off the king's funding until he agreed to it. Charles kept dissolving the Parliament, and it did not meet during the last several years of his reign. With other Protestants, Locke feared that James would favor Catholicism and make it the state religion of England, however much he protested to the contrary. While Locke is careful not to call for outright resistance against James should he become king, Locke poses a rhetorical question (*Second Treatise*, § 210) meant to suggest that James would break the faith of the social contract. On the *Two Treatises* and the Exclusion Crisis, see Ashcraft, *Revolutionary Politics*, esp. chaps. 5 and 6, and Dunn, *Political Thought*, chap. 5.

15. Dunn, *Locke*, 52–57.

16. Dunn, *Locke*, 52.

17. Dunn, *Locke*, 53.

18. "The first duty of subjects towards their magistrates is to think most honorably of their office, which they recognize as a jurisdiction bestowed by God, and on that account to esteem and reverence them as ministers and representatives of God. . . . From this also something else follows: that, with hearts inclined to reverence their rulers, the subjects should prove their obedience toward them, whether by obeying their proclamations, or by paying taxes, or by undertaking public offices and burdens which pertain to the common defense, or by executing any other commands of theirs. . . . In a very wicked man utterly unworthy of all honor, provided he has the public power in his hands, that noble and divine power resides which the Lord has by his Word given to the ministers of his justice and judgment. Accordingly, he should be held in the same reverence and esteem by his subjects, in so far as public obedience is concerned, in which they would hold the best of kings if he were given to them" (John Calvin, *Institutes of the Christian Religion*,

2 vols., ed. John T. McNeill, trans. Ford Lewis Battles, Library of Christian Classics, vol. 21 [Philadelphia: Westminster Press, 1960], bk. IV, chap. 20, §§ 22, 23, 25).

19. Calvin, *Institutes*, bk. IV, chap. 20, §§ 30–32. Calvin interweaves four possible exceptions: when God raises up an avenger by a special command; when local magistrates curb an unjust ruler (the constitutional argument); when a ruler's commands violate God's laws; and, connected to this last one, when a ruler so commands, he abrogates his power, and citizens must instead obey God (the private law theory). Cf. Michael Walzer, *The Revolution of the Saints: A Study in the Origins of Radical Politics* (Cambridge, Mass.: Harvard University Press, 1965).

20. Locke may have read Aquinas, but it is not certain that he did. His *Essays in the Law of Nature* have a Thomistic tone but do not mention Aquinas. See Ashcraft, *Locke's Two Treatises*, 16 and 34 n. 6.

21. St. Thomas Aquinas, *Summa Theologiae*, ed. Thomas Gilby, O.P., 61 vols. (London: Blackfriars, 1964–76), I–II, q. 90, a. 4: "Law is naught else than an ordinance of reason for the common good, made by the authority who has care of the community and promulgated."

22. St. Thomas Aquinas, *De Regimine Principum (On Princely Government)*, bk. I, chap. 1, in *Aquinas: Selected Political Writings*, ed. A. P. D'Entreves, trans. J. G. Dawson (Oxford: Blackwell, 1954).

23. Locke, *Second Treatise*, chap. 5.

24. Locke, *Second Treatise*, § 37.

25. Locke, *Second Treatise*, § 22.

26. Locke, *Second Treatise*, § 23.

27. Locke, *Second Treatise*, § 50.

28. Dunn would temper such a statement by arguing that Locke did not contemplate an egalitarian social revolution, partly because "egalitarian social democracy as a moral ideal would have offended against many of his deepest social and moral assumptions" but primarily because "nothing in his experience made credible the *possibility* of an achieved and stable egalitarian social structure in an economically advanced society" (*Political Thought*, 240). However, I think Ashcraft is more persuasive in his contention that Locke's *Two Treatises* was radical in intent and was so received: for instance, it was primarily addressed not to the aristocracy, but to merchants, tradespeople, and artisans; and it was not accepted by the Whigs as a defense of their Glorious Revolution of 1689, but was read as supporting the program of the Levellers (*Revolutionary Politics*, chap. 11).

29. Locke also wrote *A Second Letter Concerning Toleration, A Third Letter for Toleration*, and part of *A Fourth Letter for Toleration*, though the first is the most famous. All four letters may be found in *The Works of John Locke*, 9th ed., 9 vols. (London: Printed for T. Longman, et al., 1794), vol. 5.

30. Locke, *Letter*, 26.

31. Ashcraft, *Revolutionary Politics*, 496–97.

32. Locke, *Letter*, 49.

33. Locke, *Letter*, 50–51.

34. Ashcraft, *Revolutionary Politics*, 497. For more on the historical context of Locke's views on toleration, see chaps. 3 and 11 of Ashcraft's work.

35. Dunn, *Locke*, 84. See John Locke, *The Reasonableness of Christianity: As Delivered in the Scriptures* (Washington, D.C.: Regnery Gateway, 1965).

36. Dunn, *Political Thought*, 245, 261.

37. Dunn, *Political Thought*, 251. For examples, see 251–53.

38. See Dunn, *Political Thought*, 251–53.

39. See John Locke, *Locke on Money*, ed. Patrick Hyde Kelly (New York: Oxford University Press, 1991).

40. An example is Macpherson's reading in *The Political Theory of Possessive Individualism*.

41. The definitive biography is Alexander Altmann, *Moses Mendelssohn: A Biographical Study* (University, Ala.: University of Alabama Press, 1973; rpt., Portland, Oreg.: Littman Library of Jewish Civilization, 1998). Shorter accounts include Alexander Altmann's, "Introduction" to *Jerusalem,* by Moses Mendelssohn, (Hanover, N.H.: University Press of New England for Brandeis University Press, 1983), 3–29; and Alfred Jospe, "Introduction: Prelude to Jewish Modernity," in *Moses Mendelssohn: Selections from His Writings*, ed. Eva Jospe (New York: Viking Press, 1975), 3–46. I have relied on these works in the following summary.

42. Michael L. Morgan, "Liberalism in Mendelssohn's *Jerusalem,*" *History of Political Thought* 10, no. 2 (1989): 283.

43. Moses Mendelssohn, *Jerusalem: Or, On Religious Power and Judaism*, trans. Allan Arkush, with an introduction and commentary by Alexander Altmann (Hanover, N.H.: University Press of New England for Brandeis University Press, 1983), 85.

44. Morgan, "Liberalism in Mendelssohn's *Jerusalem,*" 283.

45. Mendelssohn, *Jerusalem,* 33.

46. Mendelssohn, *Jerusalem,* 38. The work of Locke's to which Mendelssohn is primarily referring is the first *Letter on Toleration*; he did not have *Two Treatises of Government* and many other works available to him. Cf. Altmann's "Commentary" to *Jerusalem*, 158–61.

47. Mendelssohn, *Jerusalem,* 40–41.

48. Mendelssohn, *Jerusalem,* 40–41.

49. Mendelssohn, *Jerusalem,* 41.

50. Mendelssohn, *Jerusalem,* 41, 42, 43.

51. Mendelssohn, *Jerusalem,* 44.

52. Mendelssohn, *Jerusalem,* 43.

53. Mendelssohn, *Jerusalem,* 45. Mendelssohn backs up this view with an argument based on social contracts. A society can exercise only those rights that the contracting members have a right to cede. The church, for Mendelssohn, is a relation between humans and God. Since God has no need of service or benevolence from humans, God does not contract any enforceable duties from us; religion, therefore, only gives the same duties we have toward others "a more exalted *sanction.*" Hence, the church is not the kind of society that can or needs to exert coercive force; in fact, it does not rest on a contract at all, for "there can never be a case of collision [of duty] between the church and its citizens" (*Jerusalem*, 58, 59).

54. Mendelssohn, *Jerusalem,* 44–45.

55. Mendelssohn, *Jerusalem,* 43.

56. See Mendelssohn, *Jerusalem*, 62–63, 136–37 n.

57. Mendelssohn's case for state support of religious teachers is also based on an argument, which need not detain us here, that would deny property rights to churches. Cf. *Jerusalem*, 59–62.

58. Mendelssohn, *Jerusalem*, 63.

59. See Mendelssohn, *Jerusalem*, 138, 67, 102–18.

60. Mendelssohn, *Jerusalem*, 137.

61. Mendelssohn, *Jerusalem*, 138.

62. Mendelssohn, *Jerusalem*, 135.

63. Mendelssohn's central concern is to deny that the church has any legitimate coercive power. For this same reason, he claims that "no human contract whatsoever can give the church a right to goods and property" (*Jerusalem*, 59). The upshot, it may seem, is that churches should voluntarily divest themselves of their goods, or that the state should do so for them. However, this is not the case. The key idea is that the church has no right to property by which it can *enforce* a contract. "What Mendelssohn denied were the claims, the demands, the coercive powers of the church, not the right of the church to accept voluntary contributions and own property." Mendelssohn did not think the lack of such legal rights would harm the mission of the church; he believed that churches could, and perhaps should, operate without owning property or paying ministers. He even based this claim on a rabbinic concept that religious services could not be "bought, hired, or paid for" (Altmann, *Mendelssohn*, 527–28).

64. Mendelssohn, *Jerusalem*, 73.

65. Mendelssohn, *Jerusalem*, 74–75.

66. I must acknowledge that I make such an argument from a certain social location, that is, as a citizen of a liberal order where separation from a church in most cases carries no adverse civil ramifications. From his personal experience, Mendelssohn thought it unrealistic for a religious ban to leave a person unharmed in civil affairs. Cf. Altmann, *Mendelssohn*, 465.

67. Mendelssohn, *Jerusalem*, 135.

68. Morgan, "Liberalism in Mendelssohn's *Jerusalem*," 293.

69. Morgan, "Liberalism in Mendelssohn's *Jerusalem*," 293.

70. Morgan, "Liberalism in Mendelssohn's *Jerusalem*," 294.

71. Morgan, "Liberalism in Mendelssohn's *Jerusalem*," 294.

Chapter 2

The Common Good and Religious Discourse in a Modern Liberal Society

In the previous chapter, I considered three main questions: first, whether the Enlightenment philosophies of John Locke and Moses Mendelssohn relied upon the common good in defining political obligation; second, whether they could consistently do so within a liberal framework; and third, whether religious beliefs and attachments were central to their accounts of the common good. We saw that their liberalisms contained conceptions of the common good, with religion playing a role in unifying society and in identifying rights and responsibilities. Locke focused on Christianity's role in defining the social compact as based on trust and setting limits to political authority. Mendelssohn highlighted the role of rational religion, especially his own understanding of Judaism, in promoting benevolence, tolerance, and the motivation to act for the commonweal. Locke's and Mendelssohn's modes of justification were also explored. If these classically liberal philosophers employed the common good within their political philosophies, does this incorporation show that the common good is compatible with liberalism? It does, as long as there is a conceptual coherence between common good theory and liberal theory. That is, if central tenets of one theory are at odds with central tenets of the other, the project fails. One cannot graft liberalism onto common good theory, nor common good theory onto liberalism, without showing that one is logically compatible with the other. The argument in chapter 1 has suggested this mutual compatibility by showing that liberal institutions promote aspects of the common good, such as tolerance, that benefit religious believers and, conversely, that religious convictions can strengthen citizens' commitment to the common good.

The question for contemporary political philosophy is whether this fit between liberalism and a religious account of the common good can still hold. In our contemporary political culture, we do not enjoy a clear consensus about the role of religion in our public life. As a public we are divided, and as individuals many of us are ambivalent, in naming the benefits and harms that come from the political activism of churches, the religious rhetoric of citizens, and the religious commitments of politicians. For instance, religious conviction is often a scapegoat and an element of distraction in abortion politics, as seen whenever disputants associated with prolife and prochoice advocacy groups excoriate their opponents on the grounds of their perceived religious or nonreligious motives. As explained by James Davison Hunter, the rhetoric often spirals out into sweeping, spurious generalizations: in the 1980s, for example, literature from the People for the American Way "associated the religious right with the neofascist Lyndon LaRouche, the Ku Klux Klan, and the neo-Nazi Aryan Nation," while the Christian Voice in turn called the People for the American Way a "deceitful," "militantly humanistic" organization that labors to "expunge any trace of spiritual influence from the public realm."[1] With such rhetoric, advocacy groups try to rally others to their cause through religious division; the appeals play on the deep ambivalence many Americans feel between their conviction that religion is important to their lives and the common good and their worry that religious influence in politics will compromise the freedom that makes the country strong. The advocacy groups tacitly propose that the United States cannot ensure both a vibrant public role for religion and the institutional separation of church and state: they ask Americans to choose which they care about more.[2]

How is it that liberal democracies have come to this point? If Locke and Mendelssohn represented strong and widely affirmed mediations of liberal politics and religious definitions of the common good, why has the center failed to hold? In the United States, several sociological factors are often proposed as contributors to the decline of a viable religiously grounded liberalism:

1. The increasing religious, ethnic, and cultural pluralism of modern democracies—promoted in part by immigration and the growing confidence of minority groups in claiming their civil rights—has eclipsed the cultural power of homogenous religious traditions (such as mainline Protestantism in the United States).
2. Modern communication technologies have supplanted the cultural unity provided by churches, schools, and civic organizations.
3. The creation of the welfare state, some argue, has displaced religious charities, which were the crucial loci of religion's institutional contributions to the public good.
4. The spread of capitalism, according to some, has encouraged us to base politics on satisfying material preferences. Others claim that the

shift from an agricultural economy to an industrial and then a service economy has caused geographic dislocations, the breakup of extended families, and a concomitant loss of the importance of religious traditions.

5. Advancements in the physical sciences have revolutionized our concepts of the cosmos, making plausible complete explanations of the world without reference to theistic beliefs.

No doubt each of these factors has played a role in the secularization of society and the decline of religion's cultural prominence, but my task here is not a sociological one. I am concerned with philosophical developments within liberalism, particularly with liberalism's account of political society and of religion's designated role within it. Liberalism is a political order, and as such, it has established institutions to ensure liberty, tolerance, individual rights, and social peace. However, liberalism is also undergirded by a moral philosophy, one strand of which, in trying to come to grips with pluralism, worries that views of the good—particularly but not only religious views—would divide society. Thus, some liberal philosophers argue that political institutions should refuse to base decisions upon particular views of the good; these views are salient only in the decisions of individuals, families, and voluntary groups regarding their own activities. They have argued that neither religious doctrines nor any comprehensive views of the good are proper grounds on which to delineate and publicly justify principles of justice and the shape of basic institutions in a modern democratic society. We need to inquire why such arguments are made and whether they have the effect of privatizing religion.

The most important proponent of this liberal approach has been John Rawls. Rawls's theory of justice in a well-ordered society has set the terms of debate in political philosophy for almost three decades. Rawls has generally been taken, by supporters and critics alike, as representative of modern philosophical liberalism. In particular, Rawls represents the variety of liberalism that argues for a sharp separation of political life from particular views of the good, whether religious or moral. In Rawls's view, American society and all modern democracies are marked by permanent moral pluralism; their great need is for all their members to be able to agree on basic political structures. Citizens can come to such agreement only if certain conditions obtain. Chief among these is the requirement that each person debate in terms that others can understand. This condition therefore asks that all exercise care to justify their political acts and positions in terms that others can see as rational and reasonable. Rawls calls this the ideal of "public reason."

The point of the ideal of public reason is that citizens are to conduct their fundamental discussions within the framework of what each regards as a political conception of justice based on values that the others can reasonably be expected to endorse and each is, in good faith, prepared to defend that conception so understood.[3]

Public reason straightforwardly entails that political debate, at least on "constitutional essentials," avoid any appeal to religious or comprehensive moral values. To speak and act on the basis of public reason, while an *ideal* for citizens, is a *duty* for elected officials and especially for judges.

Many of Rawls's critics counter that the ideal of public reason and the political principles that support it either unnecessarily or unjustifiably exclude the possibility of religious believers acting upon their beliefs in the public sphere. For instance, Stephen Carter discerns a general problem when contemporary philosophical liberals propose rules to govern political discourse:

> [These rules] are constructed in a way that requires some members of society to remake themselves before they are allowed to press policy arguments. To suppose that this remaking is desirable, to say nothing of possible, reinforces the vision of religion as an arbitrary and essentially unimportant factor in the makeup of one's personality, as easily shrugged off as a favorite color when, for example, one is called upon to evaluate the views of a politician who never wears it.[4]

Richard Fern specifies this charge: the Rawlsian ideal of a well-ordered society "inherently favors low-flying, minimalist conceptions of the good" and "effectively discourages" conceptions of the good that compete with its own. A result is that "some traditionally important forms of religious belief and practice"—such as resisting secular education and holding one's faith as the highest of all commitments—while "not in and of themselves clearly unjust or irrational, are placed at a serious disadvantage in a Rawlsian society."[5]

Rawls's account of a well-ordered, just, and stable society is far from uncontroversial. Since Rawls ably articulates a representative liberal account of political society, I will explore whether the charges of Carter, Fern, and others hit their mark with him. This chapter, then, will ask whether Rawlsian liberalism does indeed and of necessity privatize religion. In exploring this issue, I will use categories suggested by Paul Weithman to construe the charge that it does. For Weithman, the charge of privatization amounts to the claim that "liberalism fails to regard religious goods as public goods in these two senses. It fails to regard them as either intellectual resources to be drawn on in political argument or as social goods which effect harmony."[6] Rawls denies that he excludes religion from public life but, rather, advances the more modest claim that religion cannot usually be invoked to make certain basic political decisions. Indeed, in some important respects, Rawls's political liberalism is fully open to religious speech and to the active contributions of religious citizens. Yet significant aspects of this liberalism, in particular its ideal of public reason, are based on a narrow and misguided view of these potential contributions.

In the end, political liberalism does unduly constrain religious rhetoric and activity in political life. My argument is not that Rawls privatizes religion, but that he underestimates its potential contributions to public discourse and social unity. To further my argument, I will turn to Michael Sandel, a communitarian critic of Rawls, to see why he thinks Rawls's position inadequate and to explore the positive vision of democratic society he would offer. Though Sandel suggests a more adequate basis for reconciling the common good with democratic and pluralist institutions, he, too, fails to address important questions about the positive contributions religion can make to social unity.

SEARCHING FOR THE COMMON GOOD IN RAWLS'S POLITICAL LIBERALISM

Rawls's Concern for Stability

The essential task for society is to be *just*, *well-ordered*, and *stable*; to describe how society can be so is the aim of all of John Rawls's work. Rawls opens *A Theory of Justice* with the claim, "Justice is the first virtue of social institutions, as truth is of systems of thought."[7] Society, as an association founded on the mutual recognition of binding rules of conduct,[8] has as its highest task the establishment of political justice, which includes respect for basic rights and liberties of all citizens. Thus, stability and order are not final goods but are instrumental to achieving justice. For reasons that should shortly become clear, I will concentrate primarily on Rawls's concern for stability and its implications for religion as a source of social unity. Rawls was concerned in *A Theory of Justice* with the problem of how a pluralistic society can be stable over time. "To ensure stability men must have a sense of justice or a concern for those who would be disadvantaged by their defection, preferably both."[9] Rawls recognizes that in the actual world many people lack this sense of justice. Yet he holds that in a well-ordered society, persons will tend toward having an effective sense of justice, and he argues that his principles of justice are more likely to be stable than other (secular) principles of justice.[10]

The assumption here is that all reasonable persons can agree upon the theory of *justice as fairness*.[11] The concept of justice as fairness is that "the principles of justice for the basic structure of society" are those "that free and rational persons concerned to further their own interests would accept in an initial situation of equality."[12] Rawls tries to avoid potential disagreement arising from religious, moral, and ideological differences by abstracting from people's dearly held viewpoints. His method is to imagine citizens entering into a social contract by which they will decide the basic principles of justice for their society. In a hypothetical situation called the "original position," the parties (who could be any of us) do not know anything about their status in society or what worldviews they hold.[13] Rawls asks us, then, to imagine a situation in which we are placed behind a "veil of ignorance" and thus do not know anything about our race, ethnicity, gender, or religious affiliation, nor do we know these facts about the other parties to the contract. In this situation, what kinds of principles of justice would we all choose? Rawls thinks this method of abstraction helps us to lay aside factors that would skew a system of justice and to choose principles of justice that everyone can accept as fair.[14] But the conception of persons implied in this method has been identified as problematic for two reasons. First, persons are regarded as distinct from their social location and worldviews.

> Even if the oddly disembodied selves who populate the original position are not intended as metaphorical portrayals of our essence as people, they explicitly stand for the claim that, when it comes to thinking about justice, people should be regarded as distinct from their particularity, both their particular natural endowments and social position and their particular conceptions of the good.[15]

Second, if particular viewpoints have no bearing on the construction of justice, then Rawls's method dispenses with any criticisms of justice as fairness that are based on particular views of the good. Such criticisms, from Rawls's perspective, are not posed in the right language.

Since he wrote *A Theory of Justice*, Rawls has modified his approach, in part because of certain aspects of his Kantian theory that he came to acknowledge as problematic. Rawls now thinks it was unrealistic for him to assume that all persons could agree upon the theory of justice as fairness *as though it were a comprehensive philosophical doctrine*. By a comprehensive doctrine, Rawls means an account of human beings and what is of value to them, including nonpolitical goods and values. Rawls thinks he presented justice as fairness as a comprehensive doctrine in *A Theory of Justice* and assumed that all citizens in a well-ordered society would affirm this theory and its principles of justice. Unreasonable pluralism would be overcome when citizens realized that their considered judgments match the theory of justice. But Rawls now recognizes a major difficulty:

A modern democratic society is characterized not simply by a pluralism of comprehensive religious, philosophical, and moral doctrines but by a pluralism of incompatible yet reasonable comprehensive doctrines. No one of these doctrines is affirmed by citizens generally. Nor should one expect that in the foreseeable future one of them, or some other reasonable doctrine, will ever be affirmed by all, or nearly all, citizens.[16]

Given this long-standing pluralism of reasonable yet incompatible doctrines—the normal result of people exercising their reason in a free society—Rawls sees the need to take a different approach, one that can account for and accommodate this pluralism. The result is Rawls's development of the theory of *political liberalism*, wherein justice as fairness is presented as a strictly political conception of justice.[17] Three features make this conception strictly political: its subject is the basic structures and political institutions of society; it does not presuppose any religious or philosophical ("comprehensive") doctrine; and its content is presented as those fundamental ideas that are latent in the political culture of a modern democracy.[18]

The challenge of political liberalism "is to work out a conception of justice for a constitutional democratic regime that the plurality of reasonable doctrines—always a feature of a free democratic regime—might endorse."[19] Now we can see why religious views of the good have become a greater concern for Rawls in *Political Liberalism* than they were in *A Theory of Justice*. An account of justice cannot abstract from them and from every other point of view in a pluralist society. Pluralism as such, including religious pluralism, must be accommodated within a political liberalism. Rawls no longer hopes for liberalism to serve as the comprehensive doctrine on which citizens base their choices. Rather, he must describe how they can join together in political agreements *in spite of* their differing comprehensive doctrines. Religion is something about which people in a pluralist society disagree; citizens hold to different and incompatible religious or irreligious views. Several problems occur when citizens try to debate and decide fundamental political questions with each relying on his or her own religious views.

One problem is achieving mutual understanding. If some citizens are debating in specifically religious terms, other citizens will not be able to understand and appreciate these arguments as political arguments. Political arguments are supposed to be debates about how all citizens structure their lives together; therefore, the discussion has to occur in terms all can understand. Another problem is legitimacy. If the government defends a policy on the basis of a religious doctrine, then citizens who do not share in that belief will be hard-pressed to see the policy as legitimate. Thus, appeals to religious values in political decision making erode the legitimacy of political authority and in turn threaten the stability of society. A final problem is oppression. Since political power is coercive, citizens have the right to have this power wielded over them only for legitimate reasons. These reasons must be political; that is, they must have their basis only in the principles of justice that are appropriate to a pluralist society and that all citizens can affirm based on their common reason.[20]

We sense, then, that Rawls's theory initially leads us away from according any positive role to religion in fostering social unity. In fact, Rawls is distinctly troubled by the divisions that religion can cause in the body politic. For instance, in Rawls's historical reading, the religious strife of the Reformation not only provides the impetus for liberalism's birth, it inaugurates a new mode by which people relate their worldviews to politics. Rawls writes of the religious strife in the sixteenth and seventeenth centuries,

> What is new about this clash is that it introduces into people's conceptions of their good a transcendent element not admitting of compromise. This element forces either mortal conflict moderated only by circumstance and exhaustion, or equal liberty of conscience and freedom of thought. . . . Political liberalism starts by taking to heart that irreconcilable latent conflict.[21]

In Rawls's eyes, religion is always potentially dangerous to social unity, unless society is safeguarded by politically sanctioned tolerance and by certain ideals and constraints placed on religious language and action. Like Rawls, I affirm the importance of a climate of toleration, but I argue against the high standards to which Rawls holds religious believers in their political expressions. To prepare my argument, I need to explore Rawls's well-ordered society and its ideal of political deliberation.

Social Unity Without Moral and Religious Doctrines

Three main ideas of political liberalism guide the nature and scope of political debate in a Rawlsian well-ordered society: the *overlapping consensus*, the *priority of right*, and *public reason*. The overlapping consensus refers to the shared agreement on the basic structure of society and its principles of justice among citizens who otherwise disagree on their religious, moral, and philosophical doctrines. How is such agreement possible? Rawls's answer has two parts. The first is the argument that "the values of the political [domain] are very great values and hence not easily overridden."[22] These values ground the basic structures of political life, define basic rights and liberties, and guide the nature of public debate. Since these principles guide our public life and make it possible for us to get along as well as to flourish individually, we would not modify them except for reasons that refer to essential constitutional and political matters and that all citizens can understand and affirm. In short, the overlapping consensus is grounded by the principle of legitimacy.

The second part of Rawls's answer to how political agreement is possible points to the history of religion and philosophy. First he appeals to religious strife during the Reformation to bolster the claim that religion tends to intolerance, then he points to the historical benefits of religious pluralism to defend the overlapping consensus.[23] So when various denominations or religious confessions vie for control of political institutions, civil unrest is inevitable; yet when they agree to live together under a constitutional order, stability ensues. And the way to move toward stability is for citizens to affirm a political conception of justice from within their own doctrines. "It is left to citizens individually—as part of liberty of conscience—to settle how they think the values of the political domain are related to other values in their comprehensive doctrine."[24]

Rawls's picture of citizens coming to agreement in an overlapping consensus while still holding to diverse comprehensive doctrines is attractive in several ways. His goal is worthy: it is for members of a pluralistic society to agree on the basic ordering of their life together. His picture looks realistic—for citizens obviously do not and will not come to share one common worldview—yet it aims for more than a lowest common denominator, for it provides a framework for agreement on a conception of justice and an account of basic needs. Ultimately, Rawls hopes his theory binds us closer together; he even describes one of his principles of justice (the difference principle) as an expression of civic fraternity.[25]

Despite these attractive qualities, the overlapping consensus is a problematic ideal. First, while such a consensus seems feasible, it is in fact based upon an overly sanguine picture of social agreement about justice. As Michael Sandel has asserted, "Political liberalism must assume not only that the exercise of human reason under conditions of freedom will produce disagreements about the good life, but also that . . . [it] will *not* produce disagreements about justice." But this assumption is unwarranted, for "modern democratic societies are teeming with disagreements about justice."[26] The problem here is not that Rawls thinks it possible to achieve a workable consensus about justice in a pluralist society, but that he rules out the possibility that substantive public discussion about matters of the good could also lead to a workable consensus. Indeed, debates and agreements about justice often depend upon tacit and deep-seated cultural agreements upon matters of the good such as duties, values, and virtues.

Along these lines, Annette Baier argues that rights are parasitic upon other, less individualist moral concepts:

> Rights are only the tip of the moral iceberg, supported by the responsibilities that we cooperatively discharge and by the individual responsibilities that we

recognize, including responsibilities to cooperate, in order to maintain such common goods as civilized speech and civilized ways of settling disputes. For it takes more than rights to settle disputes about rights.[27]

If this view is correct, then liberalism must pay more attention to citizens' comprehensive doctrines and the ways they support or challenge the overlapping consensus. When debates about justice and rights come to an impasse, the only way through may be to broaden the scope of the public conversation rather than narrow it. I have in mind here, among other things, questions about who belongs to the political community—questions about the political status of animals, the natural environment, and human fetuses. Legal theorist Kent Greenawalt argues that since shared premises of justice are incapable of resolving political questions, a good liberal citizen and even a legislator can properly rely on his or her religious convictions to decide how far such beings belong to the political community and deserve protection. Greenawalt's argument entails that Rawls's overlapping consensus is insufficient for resolving many political questions.

> If the reigning theory of justice does not itself resolve the borderlines of status, it is patently false that every political issue, or every political issue involving important claims of *justice among full human beings,* can be dealt with, as Rawls seems to suppose, by derivations from the basic principles of justice plus empirical knowledge and common sense. Some very important political issues will require reference to the troublesome problems of status. If social agreement *does not exist about these,* even a shared understanding about justice will be incapable of yielding answers to these political issues.[28]

The second problem is that the overlapping consensus overtaxes some citizens. Critics like Carter and Fern argue that consensus is purchased at the price of requiring a split in citizens between the comprehensive moral and religious views that inform their lives and the purely political values that they must bring to bear in the public domain. Rawls thinks he is avoiding such a split by leaving the public domain purely political and asking citizens to validate the consensus from within their own worldviews. For political liberalism, the relation is a one-way street: citizens should affirm the consensus, or they will be considered unreasonable. In communal liberalism, by contrast, the connections between individuals' comprehensive doctrines and the public consensus on justice are multifarious. Beyond affirming the consensus as it stands, citizens can effectively appeal to their fellows using particular moral and religious claims. These claims may refer to their own beliefs, or they may connect one of their beliefs to a constitutional, historical, or philosophical reason. Citizens might also appeal to the religious and moral beliefs of those whom they seek to convince, either challenging another to act consistently within her own doctrinal view or seeking to modify her views by other arguments. Religious citizens might more effectively contribute to a public consensus on particular issues by building coalitions that at first bypass the overlapping consensus, as suggested by David Novak: "Jews and Christians must first be able to talk to each other *before* they can talk to the secular world, which is further removed from both of them. Discourse must begin with those whose traditions overlap the most."[29]

Seeing that the relationships among particular worldviews and the public domain are complex and fluid, I would modify Rawls's idea of the overlapping consensus by holding citizens not to a standard of *reasonableness*, but to one of *intelligibility*. The criterion for joining the public discourse should be that one strives to make his views intelligible to others. Ultimately, people will affirm only views that they find reasonable, but this does not justify Rawls's construction of the consensus in terms of reasonableness. Making one's position intelligible is the first step on the path to making it persuasive, so certainly Rawls's own standard includes mine; however, I find there are instances when his standard asks too much of citizens deliberating questions of fundamental justice. An intelligibility standard broadens the scope of public conversation and provides greater opportunities for citizens to shape the public conception of justice. I should stress that neither my standard of intelligibility nor Rawls's standard of reasonableness is meant to gag citizens whose rhetoric is highly idiosyncratic or even bizarre, unless their speech or actions pose an immediate threat to public order or the rights of others. Both Rawls and I are identifying standards of good citizenship. However, these standards also have implications for the kind of rhetoric and appeals that are allowable from public officials. When we come to the process for deciding policies, Rawls's approach will have more deleterious effects than are evident now. But first we must consider the significant place he provides in his liberalism for ideas of the good.

Rawls's Good Society: The Priority of Right Modified

The idea of an overlapping consensus raises questions about the content of the political values that are its locus and why they should be overriding. We come then to political liberalism's second main idea, the priority of right over the good. This idea means that principles of justice and human rights (these are the content of "the right") have a higher political and legal standing than claims based on particular moral or religious doctrines of a good and complete human life (the content of "the good"). Rawls defines a conception of right as "a set of principles, general in form and universal in application, that is to be publicly recognized as a final court of appeal for ordering the conflicting claims of moral persons."[30] In political and legal matters, principles of right override principles of good whenever the two conflict. This claim has been taken by many to mean that the state must be *neutral* regarding competing conceptions of the good, that is, "the liberal state must act to protect rights that people have to pursue and revise their conceptions of the good, and so must rule out any conceptions of the good whose pursuit would violate those rights; but beyond this the state must always refrain from acting on the basis that one conception is more valuable than another."[31] This stance can also be termed *antiperfectionism*, a view that the state should deliberately ignore the highest ideals by which people try to live their lives.

Communitarians have criticized Rawls heavily on the topic of this kind of neutrality.

> The communitarian attack has been devoted to suggesting that this claim to neutrality is an illusion; such a liberal state, by upholding a framework of rights and refraining from any further action, is in effect presupposing the validity of a distinctively liberal conception of the good. . . . [T]he exclusion of conceptions of the good from the domain of politics itself presupposes a particular conception of the good.[32]

Whether or not Rawls was committed to this view of neutrality in *A Theory of Justice* (and there are competing interpretations on this score), he moves in *Political Liberalism* to clarify that principles of good do play an important role in justice as fairness. In a political conception of justice, principles of right and good are complementary: "no conception of justice can draw entirely upon one or the other, but must combine them in a definite way."[33] What Rawls makes clear in his new political liberalism is that the theory of justice as fairness makes use of five ideas of the good: goodness as rationality, primary goods, permissible conceptions of the good, political virtues, and the good of political society.[34] The first two together compose Rawls's original thin theory of the good: they claim that citizens will find it good to privilege the fulfillment of rational desire in their account of justice and will agree that they all have certain needs that society should meet.[35] "Taken together, these two ideas provide content for the deliberations that take place in the original position; they give those deliberating behind the veil of ignorance something to deliberate about."[36]

The idea of permissible conceptions of the good indicates that some conceptions of the good are indeed constrained by principles of right. Here Rawls responds to the charge that this theory is not neutral (a term he would reject as misleading) by distinguishing different senses of neutrality. Political liberalism is not procedurally neutral, because its principles of justice are substantive. Neither is it neutral in effect or outcome, for this is impossible. Political liberalism is neutral only in its aim, and even here Rawls does not mean that the state should allow anyone to advance any conception of good at all, nor that it should try to avoid exerting any influence over citizens' choices, but just that "the state is not to do anything intended to favor or promote any particular comprehensive doctrine rather than another, or to give greater assistance to those who pursue it."[37]

Having acknowledged that the liberal state may properly influence its citizens, Rawls finds a role for a fourth idea of the good, that of political virtues. Political liberalism "may still affirm the superiority of certain forms of moral character and encourage certain moral virtues" that are important for sustaining society, such as civility, tolerance, cooperation, reasonableness, and a sense of fairness.[38] If a constitutional government strengthens these virtues and forbids practices that undermine them, it does not thereby become a perfectionist state, according to Rawls.

Fifth and finally, justice as fairness includes the idea that citizens experience political society as a good. The well-ordered society is, first of all, a good for individuals. In it, they experience as a good the exercise of their moral powers, that is, their capacity for a sense of justice and for a conception of the good. Political society also secures for citizens "the good of justice and the social bases of their mutual self-respect." Second, a well-ordered society is experienced as a cooperative good. "For whenever there is a shared final end, an end that requires the cooperation of many to achieve, the good realized is social: it is realized through citizens' joint activity in mutual dependence on appropriate actions being taken by others."[39] Citizens experience their participation in a just and democratic society as a corporate achievement of which they can be proud.

In sum, Rawls has significantly recast the priority of right to reveal political liberalism's commitment to a common good. The recast priority of right is the strongest aspect of his political liberalism. To Stephen Mulhall and Adam Swift, these ideas of the good in political liberalism (especially the fourth and fifth) "reveal Rawls to be committed to the idea that a political society can itself be an intrinsic rather than a merely instrumental good for citizens both as individuals and as a corporate body; they show that Rawls has a significant conception of a political community and of goods to be achieved in common that cannot be achieved alone."[40] Rawls argues that liberalism provides a common ground for social and political cooperation. Principles of justice act in part as constraints that make cooperation possible and the political process fair for all. Rawls goes to some pains to argue that such constraints are not meant to hinder citizens from living by their own lights; thus he responds to the communitarian charge that liberalism undermines the distinctive forms of life enjoyed by subcommunities within society. More strongly, he holds that liberal society can be thought of and experienced as a good; thus he responds to the communitarian criticism that liberalism lacks a common good. However, there are limits on the way common goods are identified and restrictions on the way political society is experienced as a good: political society may pursue common goods only to the extent that these are goods identified by a purely political process. Rawls is, in effect, trying to hold together the good society and the just society within the framework of political liberalism.

This goal parallels my own, which is to hold together the good and the just society through the framework of the common good. If my framework is to be found preferable to Rawls's as a political conception for a pluralist society, then it should be at least as open and fair as his. That is, the political process of the common good must be able to facilitate widespread participation and cooperation among the citizens of a pluralist society; and it must be fair to all members of society, including those who find it essential to their self-understandings to act publicly upon their religious beliefs. I will claim that a politics of the common good is superior to political liberalism on these counts. Before making that case, I have to show how Rawlsian liberalism falls short of these standards in the domain of public debate. This returns us to the ideal of public reason, the third main idea of his theory.

Political Liberalism's Strictures on Religious Argument

The Character and Use of Public Reason

In order to attain an overlapping consensus, citizens must agree on a political ordering of society, and they must agree to disagree about their comprehensive doctrines and the different values by which they live. Though the right is prior to the good in the political realm, society can pursue common goods, as long as they can truly be appreciated as good by all citizens. Hence, the first two ideas of political liberalism lead to a third—the idea that political discourse and decision making should be carried out on the basis of public reason. Public reason refers to the way citizens in a democratic society should explain, defend, and promote their political views: by employing reasons that are accessible to all reasonable fellow citizens and that do not rely upon comprehensive doctrines. This reason is public in three ways, says Rawls:

> as the reason of citizens as such, it is the reason of the public; its subject is the good of the public and matters of fundamental justice; and its nature and content is public, being given by the ideals and principles expressed by society's conception of political justice, and conducted open to view on that basis.[41]

Public reason has to be understood in context; its scope is narrowed in two ways. First, "the limits imposed by public reason do not apply to all political questions but only to those involving what we may call 'constitutional essentials' and questions of basic justice."[42] Second, neither do its limits apply "to our personal deliberations and reflections about political questions, or to the reasoning about them by members of associations such as churches and universities."[43] These associations compose what Rawls calls the "background culture" upon which a political society builds. Many nonpublic reasons thrive there, and properly so. However, in the political realm, elected officials and especially judges are held to the standards of public reason, as are citizens when they engage in political advocacy and voting. But Rawls points out that even here public reason is an ideal of democratic citizenship rather than a matter of law. Only in a few areas do the standards of public reason carry overriding legal weight: for instance, the Supreme Court has invalidated certain laws affecting public education and the use of public space when these laws have been enacted for nonsecular reasons or had the effect of advancing religion.[44] In such cases, the Court is employing public reason in making its decision, and it is holding public institutions to a standard of public reason in their operations.[45]

Rawls does not ascribe a certain format or set of characteristics to public reason, but he does indicate conditions of objectivity that characterize reasoning and argument within a political conception of justice. "To say that a political conviction is objective is to say that there are reasons, specified by a reasonable and mutually recognizable political conception . . . sufficient to convince all reasonable persons that it is reasonable."[46] But what constitutes reasonableness? Rawls does not have any foundational answer to this question, nor does he think we can provide one within political liberalism. But he does not thereby admit that his argument is a vicious circle. Rather, he is articulating a process for putting together a system of justice, a process he calls "political construction," in which we refine our understanding of fundamental democratic principles as we distill them from our political culture and apply them back to that culture.[47] The construction of a system of justice does not proceed purely from abstract principle or purely from social experience, but these two parts complement and correct each other; practical reason holds both together. So we might say that reasonableness is the use of practical reason in such a way that its judgments accord with the fundamental ideas of our political culture. Rawls proceeds in this way so that the political conception of justice that emerges is freestanding, or else he gets into a metaphysical morass. He thinks, then, that the circularity of political construction is virtuous, not vicious.

The use of public reason is important to Rawls because of his concern for stability. To achieve a well-ordered society over time, his political liberalism takes account of three "facts." The first, which we have already seen, is the "fact of pluralism," which is that modern democracies are characterized by a permanent pluralism of incompatible, yet not unreasonable, comprehensive doctrines. A second, related fact is the "fact of oppression," which is that a modern society could not organize itself around a shared comprehensive doctrine without an oppressive exercise of state power.[48] The third fact is that "an enduring and secure democratic regime, one not divided into contending doctrinal divisions and hostile social classes, must be willingly and freely supported by at least a substantial majority of its politically active citizens."[49]

Given this interpretation of the nature of modern democracies, Rawls thinks it essential that all citizens be able to understand the reasoning behind political decisions and policies and that they be able to affirm these within a political conception of justice. This claim is a crucial part of political liberalism: political reasons must be fully public; they must be understandable for all citizens. Rawls connects this "full publicity condition" to the liberal principle of legitimacy: "our exercise of political power is proper and hence justifiable only when it is exercised in accordance with a constitution the essentials of which all citizens may reasonably be expected to endorse in the light of principles and ideals acceptable to them as reasonable and rational."[50] Mulhall and Swift locate the liberal essence of Rawls's theory here: "At the heart of his approach is an avowedly liberal conception of the political relationship and of what makes a regime legitimate: political power is coercive, and its exercise must, if it is to respect citizens as free and equal, be publicly justifiable to them."[51]

The Constraints on Comprehensive Doctrines

Rawls hopes to achieve two grand aims by placing the full publicity condition on the political process. The first is that citizens' fundamental interests will be protected. Rawls would have us consider what happens if state decisions are enacted for reasons based on the comprehensive doctrines of lawmakers. If, for example, the government enacts a policy of restricting abortions for Christian reasons, it would follow that Jews and Muslims, among others, would have good reason to fear the passage of various other laws on the basis of Christian doctrines. Their religious liberty would be threatened. The second aim Rawls hopes to achieve is to provide a framework for political discussion and for civil disagreement.

> The point of the ideal of public reason is that citizens are to conduct their fundamental discussions within the framework of what each regards as a political conception of justice based on values that the others can reasonably be

expected to endorse and each is, in good faith, prepared to defend that conception so understood. This means that each of us must have, and be ready to explain, a criterion of what principles and guidelines we think other citizens (who are also free and equal) may reasonably be expected to endorse along with us. . . .

Of course, we may find that actually others fail to endorse the principles and guidelines our criterion selects. That is to be expected. The idea is that we have a criterion and this alone already imposes very considerable discipline on public discussion.[52]

Rawls says that comprehensive doctrines can contribute to public justification in an indirect way. He criticizes an "exclusive view" that would never allow citizens to explain their political positions in terms of their comprehensive doctrines. Rather, political liberalism is committed to an inclusive view, "allowing citizens, in certain situations, to present what they regard as the basis of political values rooted in their comprehensive doctrine, provided they do this in ways that strengthen the ideal of public reason itself."[53] The inclusive view is supported because democratic societies will fall short of the ideal case, wherein political values are widely shared and citizens conduct their discourse in terms of public reason. In one kind of case, various groups and factions will support different interpretations or applications of the principles of justice. Rawls uses the example of religious groups contesting the proper relation of the government to private religious schools, wherein each bloc affirms its own respect for constitutional principles and values, but questions its opponents' commitment to the same. Here nonpublic reason may play a helpful role. "One way this doubt might be put to rest is for the leaders of the opposing groups to present in the public forum how their comprehensive doctrines do indeed affirm those [fundamental political] values. . . . [T]heir doing so may help to show that the overlapping consensus is not a mere modus vivendi."[54] Such expressions of nonpublic reasons simply go to show how individuals or groups are supporting the overlapping consensus from within their doctrines, thus establishing their good faith in the political process and contributing (Rawls hopes) to social stability.

Nonpublic reasons may play a leading role in a second kind of case mentioned by Rawls, namely, "when a society is not well ordered and there is a profound division over constitutional essentials":

Consider the abolitionists who argued against the antebellum South that its institution of slavery was contrary to God's law. Recall that the abolitionists agitated for the immediate, uncompensated, and universal emancipation of the slaves as early as the 1830s, and did so, I assume, basing their arguments on religious grounds. In this case the nonpublic reason supported the clear conclusions of public reason. The same is true of the civil rights movement

led by Martin Luther King, Jr., except that King could appeal—as the abolitionists could not—to the political values expressed in the Constitution correctly understood.[55]

Though Rawls finds that these religious arguments "supported the clear
conclusions of public reason," I do not see how these conclusions were
clear, except in retrospect. In these cases, large segments of society were
perverting public reason, twisting it to justify the denial of basic rights to
African Americans. By their use of religious language, the abolitionists
and King were not only able to give "sufficient strength" to their appeal,[56]
as though rhetorical effectiveness were the main consideration; they were
able to claim that slavery and segregation were morally unacceptable and,
therefore, politically unacceptable. Moreover, they tried to shake Christians from their political complacency on religious grounds.

Rawls, for his part, would allow citizens to support political policies
with language based in religious and other *reasonable* comprehensive doctrines but with the proviso that they eventually translate that support into
the terms of public reason and political justice.[57] In other words, using
nonpublic reason in such cases is a temporary and remedial measure that
must ultimately bolster public reason. Even with this proviso, public reason remains flawed in two ways. First, Rawls sees these cases as excep-
tional: only in rare instances does the political exercise of nonpublic reason inspire citizens to support the democratic process and the overlapping
consensus. Except in these cases, the political use of nonpublic reasoning
threatens to undermine stability. Though his concern about social instabil-
ity is well taken, Rawls has not considered the social alienation that the
constraints of public reason might cause or, more positively, the enhanced
commitment to the common good that would result when citizens are encouraged to speak from their different comprehensive doctrines, including
religious ones, on a more regular basis. A more generous public use of
religious and moral reasoning need not threaten social harmony and can
even enhance it in the long run.

Neither does such reasoning fail to offer intellectual resources to the
public debate. On this count, we see public reason's second flaw: it stacks
the deck against those who would speak from their comprehensive doctrines, constraining them, before they speak, with the condition that their
arguments should be reasonable. To see that Rawls does institute this
constraint of prior reasonableness, consider the following restatement of
Rawls's chain of reasoning in favor of the inclusive view. First, when a
democratic society is in some way substantially unjust, political argument
based on nonpublic reasons may be used to clarify, draw attention to, and
urge support for constitutional values. Second, nonpublic reasons are valid
because public reason has broken down. We may assume public reason

has broken down, for if the majority of citizens and/or the relevant political powers were exercising public reason properly, they would not support an unjust political arrangement. Finally, political rhetoric based on comprehensive doctrines thus achieves a reorientation of other citizens' conceptions of justice: either those supporting the unjust arrangement come to see that they have been misinterpreting or misapplying principles of justice, or other previously complacent citizens become convinced that the unjust arrangement cannot endure and that they can no longer remain silent if they and their society are to be just.

If political argument based on comprehensive doctrines can achieve this end, such argument becomes vitally important to the health of a just society. Rawls's inclusive view entails that we cannot always count on public reason, at least as employed by fallible human beings. And if this is so, then we cannot decide ahead of time what kind of reorientation nonpublic reasons might effect on public reason and the content of justice. *But the ideal of public reason places a constraint of prior reasonableness on political argument from comprehensive doctrines, such that their potential to effect such changes is hampered.*

The Failure of Public Reason

Consider Rawls's treatment in *Political Liberalism* of abortion as a political issue. Although there are several important political values at stake in this issue, three are particularly salient for him: due respect for human life, the social need for reproduction and the institution of the family, and the equality of women. Rawls writes:

> Now I believe any reasonable balance of these three values will give a woman a duly qualified right to decide whether or not to end her pregnancy during the first trimester. The reason for this is that at this early stage of pregnancy the political value of the equality of women is overriding, and this right is required to give it some substance and force.[58]

I do not deny that such a right may be reasonable, politically acceptable, and even just, but I question how Rawls uses this example to prejudge certain comprehensive doctrines:

> Any comprehensive doctrine that leads to a balance of political values excluding that duly qualified right in the first trimester is to that extent unreasonable; and depending on details of its formulation, it may also be cruel and oppressive; for example, if it denied the right altogether except in the case of rape and incest.[59]

Now remember what Rawls has said about slavery and Jim Crow laws: these were unjust, even though the majority of citizens and the major institutions of society in former times believed these arrangements to be just and founded on public reason (or founded on particular reasons, especially Christian reasons, that were widely shared in society). In hindsight, we would consider it completely inappropriate for a supporter of slavery to say that a reasonable balance of political values supports the denial of rights to some human beings and that any comprehensive doctrine suggesting otherwise is unreasonable. Yet this seems an exact parallel of Rawls's claim. I am not trying to lend force to my argument by equating slavery and the practice of abortion. My point is this: In both cases, members of religious groups challenged the political status quo by marshaling arguments from their comprehensive doctrines. In the former case, we consider it fortunate that the abolitionists were able to help stir society's conscience and reorient its conception of political justice. In the latter case, we do not know how history will judge the efforts of religious opponents of abortion, but it is clear that if the political status quo represents a distortion of political justice and public reasoning, *we do not know it now*. Thus, if it is possible that particular religious and moral arguments can serve to reorient a democratic society toward more just arrangements, then we cannot rule out the possible contributions of such rhetoric on the ground of unreasonableness.

If he were to respond to my arguments, Rawls would likely disagree with my claim that in cases of social injustice, public reason has broken down. Yet I think he would be hard-pressed to give a plausible account of what happens in such situations, for he could take one of two tacks, both of which are problematic. On the one hand, he could make public reason an ideal that transcends cultural and historical constraints. This way, the ideal can be used to criticize unjust policies in any place and time. But Rawls denies that he can speak with such compass, and it would break the bounds of political liberalism to do so. On the other hand, he could affirm that the political conception of justice, which is the content of public reason, is specific to Western democracies. Yet even this context-specific approach is problematic, for the public's understanding of justice is subject to revision and development. For instance, Rawls says that public reason reflects constitutional values. But we know that the Constitution specifically allowed slavery—even though many of it framers were uncomfortable with this institution and thought (or hoped) that it would die out over time. This example shows that public reason, as it is expressed at any one time in the American political process, can be unclear, inadequate, or distorted.[60]

My analysis also challenges Rawls's rather sharp distinction of public reason from the background culture. Political arguments, decisions, and actions are always made and taken against a public culture that is influenced in important ways by religious, moral, and cultural beliefs. It is not an accurate description of the abolitionists to imply that they appealed to a freestanding ideal of public reason *through* Christian rhetoric; rather, they appealed to a set of *public* values that they believed were rather widely shared but that were at the same time eclipsed by an unjust social practice. The values-laden discourse employed by the abolitionists had several characteristics: it was historically grounded, using language that appealed to constitutional values; it was rationalist in its appeal to law, consistency, and natural law principles of human rights; and it was suffused with Christian language and images. All the same is true of the language of values spoken by Dr. King and his fellow civil rights activists.

Rawls has not demonstrated that political questions should be argued solely on the basis of public reason.[61] He does not have a good case for excluding nonpublic reasons, both because such reasons may be far more essential to social justice and social unity than he assumes and because public reason cannot be neatly dissected from the wider "background" culture. As citizens put forward their views concerning public issues, it is less important to fit these views into a terminology that liberals deem "reasonable" than to make their ideas intelligible to their fellow citizens. When the goal of public discourse is intelligibility, citizens and institutions can draw upon a wide array of strategies for building coalitions and persuading their fellow citizens. They will also feel more invested in political decisions that emerge from this process. Since the Rawlsian framework for political discourse is not adequate to these tasks, can we imagine a framework for public discussion that allows and even encourages consideration of the common good while protecting citizens' freedom to dissent and follow their own lights? This question frames the next part of the chapter.

REFORMING LIBERALISM: SANDEL'S COMMUNITARIAN POLITICS

Thus far, I have argued that Rawlsian liberalism privatizes religion to this extent: It would have citizens and officials set aside their religious (and comprehensive moral) doctrines in debating and deciding matters of political justice. In doing so, this liberalism removes from the public arena potentially important resources for guiding political reasoning and promoting the common good. Those resources comprise both the *intellectual capital* that religious traditions can bring into the public's discernment of the meaning of justice and the *social goods* by which religious institutions can promote greater harmony in society. I further describe these resources later, but we have gotten an initial sense of them in considering religious contributions to the abolitionist and civil rights movements. In fairness to Rawls, it must once again be noted that he is not excluding religious citizens and institutions from entering the public square or from addressing most political questions in religious terms; nor is he denying that religions as voluntary institutions can be positive forces in public life. However, he is saying that on questions of fundamental justice, citizens should ideally govern their speech so as to present their reasons for their political choices in secular terms. And he is saying that nonpublic reasons such as these are found in religious traditions offer nothing to political deliberations that cannot in principle be found via public reason. On these points, Rawls errs.

The problems can be most clearly seen in those cases where public reason has, in my words, broken down—especially then do the members of a pluralist society need to listen to any and all sources of wisdom as they struggle to rethink the requirements of justice. I have argued that the domain of public arguments based on citizens' religious and particular moral views is not nearly as separate from the public consensus about justice as Rawls thinks. Building social consensus on matters of justice and the common good is a difficult but feasible task, which is not helped, but rather hindered, by setting aside arguments that arise from citizens' moral and religious views. I turn to a representative communitarian, Michael J. Sandel, to see if he can cogently defend a principled role for religion in the political life of a liberal democracy.[62]

Liberalism's Flawed Foundations

In his first major work, *Liberalism and the Limits of Justice* (1982), Sandel located Rawls, as I have, in the tradition of philosophical liberalism reaching back to Immanuel Kant. Kantian liberalism, according to Sandel, "is above all a theory about justice, and in particular a theory about the primacy of justice among moral and political ideals":

> Its core thesis can be stated as follows: society, being composed of a plurality of persons, each with his own aims, interests, and conceptions of the good, is best arranged when it is governed by principles that do not *themselves* presuppose any particular conception of the good; what justifies these regulative principles above all is not that they maximize the social welfare or otherwise promote the good, but rather that they conform to the concept of *right*, a moral category given prior to the good and independent of it.[63]

We have seen that Rawls does argue for the priority of right over the good, though he also identifies five ideas of the good operative within political liberalism. Rawls's revisions do not, in Sandel's view, remove the problems with the priority of right.[64] Sandel maintains that, in order for its conception of justice to hold, modern Kantian liberalism requires that we conceive of ourselves as "stand[ing] to our circumstance always at a certain distance, conditioned to be sure, but part of us always antecedent to any conditions."[65] In other words, this liberalism does not and cannot allow us to view ourselves as socially constituted in a strong sense, each of us having a sense of self, an identity, that has been profoundly shaped by the stories and distinctive activities of our communities. Otherwise, the Kantian liberal would have to admit that justice cannot always be primary, for having this strong sense of how our very identities are bound up with the well-being of our community, we would understand that there are many aspects of social and political life where justice must take second place to considerations of the common good.

So liberalism advances a conception of the person who chooses, rather than discovers, his or her identity and who possesses fundamental rights that are not dependent on the community's understanding of what it means to belong to the community. Sandel holds that this conception is true neither sociologically nor philosophically; it matches neither the reality of how we live our lives nor our considered reflection on what it means to be a person. In most of his work, he employs only the philosophical approach, and Rawls is frequently his target. Sandel investigates the original position for an avenue into his critique. Recall that the *original position* is Rawls's term for a hypothetical situation for a social contract in which the parties do not know anything about their individual characteristics and their particular places in society. In brief, he reads Rawls as follows: Rawls assumes that the parties to the original position are mutually disinterested in each other. Rawls considers this a weaker assumption than presuming that they are mutually benevolent. That is, it is easier for us to imagine the parties being disinterested, and it does not seem to require as much of them as benevolence would (hypothetical though they are). If the parties to the original position can work out principles of justice that are acceptable to us, even though they take no interest in each other, then these principles will be more secure because they will not be based on lofty ideals smuggled into the original bargaining procedure.[66]

For Sandel, this reasoning reflects Rawls's assumptions about human nature—assumptions Sandel contests. If we reflect for a moment, it is not more demanding for us to assume the parties are mutually benevolent. And if Rawls means that it is more realistic to assume disinterest, then he is bringing empirical considerations into the original position that he intended to leave out.[67] Rawls's original position produces a philosophical anthropology, not simply a moral theory about justice. In this anthropology, Rawls privileges the fact of human distinctness over the fact that our ends can coincide with the ends of others.[68] The assumption of mutual disinterest among the parties to the original position betrays a view of human selves who enter society already individuated, which means that their personally chosen needs and goals are more determinative of their self-understanding than any needs and goals given by society or its sub-communities.

Correlative to this assumption, according to Sandel, is a denial that community can ever be constitutive of a person's identity and self-understanding. "On Rawls' view, a sense of community describes a possible aim of antecedently individuated selves, not an ingredient or constituent of their identity as such." This Kantian liberal view has important consequences for politics:

> As a person's values and ends are always attributes and never constituents of the self, so a sense of community is only an attribute and never a constituent of a well-ordered society. As the self is prior to the aims it affirms, so a well-ordered society, defined by justice, is prior to the aims—communitarian and otherwise—its members may profess. This is the sense, both moral and epistemological, in which justice is the first virtue of social institutions.[69]

Problems in Sandel's Account of the Situated Self

I have only briefly described some of Sandel's charges. The success of his critique will depend in part on the cogency of the alternative account of person and society he offers. So now I will examine what Sandel means by *a sense of community* and why he thinks constitutive attachment to community is not merely a good thing, but an essential fact of reality. Sandel does not merely recommend that we see ourselves as situated in communities; he argues that, like it or not, we cannot escape the moral fact that we are so situated.

> Certain of our roles are partly constitutive of the persons we are—as citizens of a country, as members of a movement, or partisans of a cause. But if we are partly defined by the communities we inhabit, then we must also be implicated in the purposes and ends characteristic of those communities. . . . Open-ended though it may be, the story of my life is always embedded in the story of those communities from which I derive my identity—whether family or city, people or nation, party or cause. In the communitarian view, these stories make a moral difference, not only a psychological one. They situate us in the world and give our lives their moral particularity.[70]

Sandel bolsters his claim that human selves are socially situated with the metaphysical argument that an intersubjective understanding of the self is implied in some of Rawls's theory.[71] In this argument, Sandel tries to show that philosophical liberals such as Rawls need to rely upon a more inter-subjective, socially situated notion of the human person than they are willing to admit.[72] If liberal philosophers need this moral anthropology to undergird liberal values and institutions, then citizens need it all the more if they believe that liberal institutions have barred considerations of the common good from the political process.

For Sandel, the remedy for the citizenry's alienation from politics and community life is not simply to append communitarian values to liberalism, but fundamentally to question the rights-based ethic and its underlying anthropology.

> A further clue to our condition can be located in the vision of the unencumbered self that animates the liberal ethic. It is a striking feature of the welfare state that it offers a powerful promise of individual rights and also demands of its citizens a high measure of mutual engagement. But the self-image cannot sustain the engagement. As bearers of rights, where rights are trumps, we think of ourselves as freely choosing, individual selves, unbound by obligations antecedent to rights, or to the agreements we make. And yet, as citizens of the procedural republic that secures these rights, we find ourselves implicated willy-nilly in a formidable array of dependencies and expectations we did not choose and increasingly reject.[73]

Sandel holds that a constitutive conception of community will address the frustration and anomie of citizens who have been disappointed by the liberal vision. To the liberal claim that a politics of the common good often leads to intolerance and prejudice,

> communitarians reply that intolerance flourishes most where forms of life are dislocated, roots unsettled, traditions undone. In our day the totalitarian impulse has sprung less from the convictions of confidently situated selves than from the confusions of atomized, dislocated, frustrated selves, at sea in a world where common meanings have lost their force.[74]

Such a claim requires good historical or sociological evidence. Sandel, however, does not provide such, and this leaves him open to criticism. Amy Gutmann commented in 1985:

> If Sandel is arguing that when members of a society have settled roots and established traditions, they will tolerate the speech, religion, sexual, and associational preferences of minorities, then history simply does not support his optimism. A great deal of intolerance has come from societies of selves so "confidently situated" that they were sure repression would serve a higher cause. The common good of the Puritans of seventeenth-century Salem commanded them to hunt witches; the common good of the Moral Majority of the twentieth century commands them not to tolerate homosexuals. The enforce-

ment of liberal rights, not the absence of settled community, stands between
the Moral Majority and the contemporary equivalent of witch hunting.[75]

Gutmann hit upon one of Sandel's vulnerable points—his equivocal account of constitutive community. Specifically, Sandel is not clear about the
strength of constitutive attachments. Are persons *radically* situated; that is,
are they completely dependent on the way their social context defines their
selfhood, and have they little or no freedom to choose their own values?
Sandel never makes such a claim, nor does he want to. A radically situated
subject would have no liberty at all, or liberty only as a function of living
according to communal values and rules. This communitarianism would
be fascist or communist or highly traditionalist. But if Sandel denies radical situatedness as a normative claim, then he must allow some room for
the self to question and challenge the role and values offered to it by communal traditions. If Sandel is not rejecting liberalism wholesale, then he
must retain that crucial feature of liberalism, which is to allow, as a matter
of political principle, some space for individuals to ratify, reform, or reject
their relationships to various voluntary communities. This freedom is essential to liberals, not because they do not care about the good, but precisely because they do: freedom is an essential precondition for pursuing
a good life.[76]

Sandel's "strong, constitutive sense" of community would differ from
Rawls's conception, "in that community would describe not just a *feeling*
but a mode of self-understanding partly constitutive of the agent's identity."[77] Just how strong a sense is this? In a text I cited earlier, Sandel says
that "*certain* of our roles are *partly* constitutive of the persons we are—as
citizens of a country, or members of a movement, or partisans of a
cause."[78] Yet he never gives an account of what it is about these roles that
makes them constitutive nor to what extent we are free to question these
roles. In the three types of communal roles he cites, only one—
citizenship—involves a status normally not chosen by a person. Thus, Sandel bails out before his argument reaches its natural conclusion: his talk of
constitutive community implies, on the face of it, that we are implicated
in roles given to us by the communities to which we belong and that to
flourish as persons we must embrace the content of those roles as defined
by tradition. Sandel, though, wants something weaker. We are "implicated
in the purposes and ends characteristic of those communities."[79]

Perhaps recognizing this ambiguity, in his recent book *Democracy's
Discontent* (1996), Sandel has modified his metaphor for the way we are
socially constituted:

> Self-government today . . . requires a politics that plays itself out in a multi-
> plicity of settings, from neighborhoods to nations to the world as a whole.

Such a politics requires citizens who can think and act as *multiply-situated selves.*[80]

Although Sandel does not draw out the full implications of this new metaphor, it clearly suggests that many communal memberships take part in shaping our identities. The reason we are partly constituted by those roles is because each role plays only a part; rarely in modern society is any one of a person's communal roles the sole source of his identity and goals. Sandel still takes the weaker of the two readings of "constitutive" community, but now the weaker reading has more merit to it, because it responds to an essential fact of our social order—the fact of pluralism. But the weaker reading does not simply acquiesce to this fact; it recognizes it as an opportunity for promoting the virtue of citizenship.

The metaphor of *multiply-situated selves* suggests that the valuable task of communitarian politics is not what has commonly been supposed by proponents and opponents alike: it is neither to validate every story that gives meaning to citizens' lives just because it is a story, nor is it to validate some stories as better than others. Rather, its contribution can be to tell a story about what it means to be a citizen, a story that helps citizens weave together "the various strands of their identity into a coherent whole."[81] A citizen's freedom and opportunity to connect to this overarching political story provides the critical space needed to avoid complete definition by the subcommunities to which she belongs, while the pluralism of a liberal society provides the same counterbalance against the state. Therefore, I find that Sandel's account of constitutive community requires the liberal institutions of cultural, institutional, and religious pluralism.

Until recently, Sandel has also been vague about what a politics of the common good would look like. On some issues, he comments, a rights-based politics and a common good politics might produce different rationales for similar policies. On others, they would support different policies: "Communitarians would be more likely than liberals to allow a town to ban pornographic bookstores, on the grounds that pornography offends the town's way of life and the values that sustain it."[82] Overall, he suggests that communitarians would transcend liberal-conservative debates by focusing on the empowerment of local communities:

Where libertarian liberals defend the private economy and egalitarian liberals defend the welfare state, communitarians worry about the concentration of power in both the corporate economy and the bureaucratic state, and the erosion of those intermediate forms of community that have at times sustained a more vital public life.[83]

Though this is a worthy aim, Gutmann argues that the statement does not distinguish communitarians from liberals in principle, "unless (as Sandel implies) communitarians therefore oppose, or refuse to defend, the market or the welfare state."[84]

Sandel has risen to Gutmann's challenge. In *Democracy's Discontent,* he has begun to build on his brief criticisms of an unfettered free market to argue that economic democracy is crucial to communitarian (or, as he now prefers, "republican") politics. The communitarian's concern about the growing gap between the rich and the poor is based on a conception of freedom appropriate to (multiply) situated selves. "Severe inequality undermines freedom by corrupting the character of both rich and poor and destroying the commonality necessary to self-government."[85] This concern distinguishes communitarian politics from the major options on the U.S. political spectrum:

> Civic conservatives have not, for the most part, acknowledged that market forces, under conditions of inequality, erode those aspects of community life that bring rich and poor together in public places and pursuits. Many liberals, largely concerned with distributive justice, have also missed the civic consequences of growing inequality.[86]

This *reason* for worrying about inequality is likely to make a difference in what economic policies are developed and how they are implemented.

> A politics attentive to the civic strand of freedom might try "to restrict the sphere of life in which money matters" and shore up the public spaces that gather people together in common experiences and form the habits of citizenship. . . . It would encourage "class-mixing institutions" like public schools, libraries, parks, community centers, public transportation, and national service. Although such policies might be favored by welfare-state liberals, the emphasis and justification would be different. A more civic-minded liberalism would seek communal provision less for the sake of distributive justice than for the sake of affirming the membership and forming the civic identity of rich and poor alike.[87]

But Sandel does not want and does not need to reinvent the wheel. Looking at the contemporary scene for "gestures toward a political economy of citizenship," he identifies four examples: the work of community development corporations; citizen-organized resistance to massive stores and other commercial sprawl; the New Urbanism movement in city planning; and other forms of community organizing.[88] These examples are hints, but significant ones. Along with the renewed interest in the character-forming aspects of public policies, these suggestions point toward a politics of the common good distinct from the politics of welfare liberals, libertarians, and conservatives. Sandel notes that the greatest obstacle to the effective practice of such a politics is the massive scale on which the global economy is organized, thus removing so many economic choices from the hands of local communities.[89] Nevertheless, he trusts that communitarian politics can face the challenge better than other alternatives.

Reviving Moral and Religious Argument

A final contribution Sandel has made toward a synthesis of liberalism and communitarianism is his recommendation that liberalism recover a substantial role for moral and religious argument in political deliberation. This final section explores his case. Sandel would have us free ourselves of a "sophisticated" view of judicial-political justification in order to recover a "naive" view:

> The naive view holds that the justice of laws depends on the moral worth of the conduct they prohibit or protect. The sophisticated view holds that the justice of laws depends not on a substantive moral judgment about the conduct at stake, but instead on a more general theory about the respective claims of majority rule and individual rights.[90]

According to Sandel, the sophisticated view has been given credence in political theory by contemporary liberals, and for thirty years now, it has been reflected in Supreme Court decisions regarding matters such as contraception, abortion, and homosexual relations. Those holding the sophisticated view think that by setting aside or "bracketing" moral and religious views when deciding political and legal questions, our institutions can avoid conflict among citizens and prevent the state from imposing the moral values of some upon others.

Sandel argues that this Rawlsian method of bracketing has deleterious effects for a democratic society. First, it is simply impractical. For instance, though the Court in *Roe v. Wade* attempted to stay neutral by abjuring any theory of when human personhood begins, the Court's decision to leave abortion unregulated in the first trimester "presupposed a particular answer to the question it claimed to bracket."[91] The Court made the point of fetal viability legally relevant, which is to privilege a particular theory of the fetus's moral and legal status. A defender of liberal neutrality might ask: "Then what would Sandel have the Court do? If any resolution of the case involves positing a theory, then how can the Court remain neutral in what is basically a metaphysical issue?" Sandel replies, the Court cannot remain neutral, if neutrality means refusing to think about what relevant moral doctrines might be *true*.

> Whether it is reasonable to bracket, for political purposes, the comprehensive moral and religious doctrines at stake largely depends on which of those doctrines is true. If the doctrine of the Catholic Church is true, if human life in

the relevant moral sense does begin at conception, then bracketing the moral-
theological question when human life begins is far less reasonable than it
would be on rival moral and religious assumptions. The more confident we
are that fetuses are, in the relevant moral sense, different from babies, the
more confident we can be in affirming a political conception of justice that
sets aside the controversy about the moral status of fetuses.[92]

Bracketing moral and religious views to avoid controversy is itself controversial; to set aside such considerations for the sake of fairness seems un-
fair to some. The courts fail to achieve neutrality, and so in deciding such
cases, they fall back upon tacit moral views, often smuggled in under the
guise of the "sophisticated" approach.

The other major deficiency of the bracketing method is that it erodes the
health and vitality of a democratic, pluralist society. Sandel gets at this
point through considering the legal toleration of homosexuality. In the
case *Bowers v. Hardwick*,[93] the Supreme Court let stand Georgia's antisod-
omy laws. The four dissenting justices argued for the repeal of these laws,
based, in Sandel's view, on arguments that tie toleration for intimate practices to autonomy rights alone. This "voluntarist" case for toleration "argues from the autonomy the practices reflect," while a substantive moral
case "appeals to the human goods the practices realize."[94] Sandel brings
forth other cases affecting sexual expression to show that the Court had a
precedent for protecting homosexual intimacies because of their internal
goods—goods both shared with and distinctive from those of heterosexual
unions. Nonetheless, the dissenters eschewed the substantive line of argument, leaving their case for toleration more akin to legal decisions protecting the right to possess pornography in one's home. (In fact, Sandel notes,
the New York Court of Appeals used just such a precedent in upholding
privacy rights for homosexuals.) The toleration defended in each case becomes "wholly independent of the value or importance of the thing being
tolerated."[95]

So what comes of these (no doubt) well-meaning attempts to vindicate
privacy rights and avoid social contention by demurring at substantive
moral argument? Sandel finds two difficulties. "First, as a practical matter,
it is by no means clear that social cooperation can be secured on the
strength of autonomy rights alone, absent some measure of agreement on
the moral permissibility of the practices at issue."[96] Sandel does not mean
that the courts should base their decisions on the majority's moral views
but thinks that such voluntarist decisions tend in any event to follow upon
some social consensus. To pretend otherwise is at best self-deceptive and
at worst harmful to judicial integrity.

Second, voluntarist reasoning provides a meager basis for social respect.
For instance, the New York Court of Appeals "tolerates homosexuality at

the price of demeaning it; it puts homosexual intimacy on a par with obscenity—a base thing that should nonetheless be tolerated so long as it takes place in private."[97] Such decisions are a hollow victory for citizens desiring a modicum of social respect.

> The problem with the neutral case for toleration is the opposite side of its appeal; it leaves wholly unchallenged the adverse views of homosexuality itself. Unless those views can be plausibly addressed, even a Court ruling in their favor is unlikely to win for homosexuals more than a thin and fragile toleration. A fuller respect would require, if not admiration, at least some appreciation of the lives homosexuals live. Such appreciation, however, is unlikely to be cultivated by a legal and political discourse conducted in terms of autonomy rights alone.[98]

In sum, political liberalism is counterproductive to the kinds of public discussion and political deliberation that promote a society in which citizens are truly tolerant and mutually respectful. It removes from our political deliberations those moral and religious views citizens find most germane to the debates. It restricts the range of arguments that citizens, officials, and judges can employ to deliberate and resolve difficult legal issues affecting morality. It holds up a false ideal of neutrality and an overly narrow ideal of public reason. For Sandel, political liberalism's "vision of public life is too spare to contain the moral energies of a vital democratic life. It thus creates a void that opens the way for the intolerant and the trivial and other misguided moralisms."[99] Sandel envisions "a more spacious public reason" joined to "a deliberative conception of respect." In this conception, "we respect our fellow citizens' moral and religious convictions by engaging, or attending to them—sometimes by challenging and contesting them, sometimes by listening and learning from them—especially if those convictions bear on important political questions."[100]

What Sandel offers in the place of liberalism's politics of avoidance is a politics of engagement where citizens are enabled and encouraged to bring their moral views, religious beliefs, and sources of self-understanding to bear on their political speech and action. Instead of liberalism's false neutrality, Sandel promotes a politics of the common good that addresses not only rights and justice, but also matters of the good. That is, the political process will attempt to provide conditions for human flourishing and a framework for social cooperation on common projects. But Sandel's politics would not simply update welfare liberalism: a politics of the common good would differ distinctly from the politics of welfare liberalism in that the former would be open to the goods of religious communities and traditions. As Sandel has suggested, political and legal institutions should open their deliberations to religious arguments. They should not remove from consideration arguments that can promote justice and contribute to the common good simply because such arguments are religious. In addition, these institutions should weigh the effect of their decisions on religious practices, being careful not to hinder religious freedom by making secular reasoning a condition of participation in public/political debate. Finally, I would push Sandel's framework to suggest that a politics of the common good requires the renewal or creation of structures and spaces that allow citizens to participate in the political process through their particular voluntary communities—including churches and religious institutions.

Throughout this chapter, I have tried to show that liberalism is by no means antithetical to the common good, for it embraces various ideas of the good, including the good of a just and stable society. Yet contemporary political liberalism, as articulated by John Rawls, tends to constrain religious argument and practice. Its ideal of public reason is not simply a speculation of philosophers; it typifies a great deal of argument and reasoning in our cultural, political, and legal institutions. The dominance of either philosophical liberalism's or political liberalism's canons of public discourse (as represented by Rawls's early and recent work, respectively) can have only a deleterious effect on the common good.

The question is whether liberalism can be reformed to allow a principled place for political action and argument arising from citizens' particular religious and moral commitments. I have argued in these first two chapters that liberalism can be synthesized with communitarianism to this effect, without sacrificing basic liberal rights. Moses Mendelssohn provided a model for such a synthesis, but contemporary liberals have not followed his lead. Those communitarians who want to reform liberalism rather than discard it are closer to Mendelssohn's vision than are liberals in the mode of Rawls. Michael Sandel suggests a mediation of liberalism and communitarianism as he defends the importance of religious and moral argument in political deliberation. He asserts that such accommodation of religious and moral views will bolster a deliberative respect among citizens. That assertion will be difficult to prove. As much as some citizens would welcome a more communitarian political process, others will fear that a politics of the common good will open the doors to intolerance and public discord. Therefore, to make plausible a politics of the common good, I need to address specifically the role of religious beliefs and institutions within it. Sandel does not provide much help in this regard, for the status of religion in his account is unclear. Is religion just one instance of constitutive community? Does a citizen's religious belief have the same status as her membership in a protest movement or as her ethnic identity?

Just as he has suggested but not fully articulated a communitarian politics, Sandel has only begun to show how religion can make a contribution to the common good. We need both to follow up on and to press critically his suggestions. I think it is possible to vindicate the practical and substantive contributions that religious communities can make to a liberal society, contributions that respect both liberal and communitarian principles. My exploration of the disagreement between Rawls and Sandel has brought out the main principles that must be retained in any synthesis. In order to address the specific contributions that religion does and might make to the common good, it will be useful to engage a specifically religious thinker. An author who treats religion's role in promoting the common good, in such a way that his theory effects a synthesis of liberalism and communitarianism, is the Catholic philosopher Jacques Maritain. The next chapter considers his philosophy of the common good.

NOTES

1. James Davison Hunter, *Culture Wars: The Struggle to Define America* (New York: Basic Books, 1991), 150, 151.

2. For more examples of the American ambivalence toward public religion, see Stephen L. Carter, *The Culture of Disbelief* (New York: Basic Books, 1993).

3. John Rawls, *Political Liberalism* (New York: Columbia University Press, 1993), 226.

4. Carter, *Culture of Disbelief,* 56.

5. Richard L. Fern, "Religious Belief in a Rawlsian Society," *Journal of Religious Ethics* 15, no. 1 (Spring 1987): 53.

6. Paul Weithman, "Rawlsian Liberalism and the Privatization of Religion: Three Theological Objections Considered," *Journal of Religious Ethics* 22, no. 1 (spring 1994): 6.

7. John Rawls, *A Theory of Justice* (Cambridge, Mass.: Harvard University Press, 1971), 3.

8. Rawls, *Theory,* 4.

9. Rawls, *Theory,* 497.

10. Rawls, *Theory,* 496–504.

11. The assumption owes much to Immanuel Kant (1724–1804), whose philosophical innovation was his cogent defense of an autonomous morality, totally unconditioned by empirical facts of human nature, historical events, sociological realities, or religious beliefs. Kant's philosophy figures heavily in Rawls's liberal theory, in both its initial and recent forms.

12. Rawls, *Theory,* 11.

13. Rawls describes the original position at length in *Theory*, chap. 3.

14. The two main principles of justice that would be chosen in the original position are (1) "Each person is to have an equal right to the most extensive total system of basic liberties compatible with a similar system of liberty for all," and (2) "Social and economic inequalities are to be arranged so that they are both: (a) to the greatest benefit of the least advantaged, consistent with the just savings princi-

ple, and (b) attached to offices and positions open to all under conditions of fair equality of opportunity" (Rawls, *Theory,* 302).

15. Stephen Mulhall and Adam Swift, *Liberals and Communitarians* (Cambridge, Mass.: Blackwell, 1992), 11.

16. Rawls, *Political Liberalism*, xvi. His definition of comprehensive doctrines is given on p. 13.

17. Rawls wrote several important articles in the 1980s developing the ideas that he eventually called "political liberalism." See, for instance, "Justice as Fairness: Political Not Metaphysical," *Philosophy and Public Affairs* 14 (summer 1985): 223–52; "The Idea of an Overlapping Consensus," *Oxford Journal of Legal Studies* 7 (February 1987): 1–25; and "The Priority of Right and Ideas of the Good," *Philosophy and Public Affairs* 17 (summer 1988): 251–76.

18. Mulhall and Swift, *Liberals,* 5.

19. Rawls, *Political Liberalism*, xviii.

20. In *Political Liberalism,* Rawls discusses oppression at p. 37 and legitimacy at pp. 136–40 and 216–20.

21. Rawls, *Political Liberalism*, xxvi.

22. Rawls, *Political Liberalism*, 139.

23. Cf. Rawls, *Political Liberalism*, 140.

24. Rawls, *Political Liberalism*, 140.

25. Rawls, *Theory*, 105.

26. Michael J. Sandel, review of *Political Liberalism*, by John Rawls, in *Harvard Law Review* 107, no. 7 (May 1994): 1765–94, quote at 1783.

27. Annette C. Baier, "Claims, Rights, and Responsibilities," in *Prospects for a Common Morality*, ed. Gene Outka and John P. Reeder, Jr. (Princeton, N.J.: Princeton University Press, 1993), 149–69, quote at 168. Baier's metaphor of the parasitism of rights on other moral concepts is at p. 163.

28. Kent Greenawalt, *Religious Convictions and Political Choice* (New York: Oxford University Press, 1988), 169.

29. David Novak, *Jewish Social Ethics* (New York: Oxford University Press, 1992), 78.

30. Rawls, *Theory*, 135.

31. Mulhall and Swift, *Liberals,* 216.

32. Mulhall and Swift, *Liberals,* 216.

33. Rawls, *Political Liberalism*, 173.

34. Rawls describes each of these in chapter 5 of *Political Liberalism*; my summary here relies in part upon Mulhall and Swift, *Liberals,* 216–18.

35. The primary goods fall under five headings: basic rights and liberties; freedom of movement and choice of occupation; powers and prerogatives of offices in political and economic institutions; income and wealth; and the social bases of self-respect (Rawls, *Political Liberalism*, 181).

36. Mulhall and Swift, *Liberals,* 217.

37. Rawls, *Political Liberalism*, 193.

38. Rawls, *Political Liberalism*, 194.

39. Rawls, *Political Liberalism*, 203, 204.

40. Mulhall and Swift, *Liberals,* 218.

41. Rawls, *Political Liberalism*, 213.
42. Rawls, *Political Liberalism*, 214.
43. Rawls, *Political Liberalism*, 215.
44. A three-prong test developed by the majority in *Lemon v. Kurtzman,* 403 U.S. 602 (1971) was, for about two decades, the Court's standard for judging whether a statute violated the Establishment Clause of the First Amendment. According to the "Lemon test," a statute passes constitutional muster only if (*a*) its legislative purpose is secular, (*b*) its primary effect neither promotes nor inhibits religion, and (*c*) it does not foster excessive government entanglement with religion. For one analysis of the Court's Establishment Clause jurisprudence and its recent erosion of the Lemon test, see Jeffrey W. Stiltner, "Rethinking the Wall of Separation: *Zobrest v. Catalina Foothills School District*—Is This the End of *Lemon?*" *Capital University Law Review* 23, no. 3 (1994): 823–61.
45. Public reason applies to some, but not all, parts of the public political forum. It applies to the discourse of elected officials and to citizens and parties when they engage in political advocacy. "It holds equally for how citizens are to vote in elections when constitutional questions and matters of basic justice are at stake." Most important, it applies to judges, and especially the judges of a Supreme Court, when they reason and hand down opinions. The limits of public reason "do not apply to our personal deliberations and reflections about political questions, or to the reasoning about them by members of associations such as churches and universities, all of which is a vital part of the background culture" (Rawls, *Political Liberalism*, 215–16).
46. Rawls, *Political Liberalism*, 119.
47. See Rawls, *Political Liberalism*, chap. 3; and John Rawls, "Kantian Constructivism in Moral Theory," *Journal of Philosophy* 77, no. 9 (September 1980): 515–72.
48. Rawls, *Political Liberalism*, 37.
49. Rawls, *Political Liberalism*, 38.
50. Rawls, *Political Liberalism*, 217.
51. Mulhall and Swift, *Liberals,* 190.
52. Rawls, *Political Liberalism*, 226, 227.
53. Rawls, *Political Liberalism*, 247.
54. Rawls, *Political Liberalism*, 249.
55. Rawls, *Political Liberalism*, 249–50.
56. Rawls, *Political Liberalism*, 251.
57. Rawls articulates this proviso in an unpublished paper, "Political Liberalism and Religion," presented at Yale University, New Haven, Conn., 6 October 1994.
58. Rawls, *Political Liberalism*, 243 n. 32.
59. Rawls, *Political Liberalism*, 243 n. 32.
60. On the communitarian charge that Rawls's theory is universalist and thus fails to attend to culturally and historically specific values and practices, Mulhall and Swift, writing before the appearance of *Political Liberalism*, argue that Rawls need not take a stand on his theory's cross-cultural validity and application. Moreover, they comment that, "as far as can be judged from his recent writings, he has not committed himself either way on this issue" (*Liberals,* 214). With his book,

Rawls has made clear that political liberalism is grounded in the public culture of a really existing constitutional democracy. Nonetheless; I think political liberalism faces difficulties in each direction: as a transcendent ideal, public reason undermines political liberalism; while as a culturally specific ideal, it cannot do all the work Rawls wants it to do.

61. Criticisms of Rawls's ideal of public reason that argue along lines similar to mine (and by which I have been helped) are Sandel, review of *Political Liberalism*; David Hollenbach, "Public Reason/Private Reason? A Response to Paul J. Weithman," *Journal of Religious Ethics* 22, no. 1 (spring 1994): 39–46; and conversation with David Clough.

62. For readings of the Rawls-Sandel debate alternative to the one I offer here, see Gerald Doppelt, "Beyond Liberalism and Communitarianism: Towards a Critical Theory of Social Justice," and Kenneth Baynes, "The Liberal/Communitarian Controversy and Communicative Ethics," both in *Universalism vs. Communitarianism: Contemporary Debates in Ethics*, ed. David Rasmussen (Cambridge, Mass.: MIT Press, 1990), 39–60 and 61–81, respectively. Doppelt argues that Rawls's theory is the best avenue to a communal liberalism; Baynes uses discourse ethics to analyze the broader debate (see also my description of discourse communitarianism in the introduction).

63. Michael J. Sandel, *Liberalism and the Limits of Justice* (Cambridge: Cambridge University Press, 1982), 1. In this book, Sandel gives Kantian political theory the technical name *deontological liberalism,* since the moral theory underlying it is a deontological ethic of rights and corresponding duties.

64. See Sandel, review of *Political Liberalism*, 1782–89. Sandel's three main objections to political liberalism are (1) that the political process cannot reasonably bracket all claims that citizens proffer from their religious and moral views; (2) that the "fact of reasonable pluralism" on matters of the good also applies to questions of justice, giving Rawls no good reason to rule out the possibility of political debate and consensus on moral and religious questions; and (3) that Rawls's ideal of public reason unduly restricts political discourse (1776–94).

65. Sandel, *Limits*, 10.

66. See Rawls, *Theory*, 17–20; cf. Sandel, *Limits*, 44–45.

67. Sandel, *Limits*, 46.

68. Sandel, *Limits*, 61.

69. Sandel, *Limits*, 64.

70. Michael J. Sandel, "The Political Theory of the Procedural Republic," in *Reinhold Neibuhr Today*, ed. Richard John Neuhaus (Grand Rapids, Mich.: Eerdmans, 1989), 25–26; originally published in *Revue de métaphysique et morale* 93 (1988): 57–68. This article restates arguments found in others by Sandel: his introduction to *Liberalism and Its Critics*, ed. Michael J. Sandel (New York: New York University Press, 1984), 1–11; "Morality and the Liberal Ideal," *New Republic,* 7 May 1984, 15–17; and "The Procedural Republic and the Unencumbered Self," *Political Theory* 12 (1984): 81–96.

71. In brief, Sandel argues that Rawls explicitly constructs the original position so that certain principles of justice will result. Agreement *to the principles* is purchased at the price of any discussion, deliberation, or agreement *among the per-*

sons in the original position. Rawls can achieve this agreement only if "*all* individ-uating characteristics" of the participants are excluded, which leaves them "not merely *similarly* situated . . . but *identically* situated." Rawls thus subtly shifts his metaphor from one of choosing principles to one of acknowledging them. What begins for Rawls "as an ethic of choice and consent ends, however unwittingly, as an ethic of insight and self-understanding" (Sandel, *Limits*, 131–32). I do not think this reading of Rawls's original position has to succeed in order to substantiate the more general claim that social agreements about justice subsist on richer under-standings of human persons and the common good than are found in political liber-alism.

72. In chapter 2 of *Limits*, Sandel argues that Rawls's ethic of sharing, as exem-plified by the difference principle, requires a nonliberal account of the human sub-ject.

73. Sandel, "Procedural Republic," 32.

74. Sandel, "Procedural Republic," 27.

75. Amy Gutmann, "Communitarian Critics of Liberalism," *Philosophy and Public Affairs* 14 (summer 1985): 319.

76. Rawls would certainly make this point, though it might get obscured among the many arguments he makes. For a strong statement of this point as central to the liberal moral vision, see Will Kymlicka, *Liberalism, Community, and Culture* (Oxford: Clarendon, 1989), esp. chaps. 2–3.

77. Sandel, *Limits*, 152, 150.

78. Sandel, "Procedural Republic," 27, emphasis added.

79. Sandel, "Procedural Republic," 27.

80. Michael Sandel, *Democracy's Discontent: America in Search of a Public Philosophy* (Cambridge, Mass.: Harvard University Press, 1996), 350, emphasis added.

81. Sandel, *Democracy's Discontent,* 350.

82. Sandel, "Procedural Republic," 26.

83. Sandel, "Procedural Republic," 26.

84. Gutmann, "Communitarian Critics," 318.

85. Sandel, *Democracy's Discontent,* 330.

86. Sandel, *Democracy's Discontent,* 332.

87. Sandel, *Democracy's Discontent,* 332–33. The internal quotations are from Mickey Kaus, *The End of Equality* (New York: Basic Books, 1992).

88. Sandel, *Democracy's Discontent,* 333–38.

89. See Sandel, *Democracy's Discontent,* 338–51.

90. Michael J. Sandel, "Moral Argument and Liberal Toleration: Abortion and Homosexuality," *California Law Review* 77, no. 3 (May 1989): 521.

91. Sandel, "Moral Argument," 532.

92. Sandel, review of *Political Liberalism*, 1778.

93. *Bowers v. Hardwick,* 478 U.S. 186 (1986).

94. Sandel, "Moral Argument," 534.

95. Sandel, "Moral Argument," 536. The New York case he cites is *People v. Onofre,* 51 N.Y. 2d 476 (1980).

  96. Sandel, "Moral Argument," 536–37.
  97. Sandel, "Moral Argument," 537.
  98. Sandel, "Moral Argument," 537.
  99. Sandel, review of *Political Liberalism*, 1794.
 100. Sandel, review of *Political Liberalism*, 1794.

Chapter 3

Linking Liberalism and Communitarianism Through Common Good Theory

The search for a purely political liberalism is internally incoherent and unfruitful for the common good: this was the main conclusion of the previous chapter. We as citizens ought not give up our attempts to articulate and commend comprehensive visions of a good and just society. This kind of discourse made sense to early liberals, who were more persuasive than their modern heirs in articulating the interdependence of a liberal order and the common good. Two insights are needed to understand and pursue the common good in today's liberal societies: first, liberal institutions and practices must be understood as requirements of the common good, not mere accretions to it; second, communal values and responsibilities given by the common good must be proved compatible with liberal rights. We turn now from considering how liberals and communitarians parse this debate to an exploration of how a philosopher of the common good attempts to reconcile liberalism and communitarianism. As before, the attempt to understand religion's beneficial role in public life serves as a unifying focus: synthesizing liberalism and communitarianism will pave the way for demonstrating religion's contributions to the common good.

In this chapter, I delineate what one significant strand in modern Catholic thought can offer as its contribution to an understanding of the common good. To do this, I employ the thought of Jacques Maritain because his account of the common good proceeds as both a natural law argument and a theological argument. The former, universal mode has affinities to the liberal approach, while the latter is congenial to communitarianism. These approaches are in tension, yet I hope to show how Maritain can unite them, thus strengthening his theory of the common good and contributing to a mediation of liberal and communitarian principles. This linked method will lay the ground for considering, in the next chapter, religion's role in the common good and whether Maritain's Catholic account of the common good can serve as an adequate public philosophy.

MARITAIN'S CONTRIBUTION TO THE PROJECT

Background

Jacques Maritain (1882–1973), frequently regarded as the preeminent Catholic philosopher of the twentieth century, made lasting intellectual contributions to most major branches of philosophy, including metaphysics, aesthetics, epistemology, philosophy of religion, philosophy of history, and political philosophy.[1] To situate Maritain in my project, it will be helpful to focus briefly on two aspects of his life and work: as a Catholic philosopher and as a political philosopher. As a Catholic thinker, Maritain is best remembered and appreciated for contributing to the renaissance of Thomistic philosophy. Though he saw himself as a transmitter of Aquinas's original meaning, he offered a dynamic and existentialist reading of Aquinas. This reading can be characterized as existentialist for its stress on "the act of existence as the enactment of being."[2] Far from putting aside metaphysics, Maritain wanted to revive this branch of philosophy but with the act of existence as his starting point. The act of existing discloses one's own existence and the existence of other things; it thus "grounds and centers the intelligible structure of reality," on which basis the reason can discover love, being, and God.[3]

While such an approach seems quite traditional today, Maritain's innovations were controversial to many of his contemporary fellow Catholics. In particular, some traditional Thomists thought Maritain and his ilk were importing a false individualism into Aquinas's thought. Charles De Koninck criticized "the personalists" for denying the primacy of the common good.[4] Without naming Maritain or any other writers, De Koninck argued that personalism makes single goods—the goods of individuals—superior to the common good. While there are many facets to the debate that occurred in print between De Koninck and a supporter of Maritain, Thomas Eschmann,[5] the difference between De Koninck and Maritain most salient for us lies in their views of human dignity.

> What is the real or ontological basis of this dignity? At the risk of oversimplification, we may say that for De Koninck it is the person's *rational nature*, foundation of the capacity to participate in and to adhere to freely, through knowledge and through love, an order . . . that is greater than the individual; whereas for Maritain it is above all personal *freedom*, understood as the spiritual capacity to act independently of and to transcend any given order.[6]

The difference must be interpreted in light of the disparate interests that drove De Koninck's and Maritain's projects. De Koninck focused on the person's place before God, who is the extrinsic common good of the universe (the ultimate common good that stands above and beyond the created order), while Maritain's concern was the proper relation of the person to the political common good in the face of totalitarian and communist threats to human dignity. Thus, "while De Koninck's reading and presentation are more faithful to Aquinas's position on this issue, Maritain departs from the letter of Thomas's work in order to uphold the spirit which informs it."[7]

These concerns lead us to Maritain's work as a political philosopher, where his significant achievement was to articulate a Catholic vision of a pluralist, democratic society. He stood at the creative center of the political debates of his day, serving as an apologist in two directions. First, to Catholics, he argued that the Catholic Church and its members could and should celebrate the rise of democracy around the world and promote human rights for all persons. Lifting up themes and principles from the Catholic tradition, he contended that cultural pluralism and religious liberty were central to the Church's promotion of the common good. Second, to the democratic societies of Europe and North America, he extolled the indispensable value of the Christian Gospel in birthing the democratic spirit that undergirds free and good societies. He tried to show non-Catholics that the Catholic Church was willing to engage with them in cooperative work for the common good.

Maritain's work was greatly shaped by World War II. Encouraging Europe to remain courageous against fascism and communism during the war, Maritain tried to make his work relevant to the great contest for the human spirit among the ideologies of the day.[8] His three classic books from this time are *The Rights of Man and Natural Law* (1942), *Christianity and Democracy* (1943), and *The Person and the Common Good* (1947). Maritain wrote several other political works, among them *Freedom: Its Meaning* (1940), *Scholasticism and Politics* (1940), *Principes d'une politique humaniste* (1944), and many articles on freedom, rights, politics, and the scourge of anti-Semitism, several of which are collected in *Ransoming the Time* (1941) and *The Range of Reason* (1952).[9] Capping this era of rich reflection, Maritain delivered lectures at the University of Chicago representing his mature political philosophy and natural law theory; these were published as *Man and the State* (1951).

Given a concern for Maritain's contributions to a political philosophy of democracy and the common good, his political writings from 1940 to 1951 are especially relevant to my project.[10] During that time, Maritain was trying to articulate a philosophy of human freedom that is necessarily fulfilled in the common good. He was developing a political humanism and

positioning it against what he saw as the main errors of political organization: totalitarianism, communism, and bourgeois individualism. My decision to engage Maritain's thought raises an issue that I should address
briefly before proceeding. When Jacques Maritain's name is invoked these
days, it is often done in traditionalist or neoconservative Catholic circles.
That is understandable, because Maritain flourished in the heyday of the
neo-Thomist revival and did not live much beyond the time of the Second
Vatican Council. Indeed, late in his life he wrote a somewhat dour assessment of Vatican II and its implementation.[11] And certainly the form, if not
the content, of Maritain's philosophical, theological, and ethical thought
sounds traditional today. So the reader may be wondering: Have I called
upon Maritain in order to present a "conservative" political philosophy?
The answer is no—if anything, I find Maritain's political thought during
his mature period to be progressive and remarkably foresighted on most
counts. More important, I do not wish to enter into battles over the proper
interpretation of Maritain's thought. As I did with Locke and Mendelssohn, I aim to mine Maritain's work for resources that can be used in a
theory of communal liberalism, while of course remaining sensitive to his
intentions. But I must also say that I find conservative and neoconservative
readings of Maritain's political theory largely unsatisfying. I do not think
these capture the essence and the dynamism of Maritain's thought. Over
the course of the next two chapters, we will see that Maritain is neither the
strong critic of liberalism suggested by some conservative Catholic interpreters nor the champion of liberal capitalism that Catholic neoconserva-
tives might want him to be.[12] In this investigation, we will be considering
not only Maritain's political philosophy proper, but also his theology and
epistemology as they bear on the former. We will consider the two approaches he takes in describing the common good and defending its compatibility with a pluralist democracy. Before we begin, we need to clarify
the terms Maritain uses.

Maritain's Definition of the Common Good

The common good, for Maritain, is the shared good life of a community
of free human persons. The many particular goods that fulfill human life
in its material, relational, intellectual, moral, and spiritual dimensions are
shared with others in the social whole, both because these goods are intrinsically communicative and because the shared common good is the foundation for the fulfillment of individual persons.[13] Maritain identifies three
essential characteristics of the common good. First, the purpose of the
common good is to serve persons. Therefore, the common good must recognize the fundamental rights of the person and the family, and "it must
be redistributed among persons and . . . aid their development."[14] Second,

the common good requires the exercise of political authority for its implementation, even as it is the foundation and justification of authority. In order to guide a community of persons toward the common good, leaders are invested with authority to guide and direct political society. These leaders remain accountable to the citizens as free persons and to the moral requirements of the common good.[15] Third, the common good is intrinsically moral, since persons are moral: "It is not only something useful, an ensemble of advantages and profits, it is essentially something good in itself. . . . Justice and civic friendship are its cement."[16]

When speaking of the *common good,* Maritain specifically means, unless he specifies otherwise, the *temporal, political common good.* To understand his topic, it helps to attend to each part of the phrase. First, as *temporal,* the common good is a work of persons acting on earth and in historical time; its scope and possibilities are thus limited, because we humans are limited and have our faults. The common good is distinguished from, and subordinate to, the eternal and ultimate good, which is God.

Second, the common good is *political,* which means it is a project of those who live and work together in a political society; it is a good that orients us toward a just and friendly life in society. The content of the political common good may differ from the goods of community sought by voluntary institutions such as schools, churches, and so on. The common good is often like an umbrella that protects and nurtures the goods of voluntary communities, but it does not make every goal of these communities its own.

Third, the common good, as *common,* is the result of cooperative work and is experienced as a shared good. The common good is thus different from both private and personal goods, which must themselves be distinguished. *Private goods* are those experienced only by single individuals or discrete groups, for example, the goods of camaraderie and cooperation experienced by a sports team or a coin-collecting club. Maritain, as we will see, tries to establish that the common good is superior to private goods. A group's claim to a private good must sometimes be ceded in the face of a demand made by the common good. *Personal goods,* on the other hand, are those experienced by persons (in the special interpretation of that word given by Maritain), such as the goods of freedom, wisdom, aesthetic enjoyment, spiritual growth, virtue, and sociality with others. These goods of persons, we will see, are not strictly subordinate to the common good; rather, they are goods that the common good must bolster and augment.

Finally, the common task is *good*—something beneficial, salutary, and worthy of choice. It is fundamentally a *moral good.* That is, the common good is not merely the project of meeting society's practical needs, such as constructing roads, providing public transportation, establishing laws that regulate the economy, and so forth. Rather, it incorporates these sorts of goods, which are not distinctly moral, into a larger good that persons can share because of their capacity to interact in reason, freedom, and love. This cooperation of free persons and the benefits that flow from it are the moral aspects of the common good. Maritain says the common good thus comprises

> the sum or sociological integration of all the civic conscience, political virtues and sense of right and liberty; of all the activity, material prosperity and spiritual riches; of unconsciously operative hereditary wisdom; of moral rectitude, justice, friendship, happiness, virtue and heroism in the individual lives of its members. For these things all are, in a certain measure, *communicable* and so revert to each member, helping him to perfect his life and liberty of person. They all constitute the good human life of the multitude.[17]

The Problem

It is not always clear whether, for Maritain, this description of the common good is based on a vision of society that is particularly Catholic or one that all people could in principle understand and support. On the face of it, Maritain offers his account as a guide both to cobelievers and to those fellow citizens who embrace neither the Catholic nor Christian faith. The question is whether Maritain's account can work in both directions. For in trying to occupy the creative center, Maritain may alienate both sides. His common good may presume too much harmony, shared language, and common purpose between Christians and other believers or nonbelievers. If so, its form and content will be too theological to inspire and motivate citizens who do not share his faith; indeed, some will worry that Christian or Catholic social and moral priorities would dominate the public debate. Alternatively, some Christians will feel that they have to compromise too much of their public witness in order to cooperate with non-Christians. Can he convince one group without losing the other? The question is made more complex when we notice that the general public is a very heterogeneous group. Parts of Maritain's theory may win over some citizens but alienate others.

It is precisely this challenge I want to explore in relation to Maritain's work. I think it can be shown that Maritain offers a public philosophy that uncovers a religious basis for liberalism. Liberalism, in his view, incorporates a principled place for religion in society. Moreover, the common good represents a synthesis of mutually dependent liberal and communitarian values. Maritain's account seeks its ground in both natural law and Christian theology. The theological basis for the common good is theological personalism, while the theory by which Maritain makes the common good accessible is natural law. The latter, universal method is compatible with major strands of liberalism—in that it can serve as a public frame-work—while the former, traditional-specific approach is congenial to communitarian particularism. In what follows, I hope to show how Maritain can unite the two approaches, thus strengthening his theory of the common good.

MARITAIN'S TWO APPROACHES TO THE COMMON GOOD

The First Approach: Natural Law

Maritain once wrote, "The philosophical foundation of the Rights of man is Natural Law. Sorry that we cannot find another word!"[18] Maritain was well aware of both the conceptual objections that philosophers raise about the existence of a natural law and the practical difficulties that face those trying to agree on a moral basis for political and legal rights. Yet he refused to jettison the theory of natural law in favor of legal positivism or a philosophy of pure pragmatism.

The Content and Knowledge of Natural Law

A key summary of Maritain's natural law theory appears in *Man and the State*, where he distinguishes two elements in natural law. The first is the ontological element. There is a certain real and discoverable form of human flourishing given in the nature of every person, and it provides the basis of a natural moral law. Maritain "takes it for granted that we all admit that there is a human nature, and that this human nature is the same in all." Its two features are "an ontologic structure which is a locus of intelligible necessities" and ends that correspond to those needs.[19] These presuppositions come easily to classical Thomists but are quite controversial in the light of modern psychology, anthropology, and sociology. Maritain moves to secure his claims by explaining what he means by *nature*.

Maritain defines the nature of anything by the "normality of its functioning." For example, something is recognized as a piano only because it produces certain sounds. We rely upon this inner law of normal functioning to discover how to use both artificial and natural objects.[20] The question is, then, what constitutes "normality of functioning" in the human person? Thomists typically answer this question by pointing to Aquinas's order of natural inclinations.[21] The first formal principle of practical reasoning ("good is to be done and promoted, and evil is to be avoided") is specified into secondary, material principles (guidelines to particular actions) along the order of natural inclinations.[22] These material principles are neither self-evident nor set in a definite form; the person, using practi-

cal reason, discerns that certain actions are compatible with the first principle and that others are not.

So natural law theory, in Maritain's view, is ontological, but it is not
static. While natural *law* is ontological and ideal, natural law *reasoning* is
existential and creative.

> I do not mean that the proper regulation for each possible human situation is
> contained in the human essence. . . . Human situations are something existen-
> tial. Neither they nor their appropriate regulations are contained in the essence
> of man. I would say that they ask questions of that essence.[23]

For instance, human nature reviles against genocide "as incompatible with
its general ends and innermost dynamic structure: that is to say, as prohibited by natural law." Yet this prohibition is neither "a metaphysical feature
eternally inscribed" in the human essence nor "a notion recognized from
the start by the conscience of humanity."[24] Rather, as societies over the
centuries have wrestled with problems of murder and warfare, they have
gradually and increasingly come to see that genocide is evil and incompatible with human civilization. Natural law can be described as the impulse
toward the development of conscience and civilization.

To the ontological element of natural law—its essence as rooted in
human nature—Maritain adds a second basic element: the epistemological
element, or the natural law as known.[25] Maritain's basic argument here is
that natural law is neither a written law nor a rationally deduced law, but
a law known through inclination. By the time he wrote *Man and the State*,
Maritain had arrived at a fully dynamic model of natural law. In Paul Ramsey's persuasive interpretation, Maritain abandoned claims made in his
earlier writings that natural law involves a rational apprehension of human
nature and that judgments proceeding from natural law take the form of a
deductive practical syllogism.[26] Both these claims were firmly established
in Scholastic and neo-Scholastic natural law theory, but Maritain's growing insight into Aquinas led him to discard them as mistaken. Maritain's
mature natural law theory fixes upon the way reason and will are disposed
to good action by the inclinations of our nature:

> My contention is that the judgments in which Natural Law is made manifest
> to practical Reason do not proceed from any conceptual, discursive, rational
> exercise of reason; they proceed from that *connaturality or congeniality*
> through which what is consonant with the essential inclinations of human na-
> ture is grasped by the intellect as good; what is dissonant, as bad.[27]

An important implication of this dynamic, nonconceptual view is that
natural law reasoning develops historically. We find that as we reflect, individually and collectively, on our experience of the natural law over time,

we can begin to give rational expression to its demands. Our understanding has progressed in two ways: from an inarticulate grasp to a more conscious, coherent, and rational understanding of the natural law's demands, and from foundational principles to more refined precepts.[28] The proscription of genocide and the recognition of human rights are good examples of this trend—both have been defended on natural law grounds, and both have been affirmed as basic principles in international law.

From Natural Law to the Common Good

Maritain invokes natural law in his account of the common good, though he does not draw a direct line of justification from one to the other. The following chain of claims expounds the implicit connections. First, every human being is possessed of dignity and rights, for we experience in our own lives the inclinations to preserve ourselves and to defend our kin. By further personal and collective moral reflection upon these inclinations, we are able to see that every human being is essentially the same as ourselves, and so every person is a dignified subject. Thus, the right to life and other basic rights belong to all. Next, we experience in ourselves the inclination to use our natural powers and our practical and theoretical reasoning to improve ourselves and maximize our self-potential. We are also inclined to help our family and friends fulfill their potential. By further moral reflection upon these inclinations, we are able to see that to live well with others, it is fitting to help them achieve their own potential. So the inclinations that lead us to develop ourselves intellectually, artistically, morally, physically, and so on, also support the claim that social organization should take some account of helping each member to flourish in these areas.

Next, it has become clear in the development of human social experience that various institutions are needed to help us protect ourselves, defend our basic rights, provide for our basic needs, and support our personal and collective flourishing. Therefore, every society develops patterns of social organization, embracing familial, religious, economic, and political institutions. These patterns are obviously instantiated in many different ways, but some pattern of organization and some form of authority are required. Finally, individual persons and smaller social units have to establish and adjust their relationship to larger social structures. For a society to survive, the claims individuals make upon one another and upon institutions need to be negotiated and adjudicated. For the viability of the society, and in order to protect the dignity of all, some individual claims are superseded by the claims of the community. Here is the doctrine of the priority of the common good, as well as the basis of the claim that legitimate authority must care for the common good.

Maritain's dynamic natural law theory has three main applications in his political thought. First, it recommends a *method* that explores human experience at several levels to discern what is important to us, what constitutes human flourishing. This method is open to the work of the social and biological sciences for data about the constitution and circumstances of human life; it also inquires of personal experiences that would help us fill in an account of flourishing. The method then brings these data and reflections about human nature under the framework of practical reason, which is the mental capacity we use to determine how to achieve practical ends. Natural law reasoning basically concerns determining what is good for us and how we can achieve it.

Second, natural law provides some *content*, some direction to our reflection on human nature. Fundamentally, natural law indicates that there is something to respect in human beings. While the capacities and qualities that constitute human dignity can and should be concretized in a list of human rights, Maritain reminds us that these rights are grounded in the fuller reality of the human person who is relational, free, and self-transcendent. We will investigate the content natural law theory provides for common good theory in the next chapter.

Third, because it provides a method and content accessible to rational persons, natural law theory provides a *framework* for practical political and moral discussion. That framework centers around rights as inalienable expressions of human dignity, recognizing that rights have both a communal context (they aim at the common good) and practical limitations as to their practice (they may conflict with other rights or duties). In Maritain's view, this framework makes practical discussion possible even among those who are deeply divided in their theoretical conceptions. He pointed to the consensus on a list of human rights forged by the United Nations delegates as evidence of the possibility of meaningful cross-cultural ethical and political agreements.[29] Relying upon this framework does not cause moral and political disagreement to disappear, but it does provide a basic set of ethical claims by which it is reasonable to expect persons and societies to abide.

Natural law, then, undergirds some substantial claims. Since natural law justification moves from a self-evident principle to more specific yet more contextual claims, it seems fit for articulating the common good to a pluralistic society. It lends normative weight to the requirements of the common good, while giving space for reasonable disagreement among those who would interpret it differently. However, natural law theory does not go far enough in specifying the relationship between personal flourishing (what Maritain might call the "fulfillment of our natural ends") and the common good. Nor does it indicate how religious values and commitments are to inform public values and common projects. To address these issues,

Maritain saw the need for a thicker account of the person and the common good.

The Second Approach: Theological Personalism

From the Dynamics of Personality to the Common Good

For Maritain, a theological approach to the common good is necessary if our understanding of the concept is to be complete. While this approach differs from a natural law approach, the two are in continuity in Maritain's view. One aspect of continuity is that the natural law is rooted in the eternal law of God's reason.[30] Beyond this standard Thomistic claim, Maritain appeals to the nature of God as revealed in the Christian tradition for a model of the common good. His second approach to the common good is theological, then, in three ways: it relies upon sources in the Christian theological tradition, specifically Aquinas's thought; it incorporates a Christian account of humans' ultimate end; and it appeals to the nature of God as a Trinity of Persons. Let us consider each of these characteristics.

Aquinas's interpretation of the common good is the starting point for Maritain's theological account. The first insight he gleans from Aquinas is a proper understanding of the human person in relation to the political community. Two of Aquinas's texts guide the discussion. The first says, "Each individual person is related to the entire community as the part to the whole." The second says, "Man is not ordained to the body politic according to all that he is and has."[31] The person, Maritain comments, "is in its entirety engaged in and ordained to the common good of society"; however, "he is not a part of political society *by reason of his entire self* and all that is in him."[32] The human person is engaged entirely in the common work of political society: this at minimum requires her to respect and contribute to the common good; it may require sacrifice, even the sacrifice of life (as in a war of defense or in the line of certain duties). But the person is not ordained to the common good by reason of her whole self: "there are goods and values in us which are neither by nor for the state, which are outside of the state."[33]

Maritain draws a second insight from these texts—a distinction between *individuality* and *personality*.

> The human being is caught between two poles; a material pole, which, in reality, does not concern the true person but rather the shadow of personality or what, in the strict sense, is called *individuality*, and a spiritual pole, which does concern *true personality*.[34]

The human being is not dichotomized, however. We humans are individuals by virtue of having determinate, individual bodies. We are persons by

virtue of having souls, the deepest reality of ourselves as intelligent and
loving creatures. Humans must be individuals and persons together; we
are embodied souls and ensouled bodies.[35]

This unity of the soul and body makes us persons who are free, self-
possessed, able to act and communicate. Personality is the dynamic power
of human beings that enables us to have a common good. Having a soul
makes persons whole, interior, and open: persons are not divided in themselves; they are self-aware and open to others. Personality requires communication, dialogue, relationality, and friendship. "By the very fact that
I am a person and express myself to myself, I need to communicate with
the other and with *others* in the order of knowledge and love. It is essential
to personality to seek a dialogue in which souls really communicate."[36]
Persons are naturally generous and open to others; they are also in need.
Because of their nature, persons are naturally fitted for social life, and thus
they can have a common good. "The common good is common because it
is received in persons, each one of whom is a mirror of the whole . . . [it
is] a good received and communicated."[37]

The next way this approach is theological is by incorporating a Christian
account of the person. What is the deepest nature of human personality?
Maritain answers with a theological anthropology: personality is the
human soul.

> Personality is the subsistence of the spiritual soul communicated to the human
> composite. Because, in our substance, it is an imprint or seal which enables it
> to possess existence, to perfect and give itself freely, personality testifies to
> the generosity or expansiveness in being which an incarnate spirit derives
> from its spiritual nature and which constitutes, within the secret depths of our
> ontological structure, a source of dynamic unity, of unification from within.[38]

In its theological aspect, Maritain's account of the common good is
founded on a Thomistic personalism that sets the common good in a
proper relation to humans' ultimate end. *Personalism* refers to an emphasis, a tone, in Maritain's philosophy, based on the distinction between individuality and personality.[39] The "fundamental truth" of this personalist
focus is that "the human person is ordained directly to God as to its absolute ultimate end" and hence "transcends every created common good."[40]

Maritain marshals several points of Thomistic doctrine to specify and
reinforce this claim.[41] Some of them are philosophical claims in Aquinas's
anthropology. As intellectual creatures, humans alone bear the image of
God and alone have the ability to contemplate and love God. Therefore,
they are related to God, the "separated common good," before they are
related to the "immanent common good" of the universe or to any common good of human communities. The primacy of the person's relation to

God is further strengthened by a theological appeal to the beatific vision, a "supremely personal" relation of the soul to God. In the beatific vision, the soul enters into the society of persons in the Trinity, which is the vision and model of every created common good. Significantly, this supremely personal good is implicated in a communal good—the society of the communion of saints, where all "love mutually in God."

The consequence of these Thomistic claims is that, in a certain sense, the human person has a primacy over the common good. Every person possesses an inviolable dignity due to her creation for communion with God. (Distinctive characteristics of the human person—personality, rationality, sociality, freedom, morality—are products of this deeper call to communion.) The person is superior to the common good of political society because of his dignity, with the result that the common good must serve the person's good.

The third and final aspect of Maritain's theological approach is an account of the common good modeled on the relation of Persons in the Trinity. Beginning again with the relation of person and society, he describes the political common good as "a whole composed of wholes."[42] That is to say, persons are related to the common good as complete beings—totalities of body and spirit, reason and will. They are not monads subordinated to the political body. At the same time, the political society has its own unity and value; it is not merely the assemblage of individuals. In each case, Maritain thinks that *whole* is a more dignified concept than *part*: the former term conveys unity, dignity, and a subject possessed of rights; the latter connotes division, inferiority, and a object commanded by a higher authority.

The "whole composed of wholes" idea leads to the Trinity, where both the Godhead and each Person is a whole in itself. Maritain considers the Trinity an indispensable source for understanding the true nature of the common good and the relation of persons to it, for it stands at the peak of an analogical scale of societies:

> If one wants to get the right idea of human society, it is necessary to consider how it is situated on the ontological scale between the uncreated archetype—the super-representation of the concept of society, namely, the divine society—and that which is not even a likeness of this concept, except in an improper and metaphorical sense, namely, animal society.[43]

Human society, like an animal grouping, is "a society of persons who are material individuals, each isolated within themselves," but it is also akin to its divine likeness, for its members "seek to commune with one another as much as possible here below, before perfectly communing together and with God in eternal life."[44] Seeing human society as analogous to the di-

vine society, we can see both the limitations and the possibilities of the
human common good. The main limitation is that there can never be a
perfect coincidence of personal and common goods; hence, sometimes for
the sake of the common good, persons will have to cede their claims on
individual goods. The key possibility is that the political common good
can approach and anticipate its analogue and become an honest, generous
communion in which persons identify their own good with the good of
others and of the whole.

Implications for Politics

Theological personalism helps Maritain develop his common good theory
by being able to say more about the relationship of personal goods, political goods, and the supernatural good. He holds that "the common good of
the city or of civilization . . . does not preserve its true nature unless it
respects that which surpasses it, unless it is subordinated . . . to the order
of eternal goods and the supra-temporal values from which human life is
suspended."[45] Here Maritain uses the terms *respect* and *subordination* to
express the relation of the temporal to the supernatural common good;
elsewhere he employs the more precise phrase *indirect subordination.*

> There is a common work to be accomplished by the social whole. This whole,
> of which human persons are the parts, is not "neutral" but committed to a
> temporal task; and so *persons are subordinated to this common work.* Still, it
> is essential that the common good flow back over persons—not only in the
> political order itself, but also in that other order where what is most profound
> in the person is her supra-temporal vocation and the goods bound up with it.
> In this order, too, it is essential that *society itself and its common work are
> indirectly subordinated* to the person's transcendent end.[46]

Maritain interlocks two claims here: (*a*) in the secular political order, persons are subordinated to the common work—not as individual monads,
but as persons upon whom this common good must flow back; (*b*) in the
supernatural order, society and its common good are indirectly subordinated to the person by virtue of his or her supernatural vocation. Maritain
asserts the common good's subordination to persons in light of their supernatural ends in order to remind us that the common good must serve
human flourishing; but he calls the subordination "indirect" in order to
remind us that, here and now, believers cannot manipulate the political
common good to serve their worldly ends.

Claims *a* and *b* condition each other. That is, the person is subordinated
to society in the mundane order but not in the supernatural order, because
of the person's ultimate relation to the supernatural common good. I would
say that the person's subordination to the common good also has an indi-

rect aspect, for these orders are not two-tiered, but penetrate each other. The person as person has a supernatural vocation in the midst of earthly life. This entails that the person is only indirectly subordinated to society even now; hence the requirement that the common good must flow back over the person. Correspondingly, society and its common work are ultimately subordinated to the supernatural common good, *but they are only indirectly subordinated to it in the temporal order, precisely because of society's secular purpose.*

There are two implications of this analysis. First, the ultimate and supernatural common good of religious believers appears as only a special or partial common good under the conditions of time. To enforce it as part of the political common good is illegitimate:

> To inject into political society a special or partial common good, the temporal common good of the faithful of one religion, even though it were the true religion, and which would claim for them a privileged position in the State, would be to inject into political society a divisive principle and, to that extent, to jeopardize the temporal common good.[47]

A second result, which balances the first, is that the supernatural common good does have something to do with the temporal common good. The common good of society must be indirectly subordinated, or (as I prefer to say) oriented, to the supernatural common good. This orientation must be understood within the limit set by the first result: the state must not employ its coercive power to force one view of the supernatural on the temporal common good; moreover, it ought not favor one vision of the ultimate good over another. (Limits are also set by human rights to freedom of thought, speech, religion, and association—derived in the natural law approach.) On the other hand, the political common good is oriented to the common good. This means that when social actors respect human rights, when they empower voluntary institutions, and when they enable citizens to cooperate with one another, then the temporal common good is being pursued. And when the temporal common good is pursued in this fashion, it is oriented to the supernatural common good, for it respects the dignity of persons, and it secures and strengthens the conditions that persons need in order to flourish fully (leading ultimately, in a Christian perspective, to their communion of the Kingdom of God). When citizens, voluntary institutions, and political bodies cooperate to pursue the common good in the ways just described, they do *enable* persons to achieve their own perfection, including their supernatural vocations. This empowerment is indirect, as it should be, given the nature of society.

In sum, theological personalism fills out the account of the common good in two ways. First, it specifies the complex interrelations of personal goods and the common good. The indirect subordination of persons to the common good vindicates the political priority of the common task and necessitates individual contributions and sacrifices to it; at the same time, the indirect subordination of the common good to persons validates their basic rights and transcendent dignity, and it marshals the common work to their benefit. Second, theological personalism both promotes and sets limits to the role of religion in common good. Because God is the ultimate good toward which all created common goods are oriented, the political common good, in promoting human fulfillment, must respect religious faith and remove obstacles to its practice and expression. On the other hand, the same respect for the person's transcendent orientation forbids giving political preference to any one faith. I think it is clear, then, that Maritain's theological approach furthers the articulation of the common good for a pluralistic, democratic society. This approach shows why the Christians ought to care deeply about promoting the political common good as it both distinguishes and relates their ultimate good to the good of society. To citizens who are not Christian, this theological analysis is not irrelevant, but offers them a powerful vision of a common good in which the dignity of every person is championed.

ASSESSING THE TWO APPROACHES

Reaching Multiple Audiences

We are now in a position to see how Maritain successfully intertwines the two approaches. On the one hand, we can move from natural law to theology. Natural law lies in the divine reason of the Creator: what is just is just because it corresponds to the exemplar of justice in God's reason. Yet this is not an inaccessible god, but the personal God who reveals the divine will through Scripture, personal revelation, church teaching, and God's own action in history. Because God's reason and will are united, revealed morality is in essential conformity with natural law.[48] This series of claims provides continuity between Maritain's two approaches in one direction.

We can also find continuity by working in the opposite direction, beginning with Maritain's theological commitments.[49] Maritain believes in the truth of the Christian Gospel, interpreted as a revelation of the dignity of humanity created, redeemed, and sustained by the Triune God. This faith undergirds his personalism and his belief in the evangelical inspiration of democracy. This faith also supports his conviction that people profoundly divided in their religious and ideological beliefs can nevertheless cooperate for the political common good, for Maritain believes that God's grace is offered to all, and even the "pseudo-atheist" or agnostic may respond to it:

> He may be ready to lay down his life for the cause of atheism. Yet it is not impossible that in a first act of freedom, he may decide upon the moral good and by the same token turn his life toward the Separate Good, toward the true God Whom he knows in a certain manner without knowing it. In the mysterious secret of the spirit's unconscious, such a pseudo-atheist then knows with a natural, volitional and merely practical knowledge that same God Whom he denies in his words and explicit, formulated thoughts. And what is more, without knowing it, he has faith, a merely vital and unformulated faith; and without knowing it, he has charity. (But there is within him schism and division, and therefore a particular frailty.)[50]

When persons respond in this way to the demands of justice and goodness within themselves, they build up the agreement and cooperation that sustain the "democratic faith."[51] These demands are the inner workings of the natural law.

Starting from either direction, the natural law and the theological approaches merge. Maritain never separates these approaches, though in different contexts he does stress one over the other. In *The Rights of Man and Natural Law* and *Man and the State,* he employed the natural law approach, for he was providing a philosophical defense of democratic structures. Theological concerns appear in these books as secondary notes, crucial though they are to his overall political philosophy. By contrast, *Christianity and Democracy* and *The Person and the Common Good* take the theological tack; the former is a reading of democratic culture through the lens of "Christian humanism," the latter a defense of the common good through theological personalism. Natural law principles are subsidiary in these works; Maritain simply indicates where human rights and other formal principles plug into the framework.

Maritain's linking of the two approaches advances a liberal-communitarian synthesis on the common good, in that one approach is congenial to liberalism, the other to communitarian particularism. The natural law approach is particularly akin to the method of comprehensive liberals who found the common good on natural duties within a theistic perspective. Consider a comparison to the early liberals investigated in chapter 1. Maritain bases his whole account of the common good on certain fundamental truths about persons—their God-given dignity, their possession of inalienable rights, their call to God as their ultimate end, and their need for communication and community with others. Locke and Mendelssohn similarly founded their views of common good on thick descriptions of the human person. In Locke, a notion of civil society as based on trust specifies the mutual duties of citizens and authorities. Within this social compact, natural law delineates the rights of citizens and places limitations upon rulers, while a Calvinist conception of calling mandates that each contribute to the common good. Mendelssohn held that persons have such an essential interest in their eternal happiness that society even had a role in promoting it. He conceived of persons as having natural duties to themselves, to others, and to God, and so he defined the common good as the social order that would enable persons to fulfill these duties. These conceptions of person and society are far more comprehensive than the view of contemporary liberals. They describe what the authors hold to be ultimately true about human nature and make use of religious ideas particular to Christianity and Judaism in doing so. Yet they are still liberal—and stronger, I think, than liberalisms that attempt to be purely political/procedural. As with Rawls's version, such attempts are mired in a contradiction: they cannot avoid making substantive moral claims about political obligation, which in turn rely upon truth claims about human nature.

I am not arguing that the members of a democratic society must agree upon one comprehensive view of human nature. They should, though, have opportunities for affirming the value and relevance of their particular worldviews in the public forum—opportunities to make their views intelligible to their fellows. Citizens should understand that the public dialogue welcomes their contributions as members of particular groups and traditions, but it also requires them, if they want to be effective, to engage in coalition building and "translation" from more particular to more general terminology. Maritain's particularist approach is useful as a model, for it relies on both particular communal narratives and intercommunal dialogue. Maritain's particular narrative paints a Christian vision of the common good. This story obviously matters to Christians, and especially Catholics, who are given reasons for listening to persons from other religious and cultural traditions and for cooperating with them for the common good. Yet why should this story matter to non-Christians, who have their own stories to tell of the common good? Maritain thinks it matters because the good is ultimately unified; it finally has its foundation in God. Though there is a plurality of human goods, and though the political common good can take diverse shapes, any authentic perspective on the good told by one tradition should be able to resonate with persons outside that tradition.

Maritain holds, then, that religious accounts of the common good *do matter* to the public debate in a pluralist society. David Hollenbach expresses this affirmation well:

> The God in whom Christians believe is the God of all creation, the God who built the foundations of the cosmos, and as Paul proclaimed to the Athenians in the Acropolis, the God in whom all creatures live and move and have their being. For this reason it is possible to hope that the Christian story as told in

the scriptures is not entirely foreign or strange to those outside the church. It can raise echoes and perhaps recognition among all who share in the quest for the human good.[52]

Particular communal descriptions of the human good play a key role in political dialogue. Like Sandel, Maritain affirms a politics of engagement, wherein persons speak in the public sphere from their particular religious and moral convictions, and they listen to the considered convictions of their fellow citizens. When persons engage the public debate in this way, they not only become more motivated to ensure the success of the dialogue (for they themselves are invested in it), but they have the opportunity to contribute original ideas to the evolving shape of the common good. Maritain himself identifies many public goods in the Catholic tradition, so his linked approach is a valuable precursor to articulating religion's general contributions to the common good.

Instead of limiting the appeal of his account, this linked methodology can attract audiences beyond Maritain's fellow Catholics. His argument for the common good reaches out like concentric ripples in a pond to other Christians, then to other religious believers, and finally to nonbelievers. Members of any of these groups can speak to what they find more or less persuasive in this common good theory. Through these contributions, the overarching secular understanding of the common good is *modified* as particular descriptions of the common good are proffered and pondered, and this understanding is *strengthened* as more and more citizens contribute to its shape and thus invest themselves in it. This process bears a similarity to Rawls's picture of citizens affirming an overlapping consensus from within their comprehensive worldviews but with a crucial difference: in this process, citizens have a much greater chance to shape the meaning of the common good. Through a method of engagement, they speak from their moral and political views, however these are grounded, to try to persuade their fellow citizens to prioritize certain political, social, and/or moral goals. By contrast, citizens in Rawls's overlapping consensus are constrained by the ideal of public reason: their contributions to political debate should employ reasons from their particular worldviews only if they can translate these into public reasons "in due course." From this body of politically translatable religious reasons, Rawls does not expect anything other than support for the conclusions of public reason. Thus, citizens who are motivated by religious views find their possibilities for shaping the political agenda more limited; at the same time, the common good loses the constructive and critical contributions of these citizens.

I have posed the question of whether a communal liberalism shaped by Catholic common good theory is more fair and open than political liberalism. We are now in a position to assess the issue of fairness as it applies to Maritain's and Rawls's methods. Maritain's method of engagement is fair to all citizens in a pluralist democracy, for it allows citizens to participate on an equal footing in shaping the common good and contributing to its advancement. Maritain's method is as fair to religious citizens as to nonreligious ones, for no one is prohibited, even by an ideal of virtuous citizenship, from addressing his own conception of the good to the goods at stake in the political process. Given the unnecessary restrictions that Rawls's ideal of public reason places on citizens' participation, I conclude that Maritain's political method is fairer than Rawls's. A consideration of openness—its ability actually to facilitate widespread participation and cooperation—must wait until the next chapter.

Responding to Methodological Questions in the Liberal-Communitarian Debate

On the issue of engaging versus avoiding religious differences, I have read Maritain as siding with Sandel against Rawls. But Maritain does not join in a complete communitarian rejection of liberalism. Maritain would point to liberalism's value in providing institutions and practices that enable citizens in pluralistic societies to live out the democratic faith. These contributions include, among others, human rights, institutional pluralism, open public debate, and religious toleration. Maritain's approach to liberalism is not to discard it, but to develop its full potential by describing its compatibility with a religious account of the common good. I understand this project to lead to a synthesis of liberalism and communitarianism. I close this chapter by locating Maritain's position on two methodological questions at issue between liberals and communitarians. This analysis will be complemented by a consideration of two substantive questions at the end of the next chapter.[53]

Do Principles of Justice Apply Across Cultures?

This issue concerns whether a liberal theory of justice can apply cross-culturally, "with no attention paid to the culture-specificity of the subject-matter of such theorizing."[54] Some communitarians raise this charge against liberalism.[55] I said earlier that the recent Rawls has not committed himself on this issue because he is caught in a dilemma: either public reason is culturally specific, in which case it is subject to distortion; or it is universal, in which case it undermines the shared understandings that ground political liberalism. By contrast, early liberals like Locke and Mendelssohn tended to speak with universal compass; yet they were also aware that they derived their accounts of social responsibility in part from culturally specific sources. They each had reason to believe that those religious sources were universally applicable: natural law served this purpose for Locke, while Mendelssohn employed a rationalistic interpretation of Judaism.

Maritain places himself mostly on the universal-application side of the issue, owing to his natural law theory and his understanding of pervasive grace. But I have presented three ways he tempers this universalism. First, he conceives of natural law as dynamic and developmental, so it can come to fruition differently in various cultures. Natural law always *tends* toward the same judgments, but since only its first principle is self-evident and infallibly known, there is considerable scope for culturally specific application. Natural law is "known only *in medias res*, in social contexts, or in the prism of actual cases."[56]

Second, Maritain realizes that natural law is appropriated not by persons' theoretical reason, but by their practical reason. Practical reason is shaped by particular experience. So, again, while the first principle of natural law is universally known (though by no means are all reflectively aware of it), the applications of natural law are made only in specific social and practical contexts.

Third, I have held that Maritain links his natural law approach to the common good with a specific theological approach, thus bridging a universal (liberal) and a particularist (communitarian) method. But since this theology claims to represent the "Truth," is it not unremittingly universal? For Maritain, *truth* is always universal, cross-cultural, and transhistorical; but *awareness* and *application* of truth do not have these qualities under the limiting conditions of time. Yet Maritain is no relativist: he is firmly convinced that through honest dialogue and practical cooperation, persons can share a democratic faith. The common work and shared goods that emerge from this cooperation are fitting to what is ultimately true. The values that are lived by those sharing the democratic faith are the practical, secular approximates of the supratemporal values that are realized only in the Kingdom of God. For these reasons, Maritain rejects a "spurious universalism. . . which would make all faiths have their stand, window display, and loudspeaker in a World's Fair Temple, on the condition that all of them should confess they are *not sure* that they are conveying the word of God, and that none of them should claim to be the true Faith." By contrast, a true universalism

> is just the opposite of indifference. The catholicity it implies is not a catholicity of relativism and indistinction, but the catholicity of reason, and first of all the catholicity of the Word of God. . . . True universalism presupposes the sense of truth and the certainties of faith; it is the universalism of love which uses these very certainties of faith and all the resources of the intellect to understand better, and do full justice to, the other fellow. It is not supra-dogmatic; it is supra-subjective.[57]

So Maritain indeed aims for universalism—not by abstracting from the truth-claims of particular traditions—but by urging them to engage one another in shared work and genuine interreligious dialogue. He says this dialogue would lead to a fellowship, not of beliefs, but of people who believe.[58] There is no reason to think that Maritain would exclude from the cultural conversation those whose worldviews are nonreligious or antireligious; rather, he seems to be speaking specifically of interreligious dialogue in this case. As for those who would charge that even in political contexts Maritain's view of public dialogue would privilege religious viewpoints, I can only refer to the general argument of this chapter: that Maritain's method is indeed conducive to free and fair political deliberation.

Are Judgments About the Good Objective?

The debate over moral objectivism concerns the putative liberal view that "individuals' choices of ends, values and conceptions of the good are arbitrary expressions of preference, essentially incapable of rational justification."[59] Sandel argues that Rawls privileges this voluntarist notion of agency, wherein the self gets its definitive ends through choice, over the cognitive dimension of agency, wherein the self—through a process of reflection that leads to self-understanding—discovers ends that are set before it.[60] In Rawls's defense, Stephen Mulhall and Adam Swift argue that he is not committed to a thoroughgoing subjectivism, although they detect a "quasi-subjectivism" in his neglect of the possibility that citizens debating moral matters *could* come to significant agreement on them.[61]

The debate over moral subjectivism versus moral objectivism cuts across liberal-communitarian lines. On the one side, it is easy enough to see how subjectivism fits with other liberal commitments: given the view that persons have a highest-order interest in being able to revise their conceptions of the good, it would be natural to consider those conceptions as expressions of personal preference. Yet not all liberals think this way. Contemporary perfectionist liberals are moral objectivists: they support a liberal society precisely because it fosters certain goods for persons.[62] And, as we have seen, early liberals were moral objectivists as well. On the other side, communitarians such as Sandel and Alasdair MacIntyre, accusing Rawls of subjectivism, have developed accounts of politics that rely upon rational justification of conceptions of the good. But by the same token, such accounts serve to undermine the universalism that, for early liberals, accompanies objectivism. MacIntyre, for instance, writes,

> What the good life is for a fifth-century Athenian general will not be the same as what it was for a medieval nun or a seventeenth-century farmer. But it is

not just that different individuals live in different social circumstances; it is also that we all approach our own circumstances as bearers of a particular social identity. I am someone's son or daughter, someone else's cousin or uncle; I am a citizen of this or that city, a member of this or that guild or profession; I belong to this clan, that tribe, this nation. Hence what is good for me has to be the good for one who inhabits these roles.[63]

While the narrative view of the self presented by MacIntyre acknowledges the importance of a community and its narratives in giving persons "the starting point" for their identity (as MacIntyre puts it), it can also encourage in political and religious thought a sectarian impulse that damages the common good.[64]

For his part, Maritain is an objectivist, due to his natural law theory and his theology, both of which allow for rational justification of goods and values. This complementarity of the two approaches on the question is not a happy coincidence, but results from a theological belief that the order of redemption is continuous with the order of creation. The unity of creation and redemption entails that moral norms are "justified by reference to what is good for or harmful to human beings, and moral virtues can be understood as operative habits that are perfective of human agents."[65] Thus Maritain's methodology requires us to justify and specify the content of moral norms and principles, including political principles such as justice and the common good, by reference to human flourishing. Human flourishing is an objective standard inasmuch as determining its content involves reflection upon human experience in the light of various methods of inquiry—philosophical, religious, scientific, social-scientific, and personal-experiential. When the results of these inquiries are discussed and debated, persons can come to a reasonable measure of agreement on the general content and practical implications of human flourishing.

To assert that the basic components of human flourishing hold true for all persons is not to deny that the political implications of flourishing differ across cultures. Natural law theory allows room for our insights about the specific meaning of flourishing and its concrete applications to develop and change. So Maritain's moral methodology is both universally applicable and sensitive to the real differences that exist among persons within and across cultures. His linked approach to the common good appeals to natural law for a set of moral inclinations we can recognize in ourselves and others, but it contextualizes this appeal in three ways: (1) it understands our knowledge of these inclinations to be vital, unsystematic, connatural knowledge, of which explicit awareness varies greatly among persons; (2) it recognizes that the moral virtues that bring these inclinations to fruition must be developed in virtuous communities; and (3) it is ready to supplement the political appeals derived from natural law with religious accounts of the common good.

On these two methodological issues, Maritain stakes claims that mediate the extreme options, which suggests the viability of a communal liberalism. To criticize Maritain's communal liberalism, one would have to exploit tensions in the linked method or take issue with his substantive account of persons in relation to various communities and the common good. The potential criticisms along the first line are vast, for they can come from four quarters: from those who deny the existence of a natural law; from those who question theological personalism or a theological approach altogether; from those who support natural law but not its link to theology; and from those who take a theological tack but are wary of natural law. Responses even to representative criticisms must be left aside, for my most important task has been to present the coherence and viability of the linked method vis-à-vis the debate between liberals and communitarians. The second kind of critique—pressing substantive challenges to the cogency of Maritain's account of persons and the common good—would be pursued by those who worry about the potentially divisive effects of religion in political life. We need to pursue this issue further and assess the value and potential pitfalls of Maritain's substantive public philosophy. The next chapter will explore his argument that religion contributes to social unity in a pluralist society.

NOTES

1. There is no full-length critical biography of Maritain. Important memoirs are Julie Kernan, *Our Friend, Jacques Maritain: A Personal Memoir* (Garden City, N.Y.: Doubleday, 1975); and Raïssa Maritain, *We Have Been Friends Together* and *Adventures in Grace,* vols. 1 and 2 of *The Memoirs of Raïssa Maritain,* trans. Julie Kernan (Garden City, N.Y.: Image Books, 1961). Shorter biographical surveys can be found in Deal W. Hudson and Matthew J. Mancini, eds., *Understanding Maritain: Philosopher and Friend* (Macon, Ga.: Mercer University Press, 1987), 27–90. A helpful biography situating the development of Maritain's views on mysticism and politics is part 1 of Kristopher Louis Willumsen, "The Relationship of the Mystical and the Political Dimensions of the Christian Faith in the Writings of Jacques Maritain," Ph.D. diss., Catholic University of America, 1992, 6–156, with bibliography at 503–6. There are many volumes celebrating Maritain's intellectual achievements; in addition to Hudson and Mancini's *Understanding Maritain,* see *The Maritain Volume of the Thomist,* vol. 5 (New York: Sheed & Ward, 1943); Joseph W. Evans, ed., *Jacques Maritain: The Man and His Achievement* (New York: Sheed & Ward, 1963); and Peter A. Redpath, ed., *From Twilight to Dawn: The Cultural Vision of Jacques Maritain* (Notre Dame, Ind.: University of Notre Dame Press for the American Maritain Association, 1990). A helpful new work that explores the contours of Maritain's political thought is James V. Schall, *Jacques Maritain: The Philosopher in Society,* Twentieth-Century Political Thinkers series (Lanham, Md.: Rowman & Littlefield, 1998). For comprehensive bibliogra-

phies of Maritain, see Donald Gallagher and Idella Gallagher, *The Achievement of Jacques and Raïssa Maritain: A Bibliography, 1906–1961* (Garden City, N.Y.: Doubleday, 1962); and Joseph W. Evans, "A Maritain Bibliography," *New Scholasticism* 46 (1972): 118–28.

2. Will Herberg, ed., *Four Existentialist Theologians* (Garden City, N.Y.: Doubleday Anchor, 1958), 3. The most important statement of Maritain's Thomistic existentialism is his *Existence and the Existent*, trans. Lewis Galantière and Gerald B. Phelan (New York: Doubleday, 1947). For commentary, see Raymond Dennehy, "Maritain's 'Intellectual Existentialism': An Introduction to His Metaphysics and Epistemology," in *Understanding Maritain*, ed. Hudson and Mancini, 201–33.

3. See Jacques Maritain, "A New Approach to God," in *The Range of Reason* (New York: Scribner, 1952), 86–102, quote at 87.

4. Charles De Koninck, *De la primauté du bien commun, contre les personnalistes* (Quebec: Éditions de l'Université Laval, 1943).

5. I. Th. Eschmann, "In Defense of Jacques Maritain," *Modern Schoolman* 22 (May 1945): 183–203; Charles De Koninck, "In Defense of Saint Thomas: A Reply to Father Eschmann's Attack on the Primacy of the Common Good," *Laval théologique et philosophique* 1, no. 2 (1945): 9–109. Maritain did not directly participate in this debate over personalism, but he mentions it briefly in the book he wrote to clarify his views to the reading public, *The Person and the Common Good*, trans. John J. Fitzgerald (New York: Scribner, 1947; rpt., Notre Dame, Ind.: University of Notre Dame Press, 1966), at 16 n. 6.

6. Mary M. Keys, "Personal Dignity and the Common Good: A Twentieth-Century Thomistic Dialogue," in *Catholicism, Liberalism, and Communitarianism: The Catholic Intellectual Tradition and the Moral Foundations of Democracy*, ed. Kenneth L. Grasso, Gerard V. Bradley, and Robert P. Hunt (Lanham, Md.: Rowman & Littlefield, 1995), 177.

7. Keys, "Personal Dignity," 186.

8. Maritain responded to the war not only in his writing, but in several other capacities. He marshaled prominent intellectuals to sign manifestos against Hitler, Mussolini, and Franco. Exiled with his wife and sister-in-law in New York, he delivered radio addresses to France, published political treatises that were secretly distributed through the country, and helped found a French university-in-exile. After the war, Maritain served as the French ambassador to the Vatican from 1945 to 1948, during which assignment he presided over the French delegation to the first United Nations Educational, Scientific, and Cultural Organization (UNESCO) conference.

9. The bibliographic information for works not quoted in this chapter: Jacques Maritain, *Freedom: Its Meaning*, ed. Ruth Nanda Anshen (London: Allen & Unwin, 1940); *Scholasticism and Politics*, ed. and trans. Mortimer J. Adler (New York: Macmillan, 1940); *Principes d'une politique humaniste* (New York: Éditions de la Maison Française, 1944); *Ransoming the Time*, trans. Harry Lorin Binsse (New York: Scribner, 1941).

10. Note that my focus will bypass Maritain's earlier works, some of which sounded anti-individualist, antimodern, and antiliberal notes. Prominent among

these are *Antimoderne* (Paris: Revue des Jeunes, 1922), and *Three Reformers: Luther, Descartes, Rousseau* (1925), trans. Frank Sheed (New York: Sheed and Ward, 1933). *Integral Humanism* (1936), trans. Joseph W. Evans (New York: Scribner, 1968) represents a transition between this early period and his middle, mature period, in which Maritain celebrated the virtues of democracy, pluralism, and even the American spirit. For an account of this development, see John Hellman, "The Humanism of Jacques Maritain," in *Understanding Maritain*, ed. Hudson and Mancini, 117–31. Similarly, my focus stops short of Maritain's late life, when he surprised many by leveling sharp criticisms at liberal theological trends and Church reforms arising out of the Second Vatican Council in *The Peasant of the Garonne: An Old Layman Questions Himself About the Present Time*, trans. Michael Cuddihy and Elizabeth Hughes (New York: Holt, Rinehart & Winston, 1968). Yet Maritain gives no indication in this book of a change in his political views.

11. Namely, *The Peasant of the Garonne* (see the previous note).

12. I will be making these claims more through my positive interpretation of Maritain than through an investigation of conservative and neoconservative Catholic interpreters of Maritain—from whom, I might add, there is much to be learned. For a more traditional interpretation of Maritain, see the following by Ralph McInerny, *Art and Prudence: Studies in the Thought of Jacques Maritain* (Notre Dame, Ind.: University of Notre Dame Press, 1988); "Maritain in and on America," in *Reinhold Neibuhr Today*, ed. Richard John Neuhaus (Grand Rapids, Mich.: Eerdmans, 1989), 33–45; and, with Michelle Watkins, "Jacques Maritain and the Rapprochement of Liberalism and Communitarianism," in *Catholicism, Liberalism, and Communitarianism*, ed. Grasso, Bradley, and Hunt, 151–72. I dispute the interpretation of this latter article at the end of chapter 4. A valuable exploration of Maritain within a Catholic neoconservative project is made by Michael Novak, *Free Persons and the Common Good* (Lanham, Md.: Madison Books, 1989). I agree heartily with Novak that Maritain's common good theory validates the best elements of the liberal political tradition, but my reading of Maritain and the Catholic social tradition takes me in a different economic direction than Novak, as can be seen in chapter 4. Novak is wise not to push Maritain too close to the liberal-capitalist camp: "I would be delinquent if I did not at least mention that the consonance (and serious disagreements) between Hayek's work and such works of Jacques Maritain as *Man and the State* and *The Person and the Common Good* cry out for systematic attention" (*Free Persons*, 86).

13. A good summary of Maritain's conception of the common good is reflected in the Second Vatican Council's statement that "the common good embraces the sum of those conditions of social life by which individuals, families and groups can achieve their own fulfillment in a relatively thorough and ready way" (*Gaudium et Spes: Pastoral Constitution on the Church in the Modern World* [7 December 1965], in *Catholic Social Thought: The Documentary Heritage*, ed. David J. O'Brien and Thomas A. Shannon [Maryknoll, N.Y.: Orbis, 1992], par. 74). It is no accident that the Council's definition bears the stamp of Maritain. The Council restates Pope John XXIII's description of the common good in the encyclical *Mater et Magistra: Christianity and Social Progress* (15 May 1961), in *Catholic*

Social Thought, ed. O'Brien and Shannon, par. 65. Maritain knew and worked with Pope John when the latter, as Archbishop Roncalli, was the Vatican representative to France. The two may well have shared ideas about the common good and Catholic teaching. Cf. Kernan, *Our Friend*, 138–39.

14. Jacques Maritain, *The Rights of Man and Natural Law*, trans. Doris C. Anson (New York: Scribner, 1943; rpt., bound with *Christianity and Democracy*, San Francisco: Ignatius, 1986), 95. Maritain uses the word *redistributed* for two reasons, in my view. First, it conveys that the goods that make up the common good come from persons in the first place; they are returned to them by the agents of political society. Second, the term connotes what we commonly mean by *redistribution*—welfare policies that reallocate tax moneys from the wealthier to the poorer. This kind of redistribution is required in order to secure the various rights of working persons that Maritain enumerates in this same text on pp. 169–86.

15. Maritain, *Rights of Man*, 95.

16. Jacques Maritain, "The End of Machiavellianism," in *The Range of Reason*, 142–43.

17. Maritain, *Person and the Common Good*, 52; semicolons added for clarity.

18. Jacques Maritain, *Man and the State* (Chicago: University of Chicago Press, 1951), 80.

19. Maritain, *Man and the State*, 85–86.

20. Maritain, *Man and the State*, 85–86.

21. See St. Thomas Aquinas, *Summa Theologiae*, ed. Thomas Gilby, 61 vols. (London: Blackfriars, 1964–76), I–II, q. 94, a. 2.

22. There are three categories of these inclinations: first, that we share with all living substances—self-preservation; second, those we share with animals; and third, those special to us as rational beings.

23. Maritain, *Man and the State*, 88.

24. Maritain, *Man and the State*, 88–89.

25. Maritain, *Man and the State*, 89. Maritain calls this the "gnoseological" element.

26. Paul Ramsey, *Nine Modern Moralists* (Englewood Cliffs, N.J.: Prentice-Hall, 1962), 213–23.

27. Jacques Maritain, "On Knowledge Through Connaturality," in *The Range of Reason*, 27.

28. Maritain, *Man and the State*, 94.

29. Maritain, *Man and the State*, 76–78. See also Maritain's address to UNESCO, "The Possibilities for Co-operation in a Divided World," in *The Range of Reason*, 172–84.

30. See Aquinas, *Summa Theologiae*, I–II, q. 91, a. 2.

31. Maritain, *Person and the Common Good*, 70, citing Aquinas, *Summa Theologiae* II–II, q. 64, a. 2 and I–II, q. 21, a. 4, ad 3. Maritain makes use of a few other sentences from Aquinas in establishing his own position. In Mary Keys's view, Maritain takes these sentences out of context and "seems surprisingly undaunted by the scarcity and problematic nature of the textual support for his personalist position" ("Personal Dignity," 177–78). For a faithful interpretation of Aquinas's original meaning, Charles De Koninck may have had the upper hand, though this

does not make Maritain any less useful to my constructive project of synthesizing liberal and communitarian conceptions of the common good.

32. Maritain, *Person and the Common Good*, 71.

33. Maritain, *Person and the Common Good*, 73.

34. Maritain, *Person and the Common Good*, 33.

35. This is a phrase suggested to me by Margaret Farley. As Maritain puts it, "Soul and matter are the two substantial co-principles of the same being, of one and the same reality, called man. . . . Our whole being subsists in virtue of the subsistence of the spiritual soul which is in us a principle of creative unity, independence and liberty" (*Person and the Common Good*, 36, 38).

36. My translation from Jacques Maritain, *La personne et le bien commun,* in *Oeuvres complétes Jacques et Raïssa Maritain* (Fribourg, Switzerland: Éditions Universitaires, 1982–95), vol. 9, 167–237, quote at 192. Cf. Maritain, *Person and the Common Good*, 41–42.

37. Maritain, *Person and the Common Good*, 49.

38. Maritain, *Person and the Common Good*, 41.

39. See Maritain, *Person and the Common Good*, 12–13.

40. Maritain, *Person and the Common Good*, 15.

41. For Maritain's discussion of these points, see *Person and the Common Good*, 17–28.

42. Maritain, *Person and the Common Good*, 57.

43. My translation from Maritain, *La personne*, 205. Fitzgerald's translation in the 1966 edition, on p. 58, omits key phrases in this sentence—a problem identified by David Hollenbach in "The Common Good Revisited," *Theological Studies* 50, no. 1 (March 1989): 70–94, at 86 n. 42.

44. My translation from Maritain, *La personne,* 206. Cf. *Person and the Common Good,* 59.

45. Maritain, *Person and the Common Good*, 62.

46. My translation from Maritain, *La personne,* 235–36. Maritain's French is particularly dense here, and the English translation (102–3) is difficult to follow. Therefore, I have attempted a freer translation.

47. Maritain, *Rights of Man*, 111.

48. For an analysis of this approach—a theological rationalism that grounds morality in God's reason—see Brian Stiltner, "Who Can Understand Abraham? The Relation of God and Morality in Kierkegaard and Aquinas," *Journal of Religious Ethics* 21, no. 2 (fall 1993): 221–45.

49. Cf. the following with the sequence of claims summarized by McInerny, "Maritain in and on America," 42–43.

50. Jacques Maritain, "The Immanent Dialectic of the First Act of Freedom," in *The Range of Reason*, 84. Compare how similar this argument is to Karl Rahner's well-known formulation of "the fundamental option"—the claim that persons can respond in unthematic awareness to God's uncreated grace. See Karl Rahner, *Foundations of Christian Faith: An Introduction to the Idea of Christianity*, trans. William V. Dych (New York: Seabury Press, 1978), chaps. 3 and 4, esp. 97–106.

51. Cf. Maritain, *Man and the State*, 108–14.

52. David Hollenbach, "The Common Good in the Postmodern Epoch: What

Role for Theology?" in *Religion, Ethics, and the Common Good*, Annual publication of the College Theology Society, vol. 41, ed. James Donohue and M. Theresa Moser (Mystic, Conn.: Twenty-Third Publications and the College Theology Society, 1996), 3–22, quote at 16.

53. I take my cue for these four questions from the issues that Stephen Mulhall and Adam Swift use to frame their book *Liberals and Communitarians* (Oxford: Blackwell, 1992). Their issues, five in all, are first described in their introduction.

54. Mulhall and Swift, *Liberals,* 158.

55. In particular, Michael Walzer presents a theory of egalitarian justice that departs from liberal universalism, a view he thinks the early Rawls promotes. See *Spheres of Justice* (New York: Basic Books, 1983).

56. Ramsey, *Nine Modern Moralists,* 219, describing Maritain's theory.

57. Jacques Maritain, *Truth and Human Fellowship* (Princeton, N.J.: Princeton University Press, 1957), 28, 30. Why the different capitalizations of "word of God"? In the first reference, Maritain apparently uses *word* to mean *God's teachings* generally; in the second, *Word* specifically indicates the Christian Scriptures.

58. Maritain, *Truth and Human Fellowship*, 24.

59. Mulhall and Swift, *Liberals,* 159.

60. Michael J. Sandel, *Liberalism and the Limits of Justice* (Cambridge: Cambridge University Press, 1982), 58–59.

61. Mulhall and Swift, *Liberals,* 214–15.

62. Cf. Joseph Raz, *The Morality of Freedom* (Oxford: Clarendon, 1986).

63. Alasdair MacIntyre, *After Virtue*, 2nd ed. (Notre Dame, Ind.: University of Notre Dame Press, 1984), 220.

64. Communitarian-inspired, sectarian impulses in postliberal theology are assailed by Hollenbach, "Common Good in the Postmodern Epoch"; and by Michael H. Barnes, "Community, Clannishness, and the Common Good," in *Religion, Ethics, and the Common Good*, vol. 41, ed. Donohue and Moser, 27–52.

65. Stephen J. Pope, "Knowability of the Natural Law: A Foundation for Ethics of the Common Good," in *Religion, Ethics, and the Common Good*, vol. 41, ed. Donohue and Moser, 53–63, quote at 60.

Chapter 4

Religion's Contributions to the Common Good Through the Vista of Catholicism

How are we to assess the contributions that religion does and might make to the common good? On the one hand, we could proceed by way of a social-scientific or philosophic theory about what religion is, what human needs it serves, and what social function it plays. For instance, Moses Mendelssohn relied upon a "top-down" approach when he described religion as a voluntary, noncoercive institution concerned with helping persons achieve their eternal happiness. Alternatively, we could proceed from the standpoint of a particular religious tradition, seeing what it purports to contribute to the common good and testing its compatibility with liberalism and communitarianism. While this "bottom-up" approach can speak only for the value of the religion in question, it would have implications for considering the value of religion in general: the investigation would develop questions that should be asked about the contributions of any religion to the common good, and its results could serve as part of a larger comparative investigation and as a test for social-scientific approaches. Since Jacques Maritain locates his common good theory in a particular tradition of religious inquiry, and since he focuses on the Catholic Church's role in society, it makes sense to take this bottom-up approach. Proceeding along this line has value if one accepts, as I do, the communitarian claim that in thinking about the ordering of society, we cannot completely abstract from our particular communal commitments and views of the good. Yet following upon the argument of chapter 3, we should expect to find ways that Maritain's particular theological account leads to more general claims about the value of religion to the common good.

In this chapter, I will be drawing upon Maritain, the Catholic social tradition, and commentators upon both in order to give a complete picture of the contributions Catholicism sees itself making to the common good. The following claims constitute an interpretive framework that I bring to Maritain's work, in that they comprise three general contributions that (Catholic) Christianity can make to the common good, based on claims and arguments proffered by Maritain:[1]

1. Catholicism's intellectual resources for a public philosophy include its moral anthropology, its communal orientation of human rights, and its account of mediating institutions.
2. The Christian church and its members foster conditions for social harmony though their expressions of neighbor-love and actions for justice.
3. Christians give voice to neglected human goods through a prophetic critique of society in fidelity to Jesus' option for the poor.

The intellectual resources comprise political and ethical ideas that Maritain draws from the Roman Catholic tradition. Though they are not distinctively religious, their content is grounded in theological personalism and mediated through natural law theory to a wide audience. These ideas represent Maritain's attempt to render the tradition's theological anthropology and account of society intelligible to a pluralistic culture. In his account of Christianity's community-building and prophetic roles, Maritain relies upon more distinctive religious ideas. The church and its members seek to generate commitment to the common good, not so much persuading others by rational arguments as inspiring them by example. These general contributions suggest avenues by which other religions can contribute to the common good—though, of course, other religions' understandings of their particular contributions may be quite different from the content described here. The second part of the chapter uses Maritain's public philosophy to respond to key substantive questions from the liberal-communitarian debate, vindicating the viability of communal liberalism.

INTELLECTUAL RESOURCES

An Account of Human Flourishing

The particular conception of the human person that emerges from Maritain's view of the human person, shaped by both natural law theory and personalism, has direct implications for the political common good. This anthropology suggests an account of *human flourishing*,[2] a description of a fulfilled human life, including the goods that are to "flow back" to persons from the common good in order to help them live well. Depending on the good in question, society's role may be to leave persons free to pursue it; to nurture, support, and encourage them in their pursuit of it; or to distribute it to them. Maritain holds the maximum development of the whole human person to be an essential component of the common good and the primary criterion by which we evaluate society. The common good

> involves, as its *chief* value, the highest possible attainment (that is, the highest compatible with the good of the whole) of persons to their lives as persons, and to their freedom of expansion or autonomy—and to the gifts of goodness which in their turn flow from it.[3]

But what makes for human flourishing? Recall from the previous chapter Maritain's distinction between theoretical conceptions of the good and practical matters of political and social life. He thought agreement on the former very difficult—though not impossible—to achieve in a free, pluralist society, but he held out hope for practical ethical/political agreements. Is human flourishing one of those theoretical concepts about which we can just "agree to disagree"? No, it is not. While citizens in a free society will not share the same philosophical and religious views that underpin a moral anthropology, their practical agreements must proceed from some shared or significantly overlapping agreement on what society should do for its members. Persons always act for a good, or at least for what appears as good;[4] this is true in the political no less than the personal sphere. Thus, in order to reach practical agreements, there has to be some shared account of what is good for persons and what goods the political system may properly take into account.

We have seen the main steps Maritain takes to get to an account of flourishing that can be used in political life. He describes natural law as the tendency of the human being to seek its own good and to realize its own perfection. In practice, persons act upon the natural law through their practical reason, which grasps, "in the prism of actual cases,"[5] which actions are consonant or dissonant with the self's tendencies to realize the good. It might have been useful had Maritain tried to lay out categories of action that are generally in accord with human nature, or the dimensions of human life that demand fulfillment, but these are not the matters on which he goes into detail. Yet his next step allows him to flesh out the picture of human flourishing: the norms of human functioning correspond to the rights of the human person. "The human person possesses rights because of the very fact that it is a person, a whole, master of itself and of its acts, and which consequently is not merely a means to an end, but an end, an end which must be treated as such."[6] Maritain understands human rights not merely as zones of protection for personal autonomy—although many rights imply or involve such protection—but more fundamentally as

the *inviolable claims the person may make to protect or secure the conditions of her flourishing*. As Maritain puts it:

> The notion of right and the notion of moral obligation are correlative. They
> are both founded on the freedom proper to spiritual agents. If man is morally
> bound to the things which are necessary to the fulfillment of his destiny, obvi-
> ously, then, he has the right to fulfill his destiny; and if he has the right to
> fulfill his destiny then he has the right to the things necessary for this pur-
> pose.[7]

When we turn to his human rights theory in the next section, we will see
that Maritain describes a broad array of civil, social, and economic rights.
A person who lives in a society that respects these rights would not only
be capable of functioning well, but would have the freedom and resources
for striving to live a good life in concert with others.

The Communitarian Context of Human Rights

The Catholic tradition's key contribution to human rights theory is its
proposition that *rights serve the common good*. "Just as every law—
notably the natural law, on which they are grounded—aims at the common
good, so human rights have an intrinsic relation to the common good."[8]
To see how Maritain's account of rights presents this claim of his, let us
consider his account in light of two developments that David Hollenbach
identifies in Catholic rights theory. The first is the identification of three
coequal elements of human dignity: "Respect for freedom, the meeting of
basic needs, and participation in community and social relationships are
all essential aspects of the human dignity that is the foundation of all
rights."[9] The second development is a threefold differentiation of rights
into personal, social, and instrumental rights. Personal rights are the "basic
needs, freedoms and forms of relationship" that must be protected as a
consequence of human dignity. Social rights are "expressions of the forms
of human interdependence which are indispensable for the realization of
human dignity." Finally, instrumental rights are claims on those particular
means that enable human dignity to be preserved.[10]

Maritain reflects these two developments in *The Rights of Man and Natural Law*. In the second half of the book, he enumerates a wide array of
particular human rights under three heuristic categories: the rights of the
human person as such, the rights of the civic person, and the rights of the
social/working person.[11] Now consider the first development—the identification of three essential components of dignity that rights are to protect
and ensure. Maritain's list includes rights of freedom, rights that secure
basic needs, and rights of political and economic participation.[12] Maritain

does not list these rights in any particular order or with any implication that a society should prioritize civic rights over economic and social rights. Yet he does acknowledge a temporal and causative priority of the rights of the person as such. The fundamental rights and liberties of the person belong to natural law, whereas the rights of the civic and working person "spring from positive law and from the fundamental constitution of the political community." They "depend indirectly on natural law" because they complete what natural law leaves undetermined.[13] These later categories of rights have developed as persons living in community have responded to the dynamic impulse of natural law within themselves, have asserted to one another their dignity as citizens and workers, and have arranged their institutions to respond to this dignity.

Maritain's discussion also reflects the second development in Catholic rights theory—the differentiation of personal, social, and instrumental rights:[14]

1. The fundamental rights in Maritain's list—the rights to existence, to personal liberty, and so on—identify basic needs and freedoms that are "rooted in the vocation of the person (a spiritual and free agent) to the order of absolute values and to a destiny superior to time."[15] These rights make *negative* claims on all—not to hinder unjustly the liberty of another—that remain the same no matter how a society is organized or what its level of prosperity is.

2. Yet these rights also make *positive* claims that require us to consider their correlative social dimensions. Hollenbach says that a social right makes "a claim about how the individual and the community are interrelated. Because interdependence is an essential aspect of human existence, the preservation of human dignity is a social task."[16] Examples from Maritain's list include the right to marry according to one's choice and to raise a family, the right of familial autonomy, the right to political participation, the right of association, and the right to a just wage. In Hollenbach's terms, these social rights acknowledge the way personal dignity is mediated through forms of social interdependence.

3. Personal dignity is also mediated by institutional realities. "Thus the [Catholic] tradition has come to affirm a number of conditions which must be present in . . . macro-institutions if human dignity is to be preserved."[17] These instrumental rights include, from Maritain's list, the right to property, political rights of legal equality and equal suffrage, the rights to form and join unions, and rights to economic relief and social security.

The form and content of some instrumental and social rights will vary according to the economic and social conditions of a political community.

A positive right, such as to health care, should be construed as a right not to as much medical care as one wants, nor to the most expensive care available, but to a decent level of care. What makes for a decent level of care needs to be determined by a fair social-political process involving multiple institutions (government, businesses, unions, medical societies, patient and consumer groups, etc.). In this process, citizens and decision makers would take into account such factors as the economic resources of society, what standard of care enables citizens to live decent and fulfilling lives, and what minimum level of care can be provided for all without depleting the system. Maritain clearly thinks that societies should recognize and institutionally guarantee such economic rights, though he also realizes that societies can move only as fast as economic and political realities allow.[18]

Thus, the imperatives of the common good are recognized in Catholic human rights theory: social contexts shape the application of human rights and, to some degree, their actual content. Taken together, the two developments just outlined reveal what it means for human rights to serve the common good. Though individual, social, and instrumental rights can conflict in an imperfect world, each of these three levels of rights is properly understood only in relation to the others. Both liberty and sociality are requisite to human fulfillment: while the person as a free, moral, and spiritual being transcends total communal definition, communal life is still part of her self-definition and is necessary for her maximum fulfillment. In promoting this account, Maritain contributed to Catholicism's "communitarian reconstruction of human rights."[19] Catholic social teaching since the middle of the twentieth century has reconstructed traditional liberal rights by emphasizing their communal character. A right, such as freedom from torture, is "not adequately described as a negative right to be left alone. It is a positive claim to be treated as a self-in-society, a person-in-relation-to-other-persons."[20] In recent Catholic teaching, "human rights specify the minimum standards for what it means to treat people as members of [a] community."[21] The notion of rights as empowerments takes "primacy" over the negative notion of rights as immunities, thus Catholic social teaching grants socioeconomic rights at least an equal place alongside traditional civil rights.[22] Maritain's rights theory incorporates both the common good orientation and the empowerment feature of the communitarian reconstruction.

Note two implications of the communal orientation of rights. First, rights can limit one another. The various goods promoted by different human rights have to be related to a "scale of values": in determining political priorities based on rights, we have to assess how each right contributes to human development and the common good.[23] Second, rights imply obligations. But they are not always claims against specific others; they fundamentally represent what is owed to persons as persons. Those who bear the corresponding duty may be other persons, voluntary bodies, the state, or society at large. Hence, to fulfill economic and social rights will require institutional analysis and changes.

Revitalizing Society Through Mediating Institutions

The final part of Catholicism's intellectual resources for social unity is an approach to democratic revitalization through local, or mediating, institutions. Mediating institutions, according to Peter Berger and Richard Neuhaus, stand "between the individual in his private life and the large institutions of public life."[24] Examples of these are families, neighborhoods, churches, local schools, local political structures, service groups, and all manner of associations the membership of which is voluntary. The large institutions, or "megastructures," include the modern state and "the large economic conglomerates of capitalist enterprise, big labor, and the growing bureaucracies that administer wide sectors of society, such as in education and the organized professions."[25]

There is a manifest need for institutions that mediate between the megastructures and the individual. People require the services, security, and order provided by large institutions, yet these structures are typically faceless and alienating. Healthy mediating institutions relieve the dichotomy between the public and private spheres of life, thus benefiting both individuals and society: these institutions have "a private face, giving private life a measure of stability, and they have a public face, transferring meaning and value to the megastructures."[26]

Catholic social documents of the twentieth century have stressed the value of mediating institutions in democratizing and humanizing the political, economic, and cultural spheres of life. Pope Pius XI affirmed their value by developing the principle of *subsidiarity*: "It is an injustice . . . to assign to a greater and higher association what lesser and subordinate organizations can do. For every social activity ought of its very nature to furnish help to the members of the social body, and never destroy or absorb them."[27] Certainly this stress is neither new nor particularly controversial in democratic political thought. Early liberalism sought to circumscribe the power of the state by grounding its authority in the service of citizens and by restricting its influence over important spheres of human life, such as culture, economics, and religion. Modern liberalism continued in this line, though some have criticized it for consistently favoring individual autonomy over the empowerment of mediating institutions. In response to this communitarian criticism, liberals have begun to look again at the realm of civil society, acknowledging that the liberal state should empower mediating institutions and seek their cooperation in carrying out its own tasks.[28]

Maritain's contribution to this issue was to specify the state's role in securing the interests of civil society. In *Man and the State* he writes:

> The State is only that part of the body politic especially concerned with the maintenance of law, the promotion of the common welfare and public order, and the administration of public affairs. The State is a part which *specializes* in the interests of the *whole*.[29]

The whole in this case is the political society—a body of citizens sharing a social life through a network of institutions. The state is the institution that holds the society together under a political jurisdiction; it is the "topmost part" of society.[30] This topmost status indicates the state's particular legal authority, which ultimately derives from political society and is placed at its service.

> When we say that the State is the superior part in the body politic, this means that it is superior to the other organs or collective parts of this body, but it does not mean that it is superior to the body politic itself. The part as such is inferior to the whole. The State is inferior to the body politic as a whole, and is at the service of the body politic as a whole.[31]

This theory of the state is *instrumentalist*, as opposed to *substantialist* or *absolutist*. The state is not a moral person subject to its own rights, nor is it all-competent; rather, it is an agency of political society and serves a political role constrained by the rights of citizens and the demands of the common good.[32]

This distinction of state and civil society leads to a strong commitment to pluralism, for it forbids making one institution superior in all human affairs.

> The national community, as well as all communities of the nation . . . [are] comprised in the superior unity of the body politic. But the body politic also contains in its superior unity the family units, whose essential rights and freedoms are anterior to itself, and a multiplicity of other particular societies which proceed from the free initiative of citizens and should be as autonomous as possible. Such is the element of pluralism inherent in every truly political society. Family, economic, cultural, educational, religious life matter as much as does political life to the very existence and prosperity of the body politic.[33]

Maritain combines several recurring themes to define and defend pluralism. He imagines society as a network of local communities and organizations that help their members live well. The good human life depends in part on the deep bonds forged by religious, ethnic, linguistic, and national subcommunities within a society. Yet these cultural loyalties are incomplete, and potentially dangerous, if severed from a political framework that orients them toward the larger society.[34] Pluralism is not only the freedom to be distinct but an empowerment to participate in the common good. Maintain offers not only these anthropological and political grounds for pluralism, but suggests a theological one as well: while each human association is analogous to the ultimate common good of human communion in and with God, [35] the plurality of associations is a consequence of human finitude and a guard against hubris. In sum, pluralism is central to the common good because different communities center on the pursuit of different components of the complex human good; because institutional diversity facilitates extensive participation in social life; and because no one association can claim to be the perfect community.

The intellectual resources of Maritain's common good theory are pertinent to political debate and decision making. His conception of human flourishing can be offered in public discussions about the sorts of human goods that policies should support. His account of human rights presents normative proposals for granting institutional recognition to social and economic rights and for keeping the application of personal rights within a framework of communal responsibilities. And his account of mediating structures has various implications for promoting cooperation between governmental and voluntary institutions in pursuit of the common good.

All of the resources are ultimately derived from the conception of the common good that Maritain derives through theological personalism and natural law theory. Because his personalist anthropology and sociology can be mediated through natural law theory, as I explained in the previous chapter, their explicitly religious ideas play a background role in the presentation of these intellectual resources. Maritain can articulate them to fellow Catholics and Christians using such theological resources as doctrinal themes, church teachings, classic theologians, and Scripture. In presenting these ideas to a wider public, Maritain does not hide their theological roots, but neither does he present them as the reasons for which his political ideas should be found persuasive. Maritain may provide theological warrants in order to make his presentation complete, coherent, and therefore intelligible; but the way he tries to convince his non-Christian readers is with appeals to fundamental and widely shared ethical principles like human dignity and to the society's collective commitment to "the democratic faith." What he asks of these readers in return is to compare his political ideas with their own, to respond in an intelligible manner, and, if they find his account persuasive, to live out its ethical and political vision in cooperation with others.

CONDITIONS FOR SOCIAL HARMONY

Beyond the intellectual resources it can offer the public debate, religion can work to promote social harmony. Here, again, we are considering Maritain's account of Catholicism's or Christianity's contributions. Maritain holds that the Gospel, the church's proclamation of Jesus' message and his person, works as a leaven in society, inspiring justice and civic friendship.[36] The leavening occurs when the church and individual Christians act out of love for their neighbors—their concrete actions contribute to social and intellectual solidarity. Maritain wants to convince us that a public role for religion is essential for realizing a just and good society and that religion can serve this good without becoming divisive. In contrast to the intellectual resources, this account of religion's goods will seem quite theological at points. Yet we should remember that Maritain's whole presentation is framed by his commitment to a free society that is personalist, communal, and pluralist.[37]

In addition to those marks, Maritain holds that a society of free persons must also be "theist," or "vitally Christian."[38] The mere suggestion of this characteristic challenges the liberal component of his theory and may alienate some of Maritain's potential liberal supporters. Nonetheless, he can defend this claim and remain a liberal, because the theist character of society expresses itself primarily at the level of autonomous civic institutions.

> Civil society is organically linked to religion and turns consciously towards the source of its being by invoking divine assistance and the divine name as its members know it. Independent in its own temporal sphere, it has above it the kingdom of things that are not Caesar's, and it must cooperate with religion, not by any kind of theocracy or clericalism, nor by exercising any sort of pressure in religious matters, but by respecting and facilitating, on the basis of the rights and liberties of each of us, the spiritual activity of the Church and of the diverse religious families which are grouped within the temporal community.[39]

Civil society's orientation toward the supernatural common good requires three activities: to acknowledge the presence and guidance of the divine, to respect the rights and liberties of believers, and to respect and facilitate the "spiritual activity" of all religious communities. Maritain is speaking of civil society broadly here and has not yet delineated the particular role of the state. In general, it seems society should approve both "civil religion" (by acknowledging the Creator and natural law) and the vital role of religious communities in private and public life.

Maritain obviously does not intend for the theist character of society to threaten religious pluralism. But can a theist society, even of the sort he describes, safeguard true religious pluralism? The answer depends upon the willingness of its citizens and its authorities to safeguard religious liberty. Maritain has just made the point that juridical protection of religious liberty is entirely compatible with the society he envisions. But society cannot rely upon laws alone. Religious liberty will be secure in the long run only if citizens practice what Hollenbach calls "intellectual solidarity." This "virtue" or "spirit" is "a willingness to take other persons seriously enough to engage them in conversation and debate about what they think makes life worth living, including what they think will make for the good of the polis."[40]

> Intellectual solidarity entails engagement with the other through both listening and speaking, in the hope that understanding might replace incomprehension and that perhaps even agreement could result. Since it is *mutual* listening and speaking, it can only develop in an atmosphere of genuine freedom. But also because it is mutual, this freedom will not be that of an atomistic self. Where such conversation about the good life begins and develops, a *community* of freedom begins to exist. And this itself is a major part of the common good.[41]

While intellectual solidarity is a virtue that citizens and groups must bring to the public sphere, the structure of public space can reciprocally strengthen and promote this practice. Hollenbach looks for conversation about the common good to "develop freely in those components of civil society that are the primary bearers of cultural meaning and value—universities, religious communities, the world of the arts, and serious journalism."[42] Political deliberation needs to draw and build upon the public discourse occurring in these institutions.

In such encounters, says Hollenbach, all parties are challenged. "Religious believers must enter this discourse prepared to listen as well as to speak, to learn from what they hear, and, if necessary, to change as a result of what they have learned."[43] Nonreligious persons have to be open to the positive contributions religious traditions make to public life through their culture-shaping narratives and symbols.[44] In practicing intellectual solidarity, believers and nonbelievers are challenged to change and grow, perhaps to admit that they do not possess the whole truth, or at least that their understanding of the truth can be broadened through mutual exchange. The common good is likewise advanced in this exchange, and society stands to lose if the debate is restricted to the terms of public reason:

> For society to try to exclude religious narratives and symbols from public life simply because they are identified with religion would be to impoverish itself intellectually and culturally. It would *a priori* cut itself off from one of the

most important forms of intellectual exchange necessary in a community of freedom.[45]

Neither Maritain nor Hollenbach are Pollyannas when they maintain that a pluralistic society can have a genuine civic conversation about the common good. And neither of them are engaging in special pleading for their own religious community—the Roman Catholic Church—when they argue that religion makes a vital contribution to this conversation. Churches, as communities of spiritual discernment and moral reflection, can begin conversations about the common good within their own communities and then reach out to include other persons and institutions. At their best, churches inject into the public conversation social visions richer than those of bureaucrats and political interest groups; in the United States, these visions are grounded in the biblical and republican traditions of the public culture.[46]

Ecclesial commentary on political issues provides a moral counter to policy discussions based on cost-benefit analysis and public opinion polls. Several sociological studies confirm the importance of churches in promoting civic concern and facilitating civic participation. One recent study demonstrates the strong correlation between participation in religion and in civic life.[47] Churchgoers are significantly more likely than nonchurchgoers to vote, volunteer, and donate their time to civic organizations, because their church involvement helps them develop civic skills and nurtures their voluntaristic motivations. In Hollenbach's estimation, these findings suggest that "an active presence of religious communities in the public life of the country can strengthen rather than threaten democracy. If one fears that public life is becoming increasingly fragile, the prescription would appear to be more church involvement in public life, not less."[48]

PROMOTING HUMAN DIGNITY AND NEGLECTED GOODS

The Christian church's second contribution to social unity leads to its third—promoting human dignity and drawing attention to those human goods that are neglected by the larger society. The Gospel not only inspires the intellectual solidarity of a free community, but it requires Christians to act concretely for the well-being of others. Thus, intellectual solidarity leads to social solidarity.

A virtuous community of freedom must address not only the heights to which human culture can rise but also the depths of suffering into which societies can descend. There are strong currents in American life today that insulate many of the privileged parts of civil society from the suffering that exists in other parts of the body politic. Though it is obvious that individuals and groups can never share the experience of all others, encouraging commitment to the common good nevertheless calls for new ways of overcoming this insularity in at least incremental ways. Here again, universities, churches, the arts, and journalism can play important roles in opening up avenues to enhanced social solidarity.[49]

Beyond what it can do in concert with and in the same vein as other civic institutions, the Christian church makes a distinctive contribution to social solidarity, which Maritain describes as "existing with the people."

"To exist with is an ethical category," Maritain writes. "It does not mean loving someone in the mere sense of wishing him well; it means loving someone in the sense of becoming one with him, of bearing his burdens, of living a common moral life with him, of feeling with him and suffering with him."[50] The *people* are "the mass of non-privileged ones . . . that moral community which is centered on manual labor . . . [with] a certain way of understanding and living out suffering, poverty, hardship and especially work itself . . . a certain way of being 'always the same ones who get killed.' "[51] Because the people, the poor, were those whom Christ loved, and because they are the "mass" in which the vital life of a new civilization takes root, the church and its members are bound to them.

> The Church is the Kingdom of God "in a state of pilgrimage and crucifixion." Concerned, not with managing temporal matters, but with guiding men toward supernatural truth and eternal life, the Church as such, in her very life and spiritual mission, exists and suffers with the people; nor can she do otherwise. . . .
>
> The proper order of the Church is the spiritual order. Now, in the temporal order, the Christians, as members of the earthly community, have to exist with the people and suffer with the people, this time with respect to the temporal aims of the history of mankind, and in order to work with the people toward their achievement.[52]

The force that impels the Christian to live and suffer with the people is love. Called *agape* in the New Testament and *caritas* (charity) in medieval theology, this love is a self-giving, other-regarding concern for the well-being of one's neighbor.[53] As such, it has a decidedly social impact. The Gospel leavens and ferments the social order through active expressions of love. In Maritain's eyes, love underlies every authentic human action for justice and exerts a moral power that orients social activism to its proper end, which is the common good.[54]

Maritain described this moral power in a letter to his friend Saul Alinsky, the community organizer and social activist. Alinsky organized the

disenfranchised (the working poor and African Americans) to shame vig-
orously and annoy relentlessly the elites until they agreed to give the pro-
testers a share of their power. Maritain approved of Alinsky's organizing
methods and commented favorably upon them in several of his works.[55]
But he also urged his friend to recognize that love remains the proper basis
of protest power.

> In the temporal realm (civilization) it is normal to aim primarily at power in
> the ordinary sense (implying coercion, pressure), but such power will inevita-
> bly become corrupted if the only incorruptible power, the power of love, is
> not quickening the whole business.[56]

Maritain suggested to Alinsky that there was an "essential complementarity" between his aggressive protests and Martin Luther King's strategies
of passive resistance.

> The Montgomery bus affair—inspired by Gandhi and the Gospels—implied
> in actual fact a certain conquest of power. Your own bus affair for Negro reg-
> istration—inspired by your ideas about power—implied in actual fact the ex-
> ercise of *moral power* (the only power and weapon by which oppressed black
> people can *immediately* manifest *superiority* with respect to white people).[57]

Thus Maritain urged his friend to meet and work with activists like King,
since he thought their methods were complementary and were inspired by
the same love: "Your own case, my dearest Saul, . . . [a]ll your fighting
effort as an organizer is quickened *in reality* by *love for the human being,
and for God*, though you refuse to admit it."[58]

The case of political organizing for civil rights is a concrete example of
love expressing itself in action for justice. And it is the kind of work by
which churches and religious institutions can distinctively promote the
common good. In a Catholic common good perspective, at least three special traits characterize the church's expressions of neighbor-love. Here I
write not specifically of Maritain's ideas, but of claims in the recent Catholic tradition that have an affinity with Maritain's thought and may even
owe some debt to it.

First, the nature of the church's existence with the people is an option
for the poor.[59] When the church opts for the poor, it allows its preaching
and theologizing to be shaped by the perspective of the poor—which becomes the church's perspective as it shares in their life. The option for the
poor is "preferential" in that it entails making service among the op-
pressed a pastoral priority.

Second, the option for the poor involves a prophetic critique of social
structures. *Sin* and *conversion* become terms that apply to the social realm
as well as to the personal, and the option for the poor becomes fundamen-

tal to an ethical assessment of society—how a society treats the poor is an essential measure of how well it abides by the requirements of the common good. The U.S. Catholic Bishops state: "The prime purpose of this special commitment to the poor is to enable them to become active participants in the life of society. It is to enable *all* persons to share in and contribute to the common good."[60]

The church's evaluation of society draws attention to all those human needs and yearnings that call for fulfillment. The church's vision of human flourishing is capped by the aim of spiritual freedom and self-transcendence—what Maritain calls "the conquest of freedom."[61] The person's freedom is ultimately fulfilled beyond society, in the society of the Godhead, but human society is not thereby denigrated. For even as self-transcendence is the fruit of the common good, it is also its precondition.

> The self is inherently relational and achieves depth and solidity only by going beyond itself in solidarity and community. Christians call the move from private interests to other-relatedness conversion—a turning to the neighbor in love, based on a recognition that the neighbor is a gift rather than a threat.[62]

So we conclude Maritain's substantive account of the common good where it began—with an account of human flourishing. But between the first introduction of that concept and this point, we have seen that churches need not and should not limit themselves to offering ethical, political, and philosophical ideas to the public debate, important though that is. A religious tradition can provide conditions for social harmony in several ways: infusing its values into society through its character-shaping activity; cooperating with public and voluntary institutions to provide the cultural, economic, and spiritual conditions for persons to achieve their fulfillment in community; promoting public discussion about justice and the good; building intellectual solidarity through its willingness both to challenge others and to learn from them; loving neighbors concretely; sharing the life of the people, especially the poor; acting to empower the disenfranchised so that they may fully participate in social life; and reminding persons of their call to life with God, who is the deepest basis of their worth and their liberty.

These aspects of religion's contribution to the common good are those promoted by the Catholic tradition. My exposition has focused on how Catholics and the Catholic Church understand their own contributions to the social task, even though they understand most of these obligations to be incumbent upon the entire Christian church. Other religious traditions would articulate many of their contributions along the same lines, though obviously with distinctive accents and plenty of differences. In every society, any religious group may present its understanding of the role it can play in promoting the common good. The common good welcomes and urges every group and tradition to do so. All that is required for a group to participate is that it acknowledge the right of equal participation for all others.

We should not expect the contribution of religion to be monolithic, for "religion" exists only as concrete religions. But we should expect religions to draw our attention to values that are not material, conventional, and convenient. We should expect them to witness to a value, a source of good, that lies beyond what humans can know and achieve through rational and technical mastery. To know our limitations, to be awed by the thought that we are not ultimately in control of the world or even our own lives—this alone may work a salutary effect on discussions about the common good in a world too often given to pretensions of control and domination.

RESPONDING TO SUBSTANTIVE QUESTIONS IN THE LIBERAL-COMMUNITARIAN DEBATE

One way to assess the value of Maritain's common good theory as a substantive public philosophy is to locate it in the context of the liberal-communitarian debate. If his theory successfully mediates the political principles of these philosophies, we will have good reason to believe that it can make constructive contributions to debates about justice and public goods. Our confidence would be based in the theory's ability to articulate a compelling vision of political community that commands the allegiance of citizens while not causing them to risk loss of their distinct identities as informed by local subcommunities. Beginning with the previous chapter, I have been arguing that Maritain's theory succeeds in this regard. Now I will explicitly locate Maritain's position on two substantive political questions in the liberal-communitarian debate.

How Far Is Individual Identity Constituted by the Community?

In trying to locate Maritain's position on two substantive questions in the liberal-communitarian debate, the first issue concerns the communal constitution of individual ends. To what extent are personal conceptions of the good shaped by one's community? Alternatively, how free is the person in choosing his own ends, values, and conceptions of the good? Communitarians generally argue that the Rawlsian conception of the self leads to two errors:

> the philosophical error of assuming that any individual's ends, values and identity (regardless of their content) can be thought of as existing indepen-

dently of the wider communities of which he or she is a member; and the substantive error of failing to acknowledge the true significance of those particular human goods whose content or focus is inherently communal (in particular the good of political community).[63]

John Rawls denies the charge of asocial individualism but still affirms a political conception of the citizen as having enough distance from his communal attachments that he can revise his own views of the good.[64]

Maritain would side with Michael Sandel against Rawls, arguing that certain communal roles are constitutive of our identities. In particular, one's citizenship in political society and one's membership in a faith community are usually tightly bound with one's self-understanding (a descriptive claim), and in any case, they should be (a normative claim). For example, as a U.S. citizen and a Roman Catholic, I cannot just "become," say, a Canadian Protestant by an act of will. I can nationalize in a new country and join a new church, but these changes will be preceded and accompanied by significant disruption to my sense of self.[65] Most likely, I would not undertake such changes in affiliation without having been through a process of questioning myself and my communal roles because I find the practices and goals of my current communities at some variance with certain longings within me. Now this possibility may seem to justify the Rawlsian claim that we can and should take a great interest in being able to revise our conceptions of the good. But what is missing in the Rawlsian picture is an awareness of two realities: first, that such revisions will most likely occasion disruption, pain, and loss, because in fact these communal identifications are deeply constitutive; and second, that such revisions are almost never independent undertakings but require the guidance of others who belong to the new communities. Even if I make such a change, the religion and nationality under which I was raised will always, or for a long time at least, bear on my self-understanding—on the questions I ask of myself; on my deeply inculcated habits, values, and feelings; and on how I understand and take on the responsibilities that attend my new membership.[66]

As a description of how people usually change their affiliations, the preceding is neither controversial nor original. But Maritain does bring something new to the liberal-communitarian debate with the normative conclusions he draws from this description. Maritain is not giving a simple "both/and" answer to the question of whether or not persons are encumbered by their communities; rather, he is considering the human person in a complex way, which yields a complex answer: as persons, we are the subject of rights that provide a significant buffer from any community's claims on us as we strive to achieve our ends; yet as individuals, we receive and understand these ends only in communal contexts.

Maritain also advances the debate by beginning to specify the relative importance of various communities in shaping our identities and ends. Consider this quotation:

> The development of the human person normally requires a plurality of autonomous communities which have their own rights, liberties and authority; among these communities there are some of a rank inferior to the political state, which arise either from the fundamental exigencies of nature (as in the case of the family community) or else from the will of persons freely coming together to form diverse groups. Other communities are of a rank superior to the State, as is above all the Church in the mind of Christians, and as would also be, in the temporal realm, that organized international community towards which we aspire today.[67]

Taking this text along with other indications from Maritain's works, we can identify two ways of ranking the relative importance of communities. The following are heuristic categories I bring to Maritain's thought.

The first is a *scale of authority*, which indicates the relative binding weight of institutions in the political realm. Individual citizens and voluntary communities (based on the shared interests of their members) are at the bottom of this scale, subordinate to higher orders of government. Next in the line of political authority come local governments, then state or regional governments, and then the national government (the state). Above these should be placed an organized and effective international agency to govern the relations among nations. Finally, the family and the church have a special status. In one sense, they are off the scale, because they are authoritative in their own realms: the domestic and the spiritual. In another sense, as small, mediating institutions, they belong at the first level with other voluntary institutions. The upshot of this dual placement is that government has a circumscribed authority over them. It may properly intervene to protect family or church members in harm or to proscribe destructive or violent acts by these groups; however, the church has primary authority in guiding its members in their spiritual lives, and parents have primary authority in raising and educating their children. More broadly considered, governmental authority is circumscribed throughout this scale by two factors: (1) authority is exercised at each level for the sake of the whole—for the sake of the common good and for the care of the lower levels; and (2) the principle of subsidiarity works to push responsibility and accountability down the scale.

The second ranking is a *scale of perfection*, which indicates the relative value of communally supplied aims. We can approach this scale developmentally. As children, we are first aware of and enmeshed in family ties. As we become older, we grow in awareness of our ethnic, racial, and national heritage, though the extent of their value to us depends a great deal on how our family understands and expresses these relations. We also begin to get involved in local voluntary communities, such as schools, clubs, sports teams, and churches. As we grow into adolescence and early adulthood, we begin to grasp that we are part of a political society and, if we belong to a local church, that we also belong to a larger church—to a denomination, a religious heritage, and a transhistorical spiritual community. Because this scale is developmental, the earlier communities may well have a deeper and more lasting impact than the later institutions: the "lower" communities are usually the most constitutive of our identities, so we must reckon well the importance and value of the ends and practices we learn in them.

All of these communities set before us ends and practices that serve to constitute our identities. Yet Maritain argues that the ends and practices of the "higher" communities—political society and the church—have special weight for several reasons.[68] These roles engage more of our reason and freedom. They require us to communicate and cooperate with others in the fullness of their personalities. Our participation in these institutions usually involves many aspects of our lives, which helps us to integrate the many facets of our characters and personalities. Finally, the practices of these institutions aim at the fulfillment of higher and more complete personal goods. Maritain thinks the church is the highest of these communities because it engages us as full persons, in cooperation with other persons, for the highest good, a good that completes us and calls us to wholeness.

A normative ramification of both scales is to ennoble politics. Political goals are not more valuable than those of families and voluntary associations, but political institutions make special contributions relevant to their authority. Politics should facilitate the activities of voluntary communities, provide conditions for cooperation among them, and build its own work upon the structure of social life they establish. In these ways, politics provides the grounds for the flourishing of persons in all levels of community.

Can Government Remain Neutral Between Conceptions of the Good?

The second question concerns the charge that philosophical and political liberalisms, while claiming to be neutral among competing conceptions of the good, in fact rely upon particular and sometimes thick views of what is good for persons. Some liberals link neutrality to antiperfectionism, which is the principle that the state should deliberately ignore the highest ideals by which people try to live their lives. Communitarians fear that a liberal society committed to these ideals "might discriminate against conceptions of the good held by its citizens in ways other than those explicitly needed to protect the autonomy of all citizens."[69] An example of this criticism is my argument in chapter 2 that Rawls's ideal of public reason constrains religious argument. What lines of defense can a liberal take? If she is a moral subjectivist, she has to claim that the state must remain neutral because we cannot know which forms of life are better for persons. A moral objectivist liberal could defend state neutrality in one of several ways: (*a*) because ways of life must be freely chosen, (*b*) because state interference distorts choices and their costs, (*c*) because what matters most is to live in a society on whose form we can all agree, or (*d*) because the state is clumsy and even dangerous when given the power to promote conceptions of the good. (Rawls, for example, is a moral objectivist who defends a form of neutrality based largely on claims *c* and *d*.)

Maritain would join communitarians in criticizing the effect the neutrality principle (promoted by the ideal of public reason) has on political discourse and on the political participation of those who rely on religious views of good. To assess the extent to which Maritain is a perfectionist, we need to note the kind of ideals at stake (whether they are religious or moral) and the type of state action allowed (whether it is to condone, acknowledge, or promote particular behavior). On religious matters, Maritain is cautious in his perfectionism. He would not keep politics immune from the influence of citizens' perfectionist religious ideals, though he would be wary of the state's advancing them. The form of protection he offers citizens from state coercion in matters of religion is based, I would say, on claims *a* and *d:* religious belief must be free belief, and the state's privileged enforcement of particular religious claims would be counterproductive, dangerous, and unjust. On the other hand, Maritain believes that this stance allows room for some healthy acknowledgment of a nation's religious heritage(s) in the public square. In the United States, for instance, "thanksgiving and public prayer, the invocation of the name of God at the occasion of any major official gathering," are in keeping with the great inspiration of the U.S. Constitution—that human society cannot "stand aloof from God and from any religious faith."[70]

As an objectivist and a Christian believer, Maritain cannot completely leave the perfectionist ideals of the church in a realm isolated from political life. He holds that there must be appropriate cooperation of church and state, guided by a recognition of their separate primary realms and their different means. Maritain first notes that a pluralist society is demanded by the common good and that the obligations of the body politic toward the truth take hold at the level of citizens and their voluntary institutions.[71] With these caveats in mind, he describes the reciprocal obligations of church and society. The obligation of the church to political society is to advance the common good and the values that support freedom. The church's means to this end are "moral influence and authority," that is, preaching and teaching.[72] The state should call upon the church's help in carrying out various tasks of the common good, such as educating citizens and meeting their welfare needs. The state for its part must assist the church in its mission, not its clerical but its spiritual mission. It does so by guaranteeing the full freedom of the church and by working in partnership for the common good.[73] When Maritain speaks of "the Church" in this regard, he generally means the Catholic Church, whose valuable role in a democratic society he is eager to defend. But it seems to me that these comments apply just as well to churches in the plural; in fact, Maritain's view of church-state relations is stronger when he keeps the pluralist principle at the forefront. So Maritain's perfectionist state acknowledges the value of religious belief, both in individuals' lives and in the life of society, though it promotes those ideals only indirectly—by fostering the conditions in which churches can succeed in their spiritual missions and by actively cooperating with churches for the social welfare.

On moral ideals, Maritain differs from many contemporary liberals, for he would have the state facilitate the political pursuit of a substantive common good, one that embraces moral virtues and values. Hence the state should promote certain moral ends, though at the same time it should take care to respect the consciences of citizens who act upon moral codes that derive from their particular traditions. The state should not unduly burden these citizens, and it should acknowledge the positive values in particular moral traditions whenever possible. Even when these moral codes clash with the duties of natural law, Maritain would restrain the state:

> The legislation of the Christian society in question could and should never *endorse* or *approve* any way of conduct contrary to Natural Law. But we have also to realize that this legislation could and should *permit* or *give allowance to* certain ways of conduct which depart in some measure from Natural Law, if the prohibition by civil law of these ways of conduct were to impair the common good, either because such prohibition would be at variance with the ethical code of communities of citizens whose loyalty to the nation and faithfulness to their own moral creed, however imperfect it may be, essentially matter to the common good, or even because it would result in a worse conduct, disturbing or disintegrating the social body, for a great many people whose moral strength is not on a level with the enforcement of this prohibition.[74]

Maritain is not having the state enforce perfectionist moral ideals, for the natural law is not a perfectionist code; it is rather a human dynamism to act for the good. Moreover, he would not have the state proscribe all acts that go against natural law but only the more egregious and harmful of these. As I read this text, Maritain grants a presumption of acceptance to those moral codes that lead to actions contrary to natural law, *because it*

is beneficial to the common good that persons adhere faithfully to their
moral and religious traditions, even when these are in some tension with
a Catholic and natural law account of the common good.

In sum, Maritain's perfectionism builds in safeguards that distinguish it
from a thoroughly communitarian perfectionism, while it differs from liberal perfectionism in focusing on a broader range of goods for personal
well-being than the good of autonomy. Maritain and other perfectionists,
be they liberal or communitarian, can equally affirm that "what matters is
that people live valuable lives, and . . . it is appropriate that we should use
politics to help them do so."[75]

MARITAIN AS A COMMUNAL LIBERAL

As with the methodological questions, Maritain, in my interpretation,
takes mediating positions on these substantive questions from the liberal-
communitarian debate. We are now in a position to assess Maritain's overall status as a communal liberal.

It is clear that Maritain's common good theory is committed to both
liberal and communitarian principles and practices. How are these ultimately related to each other? Michelle Watkins and Ralph McInerny suggest four options for interpreting Maritain.[76]

1. Maritain could be a "true liberal," supporting communitarianism
   only in rhetoric.
2. He could be "genuinely and theoretically committed to the conceptual schemes of both communitarianism and liberalism in one way or
   another."
3. He could be a "true communitarian," supporting liberalism only in
   rhetoric.
4. He could be a communitarian "with respect to the *ideal* political
   order," while "somewhat committed to liberalism at the practical
   level."

They discard the first three options as untenable, leaving the fourth. In
their interpretation, Maritain is mainly communitarian at the theoretical
level, given the thick, theological underpinnings of his theory, but he also
works into his theory revised liberal commitments to individual freedom
and human rights. At the practical level, Maritain is still communitarian,
but he also "grants certain concessions to liberalism—concessions he
deems necessary because of the exigency of pluralism and of the tendency
of political power to be misused."[77]

Watkins and McInerny think Maritain's theory would have been stronger had he given up some of his liberal themes and been more consistently communitarian, especially at the theoretical level. Commenting on Maritain's references to "primordial rights," rights of the prepolitical or precommunal person, they write:

> In essence, this means that the person is granted rights simply for being a human being. However, as Maritain explains it, it is the community and the political life that enable the person to be human and to fulfill or perfect this human nature. Why then the necessity of demanding from the community and the state the rights of a person qua human being when it is the community and the state that enable this person to become human in the first place?[78]

Watkins and McInerny go awry in this interpretation and thus in their wish that Maritain forgo his liberal theoretical commitments. It is *not* the case for Maritain that the community and the state enable the person to become human in the first place. In Maritain's theological view, one's humanity and human dignity are precommunal, because they are God given; they obtain because humans are created in the image of God and with a capacity to commune with God. The community and the state enable the person fully to live out the capacities he or she has as a human being. It makes sense to identify prepolitical rights as a way to protect inalienable human dignity. Maritain thinks these rights are necessary because any human community can become corrupt and twist the meaning of human dignity.

Thus the human person is not granted all his rights qua member of a community; if he were, a political community would be justified in denying basic rights to those who are not members of the community—such as a foreign national or an undocumented ("illegal") immigrant. Watkins and McInerny could respond that such persons are granted rights in a nation by virtue of their membership in the international community, but their argument about rights goes deeper than political jurisdiction. "It would be more appropriate . . . to think of the person as being granted goods and 'rights' qua member of a community rather than simply qua human being," for "human nature is fulfilled in community where the opportunity is given to know and love, to develop morally and intellectually."[79] Yet many human beings, such as newborns, anencephalic newborns, late-term fetuses, and persons with profound mental retardation, are not able (or yet able) to take advantage of these opportunities or are severely limited in this regard. Given that such persons live in our midst and are part of the human race, I consider it dangerous to muse, "If human beings are defined by their political and communal interactions, one wonders if they truly have a prepolitical status."[80] As I have shown, humans do, for Maritain, have a prepolitical status. This claim sets Maritain apart from full-fledged narrative communitarians, and it explains why he makes room at the theoretical level for liberal principles such as freedom and human rights.

Watkins and McInerny's distinction of theoretical and practical levels in Maritain is accurate (for Maritain himself draws the distinction), as is their identification of his liberal and communitarian commitments at both levels. But if we now see his principled commitment to freedom and rights as a check on communal definition of personal identity, then we will not call his practical commitment to rights a concession to liberalism. Maritain grounds rights in his anthropology, in which autonomy plays only a part. Consider an essential element of Maritain's assessment of liberalism that Watkins and McInerny never mention—his critique of bourgeois individualism and laissez-faire economics. If Maritain were committed to rights mainly because of worries about the abuse of state power, he would support a liberal or neoliberal economics. As it is, Maritain affirms economic rights and supports appropriate state action to ensure these rights. Such a view can only emerge from a theoretical position that affirms human rights as expressions of precommunal human dignity (which does not require society to "grant" them) yet gives them a strongly communal construction at the practical level (which recognizes the communal aspects of human dignity and sets individual rights in proper relation to the common good).

So in the end, I would take Maritain as genuinely and theoretically committed to both liberalism and communitarianism (Watkins and McInerny's second option), while bringing liberal commitments to the fore at the practical level (from their fourth option). Watkins and McInerny's objection that the second option involves too much inconsistency can be dispensed by refusing to define liberalism and communitarianism as extremely and monolithically as they do.[81] The reason liberal practices come to the fore at the practical level is, first, because Maritain's personalism entails a wide array of rights and social-support structures and, second, because he emphasizes civil society as the arena in which communities make a great many of their contributions to the common good. In other words, the way Maritain wants the communitarian side of his account to flower is through the free activity of mediating institutions in civil society—not mandated or supplanted by the state, but supported and enhanced by government action. In my judgment, Maritain's theory successfully mediates the philosophical and practical principles of the two schools, therefore it deserves the name of "communal liberalism."

NOTES

1. My articulation of these claims has been influenced by two authors. Paul Weithman, as was shown in chapter 2, construed the claim that religious goods can serve as public goods in two senses: they can be regarded "as either intellectual resources to be drawn on in political argument or as social goods which effect

harmony" ("Rawlsian Liberalism and the Privatization of Religion: Three Theological Objections Considered," *Journal of Religious Ethics* 22, no. 1 [spring 1994]: 3–28, quote at 6). David Hollenbach identifies three Catholic contributions to American public life: a focus on the renewal of civic society to counter the dominance of the state and the free market; a promotion of civil conversation "that can yield shared understandings of the social good, even shared religious understandings"; and a "challenge to the primacy assigned to self-interest" with a view to creating genuine community ("Afterword: A Community of Freedom," in *Catholicism and Liberalism: Contributions to American Public Philosophy*, ed. R. Bruce Douglass and David Hollenbach [Cambridge: Cambridge University Press, 1994], 323–43, quote at 324). Weithman thus indicates the categories under which a religion would have to vindicate its status as a public good, while Hollenbach suggests some potential public goods offered by Catholicism. My framework draws upon both ideas.

2. This term was not used by Maritain, but it is one that has been used more recently by philosophers in the Aristotelian and Thomistic traditions, including authors as disparate as Martha Nussbaum and John Finnis. For both, the term basically refers to a fulfilled, happy, truly human life. An account of human flourishing picks out those capabilities that persons should have and those activities in which they should engage in order to live fulfilled lives. These capabilities and activities are, at a fundamental level, shared by all human beings; thus Nussbaum's and Finnis's accounts of flourishing are objective and cross-cultural. Though they share the belief that there is an objective meaning to human flourishing, Nussbaum and Finnis disagree on several matters: for instance, on how they would arrive at this account (Nussbaum by practical, commonsense reasoning in the style of Aristotle; Finnis from within a particular style of natural law reasoning) and on how the account should be specified (e.g., Nussbaum and Finnis squared off over the legal question of whether there can be a rational basis for laws that discriminate against homosexual citizens). See Martha Nussbaum, "Aristotelian Social Democracy," in *Liberalism and the Good*, ed. R. Bruce Douglass, Gerald M. Mara, and Henry S. Richardson (New York: Routledge, 1990), 203–52; John Finnis, *Natural Law and Natural Rights* (Oxford: Clarendon, 1980), and John Finnis and Martha Nussbaum, "Is Homosexual Conduct Wrong? A Philosophical Exchange," *New Republic* (15 November 1993): 12–13.

3. Jacques Maritain, *The Rights of Man and Natural Law*, trans. Doris C. Anson (New York: Scribner, 1943; rpt., bound with *Christianity and Democracy*, San Francisco: Ignatius, 1986), 94.

4. Cf. Thomas Aquinas, *Summa Contra Gentiles*, bk. III, chaps. 3–4, in *Introduction to St. Thomas Aquinas*, ed. Anton C. Pegis, Modern Library (New York: Random House, 1945), 432–35; and *Summa Theologiae*, ed. Thomas Gilby (London: Blackfriars, 1964–76), I–II, q. 8, a. 1. That the will always aims for a real or perceived good does not eliminate the possibility of error or moral evil: it is essential for the reason properly to apprehend and order the objects of the will. Cf. *Summa Theologiae*, I–II, q. 19.

5. Paul Ramsey, *Nine Modern Moralists* (Englewood Cliffs, N.J.: Prentice-Hall, 1962), 219.

6. Maritain, *Rights of Man*, 144, 145.

7. Maritain, *Rights of Man*, 145.

8. Jacques Maritain, *Man and the State* (Chicago: University of Chicago Press, 1951), 101.

9. David Hollenbach, *Justice, Peace, and Human Rights* (New York: Crossroad, 1988), 95.

10. David Hollenbach, *Claims in Conflict: Retrieving and Renewing the Catholic Human Rights Tradition* (New York: Paulist Press, 1979), 94–100; quotes at 95 and 96.

11. Maritain, *Rights of Man*, 152–86.

12. Examples of rights of *freedom* on Maritain's list are those to existence, personal liberty, religious liberty, free choice of one's work, and the freedom and integrity of the family. Examples of rights that secure *basic needs* are those to property, work, a just wage, unemployment insurance, and social security. Examples of rights of political and economic *participation* are those to political participation, political equality, equal suffrage, freedom to form and join political parties and labor unions, free expression, and the freedom of labor groups. See the summary of rights in *Rights of Man*, 186–89.

13. Maritain, *Rights of Man*, 161.

14. In what follows, I fit Maritain's description of human rights into Hollenbach's interpretive framework. See Hollenbach, *Claims in Conflict*, 94–100, esp. the chart on p. 98.

15. Maritain, *Rights of Man*, 159.

16. Hollenbach, *Claims in Conflict*, 96.

17. Hollenbach, *Claims in Conflict*, 96–97.

18. Maritain takes stock of such considerations in describing two rights of the instrumental variety. One is the right to joint ownership and management of business enterprises "wherever an associative system can be substituted for the wage system"; the other is "the right to have a part, free of charge, depending on the possibilities of the community, in the elementary goods, both material and spiritual, of civilization." Both of these rights come with conditionals that indicate that the content of the right depends on how much progress the society has made in economic development and economic democratization (Maritain, *Rights of Man*, 188–89).

19. David Hollenbach, "A Communitarian Reconstruction of Human Rights," in *Catholicism and Liberalism*, ed. Douglass and Hollenbach, 127–50.

20. Hollenbach, "Communitarian Reconstruction," 145.

21. Hollenbach, "Communitarian Reconstruction," 140, emphasis deleted.

22. Hollenbach, "Communitarian Reconstruction," 141.

23. Maritain, *Man and the State*, 106.

24. Peter Berger and Richard Neuhaus, *To Empower People: The Role of Mediating Structures in Public Policy* (Washington, D.C.: American Enterprise Institute, 1977), 2.

25. Berger and Neuhaus, *To Empower People*, 2.

26. Berger and Neuhaus, *To Empower People*, 3.

27. Pope Pius XI, *Quadragesimo Anno: On Reconstructing the Social Order*

(15 May 1931), in *Catholic Social Thought: The Documentary Heritage*, ed. David J. O'Brien and Thomas A. Shannon (Maryknoll, N.Y.: Orbis Books, 1992), par. 79. The term *subsidiarity* derives from the Latin *subsidium*, meaning "help, aid, support." Cf. the use of this principle by the National Conference of Catholic Bishops in *Economic Justice for All* (18 November 1986), in *Catholic Social Thought*, ed. Shannon and O'Brien, pars. 99–100.

28. A useful earlier work on mediating structures is Michael Novak, ed., *Democracy and Mediating Structures: A Theological Inquiry* (Washington, D.C.: American Enterprise Institute, 1980).

29. Maritain, *Man and the State*, 12.

30. Maritain, *Man and the State*, 10.

31. Maritain, *Man and the State*, 13.

32. Maritain, *Man and the State*, 13.

33. Maritain, *Man and the State*, 11.

34. See Maritain's distinction of a national community and a political society in *Man and the State*, chap. 1.

35. David Hollenbach, "The Common Good Revisited," *Theological Studies* 50, no. 1 (March 1989): 70–94, cited at 87.

36. See Jacques Maritain, *Christianity and Democracy*, trans. Doris C. Anson (New York: Scribner, 1944; rpt., bound with *The Rights of Man and Natural Law*, San Francisco: Ignatius, 1986), esp. 25–46; and Matthew J. Mancini, "Maritain's Democratic Vision: 'You Have No Bourgeois,' " in *Understanding Maritain: Philosopher and Friend*, ed. Deal W. Hudson and Matthew J. Mancini (Macon, Ga.: Mercer University Press, 1987), 133–51.

37. Maritain, *Rights of Man*, 104.

38. Maritain, *Rights of Man*, 105, 107.

39. Maritain, *Rights of Man*, 106.

40. David Hollenbach, "Contexts of the Political Role of Religion: Civil Society and Culture," *San Diego Law Review* 30 (1994): 879–901, quote at 892. Cf. Hollenbach's other formulations of the notion of intellectual solidarity in "Afterword," at 334; "Civil Society: Beyond the Public-Private Dichotomy," *Responsive Community* 5, no. 1 (winter 1994–95): 21; "Virtue, the Common Good, and Democracy," in *New Communitarian Thinking: Persons, Virtues, Institutions, and Communities*, ed. Amitai Etzioni (Charlottesville, Va.: University of Virginia, 1994), 150.

41. Hollenbach, "Afterword," 334.

42. Hollenbach, "Civil Society," 22.

43. Hollenbach, "Contexts of the Political Role," 895.

44. Hollenbach, "Contexts of the Political Role," 895–96.

45. Hollenbach, "Afterword," 338.

46. See Robert N. Bellah, Richard Madsen, William M. Sullivan, Ann Swidler, and Steven M. Tipton, *Habits of the Heart: Individualism and Commitment in American Life* (Berkeley: University of California Press, 1985; rev. ed., 1996), chap. 2 and passim. The methods and claims of this book have been widely and variously assessed. One may begin with John F. Wilson, Barbara Hargrove, and Julian N. Hartt, reviews of *Habits of the Heart*, by Robert N. Bellah, et al., in *Reli-*

gious Studies Review 14, no. 4 (October 1988): 304–10. Bellah and his colleagues respond to various criticisms in the introduction to the revised edition.

47. Sidney Verba, Kay Lehman Schlozman, and Henry Brady, *Voice and Equality: Civic Voluntarism in American Politics* (Cambridge, Mass.: Harvard University Press, 1995).

48. Hollenbach, "Contexts of the Political Role," 888. Hollenbach offers more extensive reflections on the study of Verba, Schlozman, and Brady in "Politically Active Churches: Some Empirical Prolegomena to a Normative Approach," in *Religion and Contemporary Liberalism*, ed. Paul J. Weithman (Notre Dame, Ind.: University of Notre Dame Press, 1997), 291–306.

49. Hollenbach, "Civil Society," 22–23.

50. Jacques Maritain, "To Exist with the People," in *The Range of Reason* (New York: Scribner, 1952), 121; originally published in *Esprit* (12 February 1937).

51. Maritain, "To Exist with the People," 122.

52. Maritain, "To Exist with the People," 125, emphasis deleted.

53. For a masterly account of Christian neighbor-love, see Gene Outka, *Agape: An Ethical Analysis* (New Haven, Conn.: Yale University Press, 1972). For a synthetic analysis of Maritain's view, see William L. Rossner, S.J., "Love in the Thought of Jacques Maritain," in *Jacques Maritain: The Man and His Achievement*, ed. Joseph W. Evans (New York: Sheed & Ward, 1963), 237–58.

54. Love can be seen as the underlying basis of authentic human acts in a theological view that understands God's grace as pervasive and offered to all persons and that understands persons as having the power of responding to that grace in a fundamental option of the will. Note my comparison of Maritain to Karl Rahner in chap. 3 herein, n. 50.

55. Alinsky describes his strategies and organizing philosophy in *Reveille for Radicals* (Chicago: University of Chicago Press, 1946) and *Rules for Radicals* (New York: Vintage Books, 1972). Alinsky said that he wrote the first book due to Maritain's encouragement. Maritain approvingly cites Alinsky's methods in *Man and the State*, 66–68, and in *The Peasant of the Garonne*, trans. Michael Cuddihy and Elizabeth Hughes (New York: Holt, Rinehart & Winston, 1968), 41.

56. Jacques Maritain, letter to Saul Alinsky, 14 September 1964, in *The Philosopher and the Provocateur: The Correspondence of Jacques Maritain and Saul Alinsky*, ed. Bernard Doering (Notre Dame, Ind.: University of Notre Dame Press, 1994), 106. Doering's introduction gives a history of the two men's personal and professional interactions.

57. Maritain to Alinsky, in *Philosopher and Provocateur*, ed. Doering, 106.

58. Maritain to Alinsky, in *Philosopher and Provocateur*, ed. Doering, 106. Alinsky, a Jewish agnostic, never came to explicit belief in God, but Maritain often told him that he saw a tacit faith implicit in Alinsky's tireless work for justice.

59. For a history of the concept, see Donald Dorr, *Option for the Poor: A Hundred Years of Vatican Social Teaching* (Maryknoll, N.Y.: Orbis Books, 1983).

60. National Conference of Catholic Bishops, *Economic Justice for All*, par. 88. The Bishops call the option "fundamental" rather than "preferential" in order to emphasize the society-assessing function of the option.

61. See Jacques Maritain, "The Conquest of Freedom," in *The Social and Polit-*

ical Philosophy of Jacques Maritain, ed. Joseph W. Evans and Leo R. Ward (New York: Scribner, 1955), 10–27.

62. Hollenbach, "Afterword," 341.

63. Stephen Mulhall and Adam Swift, *Liberals and Communitarians* (Oxford: Blackwell, 1992), 158.

64. Rawls identifies two highest-order interests: (1) the "capacity to form, to revise, and rationally to pursue a conception of one's rational advantage or good"; and (2) the "capacity to understand, to apply, and to act from the public conception of justice." These interests correspond to the two moral powers predicated of citizens in a political conception of justice—capacities for a sense of justice and for a conception of the good (John Rawls, *Political Liberalism* [New York: Columbia University Press, 1993], 19; cf. § I.5 and § II.5).

65. Maritain would appreciate the truth of this statement given his and Raïssa's conversions to Roman Catholicism from their Protestant and Jewish backgrounds. See Julie Kernan, *Our Friend, Jacques Maritain* (Garden City, N.Y.: Doubleday, 1975), chaps. 2 and 3.

66. For an interesting exploration of constitutive attachments and what it means to change them, see the imaginary dialogue between two graduate students, a liberal and a communitarian, in act III of Daniel Bell, *Communitarianism and Its Critics* (Oxford: Clarendon, 1993), 90–113.

67. Maritain, *Rights of Man*, 105.

68. Cf. Maritain, *Rights of Man*, 103–4.

69. Mulhall and Swift, *Liberals,* 159.

70. Maritain, *Man and the State*, 184.

71. Maritain, *Man and the State*, 169, 166.

72. Maritain, *Man and the State*, 162. Cf. Mendelssohn's similar views of the church's means for promoting the common good in chap. 1 herein, esp. under "The Church's Role in Political Affairs" and "The Role of Churches in the Common Good."

73. Maritain, *Rights of Man*, 110–13.

74. Maritain, *Man and the State*, 167–68.

75. Mulhall and Swift, *Liberals,* 288, describing the view of Joseph Raz in *Morality of Freedom* (Oxford: Clarendon, 1986).

76. Michelle Watkins and Ralph McInerny, "Jacques Maritain and the Rapprochement of Liberalism and Communitarianism," in *Catholicism, Liberalism, and Communitarianism: The Catholic Intellectual Tradition and the Moral Foundations of Democracy*, ed. Kenneth L. Grasso, Gerard V. Bradley, and Robert P. Hunt (Lanham, Md.: Rowman & Littlefield, 1995), 151–72, quotes at 161.

77. Watkins and McInerny, "Jacques Maritain," 166.

78. Watkins and McInerny, "Jacques Maritain," 168. Cf. this statement to Alasdair MacIntyre's argument against the existence of human rights: "It would of course be a little odd that there should be such rights attaching to human beings simply *qua* human beings in light of the fact . . . that there is no expression in any ancient or medieval language correctly translated by our expression 'a right' until near the close of the middle ages. . . . From this it does not of course follow that there are no natural or human rights; it only follows that no one could have known

that there were. . . . [T]he truth is plain: there are no such rights, and belief in them is one with belief in witches and in unicorns" (*After Virtue*, 2nd ed. [Notre Dame, Ind.: University of Notre Dame Press, 1984], 69).

79. Watkins and McInerny, "Jacques Maritain," 169.

80. Watkins and McInerny, "Jacques Maritain," 169. I am sure Watkins and McInerny would affirm the humanity and human dignity of such persons and endorse humane and human treatment of them, yet I think this affirmation would force a reconsideration of their argument denying the prepolitical status of persons and their rights.

81. Watkins and McInerny argue that this second option entails incompatible views of human nature and political society. Of the latter, they write: "According to liberalism, the political community as a whole is to remain neutral with respect to any substantive conception of the good, whereas communitarianism requires it to be committed to a particular conception of the good" ("Jacques Maritain," 163). As we have seen through these first four chapters, any description of liberalism and communitarianism must take some note of the varieties of each and must qualify such general definitions as this one. Moreover, I have demonstrated how key liberal writers incorporate communitarian themes, foundations, or ideas, and vice versa.

Chapter 5

Creating a Politics of the Common Good: A Case Study of the Abortion Debate

I have considered in some depth Jacques Maritain's linked natural law–theological approach to the common good, as well as his substantive account of the common good, including its essential threefold role for religion. I have argued that Maritain's common good theory successfully mediates liberal and communitarian principles into a *communal liberalism*. Communal liberalism, as I have presented it, understands political society as a cooperative association constituted both by individual citizens and by the mediating institutions in which they participate. It holds that politics can and should focus on the pursuit of a common good both substantive and procedural. In promoting substantive aspects of the common good, communal liberalism reveals its communitarian commitments to a view of the person as constituted by communal attachments and to a politics based on public deliberation about matters of personal and social flourishing. Communal liberalism's account of the procedural elements of the common good places limitations on a political community's ability to shape an individual's total conception of the good and his or her role in society. The theory's liberal commitments to human rights, institutional pluralism, and equal participation are measures that provide social space for persons to evaluate critically and to modify their relationships to political and voluntary communities. I have argued that this account of political society is more fair to all citizens than a society based on Rawlsian political liberalism. Moreover, it is superior to Michael Sandel's communitarianism in its redefinition of liberal political institutions such as rights and in setting clearer limits to a community's power to shape and set an individual's life goals.

Now, in this final chapter, I want to demonstrate that communal liberalism is also more open than political liberalism—that it surpasses Rawlsian liberalism in its ability to articulate avenues for cooperation among diverse citizens and groups in a pluralist, democratic society. The ground for this argument has been laid by my exposition and interpretation of Maritain's substantive account; the present task is to show that this account has some practical value in politics and that it can survive challenges that would question the coherence or value of the theory. The first part of this task will be to apply Maritain's account of religion's intellectual resources to the moral, social, and political debate over abortion. My focus here will be the debate that occurs in the United States. The second part will draw on his description of the church's contributions to the common good in order to analyze the moral and political responsibilities of churches vis-à-vis the issue of abortion.

I have chosen to consider the abortion debate because it can serve as a litmus test of a theory of the common good: To what extent is such a theory able to identify points of agreement in the debate over this issue and point the way toward constructive action between opposed parties? Some define abortion as a purely private moral issue; others consider it merely a political issue, a contest over political rights. I consider both of these approaches inadequate. My thesis is threefold. First, abortion is both a moral and a public issue, thus it must be a topic of society's debate about the common good. Second, some rapprochement in the abortion debate is practically possible, and common good theory offers a framework for pursuing and acting upon points of agreement. And third, religious believers and institutions can positively contribute to the public deliberation over this issue. The abortion debate is not advanced by trying to marginalize religious voices; a liberal society that seeks the common good excludes them to its own detriment.

In considering the abortion issue, we do not receive direct guidance from Maritain. To my knowledge, he never addressed abortion as a moral or political issue in his written corpus; it simply was not a topic of scholarly concern for him. But the approach to the common good that I have developed in dialogue with him can help a pluralist society deal with social, moral, and political disagreements as deep as this one. Let me be clear on two matters. First, some of my specific judgments differ markedly from those that Maritain, in his time and place, would likely have advocated. Second, my ethical approach to the abortion issue is not offered as a distinctively Roman Catholic moral approach. If I were to address specifically the moral and personal question of abortion, my approach would be developed in closer dialogue with Catholic moral theology and Catholic Church teaching. Therefore, I am not trying to marshal Catholic ethics in favor of a certain resolution of the abortion question, nor am I suggesting that most or even many American Catholics would find my approach to the political issue of abortion agreeable. Rather, I try to offer a common good approach to the *political* question of abortion that takes serious account of the possibilities for communal liberalism in the Catholic tradition. My approach does not naively aim to achieve social consensus on such divisive issues but, instead, to articulate avenues for cooperation and conversation. In this way, it may serve to promote community in society, even as it challenges particular moral and religious traditions when they fall short of the ideals of communal liberalism.

Before I proceed, something should be said about matters of terminology. In the current U.S. political climate, the language one uses when referring to abortion supporters, abortion opponents, and unborn fetuses is quickly taken as an indication of what side of the issue one stands on. Sometimes people do want their language to be so read and heard, yet this situation makes it difficult and uncomfortable for those who want to take a moderate or neutral stance on the issue or who want to engage in conversation with a variety of opponents, proponents, and moderates. Since my goal is to lay out a framework for that inclusive conversation, I hope at least to use terminology that does not hinder further conversation. I also hope that the tone and context of my discussion makes clear that whatever terminology I employ is meant neither to marginalize someone whose views may differ from mine nor to be taken as a shibboleth for my own complex views on abortion. With those intentions clarified, let me mention a few specific decisions on terminology. When speaking of the main contestants in the U.S. political debate over abortion, I use the terms *prochoice* and *prolife* because these are how the parties label themselves. When speaking of a group's or an individual's evaluation of abortion, it may be appropriate to use the terms *proabortion* or *antiabortion*. Yet I consider both sets of terms simplistic, given the moral complexity of abortion; so I use them with caution and, wherever possible, employ more nuanced descriptions. In regard to the fetus, or unborn child, the language is even more emotionally charged—prolifers usually see *fetus* as a medical term that depersonalizes the child whose life is at stake, while prochoicers tend to see *unborn child* as a term that is used to personalize someone who is not a person. It is not feasible to split this difference down the middle, and no synonyms that could nuance the discussion present themselves. At the risk of being insensitive to those who identify with the prolife cause, I employ the term *fetus* because it is the standard medical term for a child in utero. However, as I will soon explain, all parties to the political discussion should be clear on the fact that the fetus is a human life; therefore, I often speak in what follows of *human life* and *the life of the fetus*.

THE ABORTION DEBATE AND THE LIMITS OF LIBERALISM

Since the 1970s, abortion—as a moral issue, a medical practice, and an item of public policy—has been a deeply contentious topic in American public life. The practice of abortion and the debate over its morality existed long before the *Roe v. Wade* decision of 1973.[1] But in recent years, the debate between Americans who support abortion rights and those who want to restrict or eliminate the practice seems intractable. The *Roe* decision ushered in or at least marked a new stage in the debate, in which abortion became a central issue in national politics, accompanied by aggressive political advocacy and occasionally bitter rhetoric by groups on both sides of the issue. I contend that the *Roe* decision was a legal manifestation of the political-liberal approach to public policy and, therefore, that *Roe* provides an inadequate framework for achieving cooperation and promoting conversation on an issue fraught with moral and religious implications. We saw in chapter 2 the inadequacies of the political-liberal approach in John Rawls's treatment of abortion. Rawls thought that "any reasonable balance" of the values at stake in abortion would lead to a duly qualified right to abortion in the first trimester. In the early stages of pregnancy, the political equality of women is an overriding value, so there must be a "duly qualified right" to abortion during the first trimester of pregnancy.[2] The flaw I identified in Rawls's treatment was not his assertion of a right to abortion per se, but the way he arrived at it. One problem is that his conclusion has no clear basis in his theory of political liberalism—he gives no indication as to how he weighed the competing values and came to his conclusion. The equality of women is a value clearly grounded in his political conception of citizens and their basic moral powers, but its overriding character vis-à-vis other values is asserted, not argued. A second problem is his labeling of comprehensive doctrines that arrive at more restrictive conclusions as unreasonable. Rawls unfairly rules out the potential contributions that particular comprehensive doctrines can make to political debate, and he neglects the possibility that public reason can itself be limited and mistaken.

The balance of political values that Rawls considers reasonable and supported by public reason is basically the current law of the United States as defined in *Roe*. This ruling established that the abortion decision must be left to the pregnant woman and her physician during the first trimester of pregnancy. The fifty states may regulate abortion at two later stages of pregnancy: after the first trimester, a state "may, if it chooses, regulate the abortion procedure in ways that are reasonably related to maternal health"; and after the stage of fetal viability, it "may, if it chooses, regulate, and even proscribe, abortion except where it is necessary, in appropriate medical judgment, for the preservation of the life or health of the mother."[3]

The first kind of regulation is justified by the state's interest in the mother's health, and the second by the state's interest in "the potentiality of human life."[4] In practice, *Roe* effected a nationwide policy of abortion-on-demand during the first trimester of pregnancy and generally unlimited access to abortion up to the point of viability (which falls between about twenty-four and twenty-eight weeks, approximately at the beginning of the third trimester). Late-term abortion for various medical reasons is legal in many states, though few hospitals and clinics actually perform late-term procedures. The attempts of several states to enact regulations or proscriptions according to *Roe*'s guidelines were generally thwarted by the courts until the 1992 decision *Planned Parenthood v. Casey*, which eliminated the trimester framework but preserved the right to abortion.[5]

The reasoning of Justice Harry Blackmun's majority opinion in *Roe* shows promise, in a communal liberal perspective, for it makes substantial use of a philosophical, religious, and legal history of abortion. In its final judgment, however, the opinion shows itself to be a political-liberal document. The upshot of the philosophical and religious history, for Blackmun, is that the issue of human life's beginning is a metaphysical question incapable of resolution. Religious and philosophical opinions are marshaled to support the need for a political resolution that is *independent* of those opinions:

> We need not resolve the difficult question of when life begins. When those trained in the respective disciplines of medicine, philosophy, and theology are unable to arrive at any consensus, the judiciary, at this point in the development of man's knowledge, is not in a position to speculate as to the answer.[6]

I have criticized liberalism for failing to account religion as an intellectual resource or a contributor to social unity. On the first count, the Supreme Court's decision does use religious ideas as a resource of sorts: Blackmun surveys such ideas in his explanation of historical attitudes toward abortion and again in a brief account of the diversity of current opinion on the beginning of life. Of course, the Court did not base its decision on a religious doctrine, nor should it have. The judiciary of a liberal democracy should base its decisions on a constitution that has been established and can be modified by democratic consent. However, the religious opinions of society are important to judicial reasoning: the courts should be cognizant of the religious ideas that have shaped the political and legal culture and that might play a role in shaping policies that are left open to states and citizens by their constitution. The Supreme Court seems aware of this role, and thus Blackmun thought it important, or at least useful, to discuss religious opinions of abortion in his opinion. But this discussion has remarkably little payoff: Blackmun did not draw a connection between

the religious/philosophical history and his identification of viability as a
constitutionally significant turning point.

The decision also shows some promise on the second count, in that it
does envisage leaving space in the political process for citizens in the various states to shape local decisions about the scope of the abortion right—
about how it may be regulated after the first trimester in the interest of
maternal health and whether and how much it may be regulated after viability. Yet in subsequent decisions the Court interpreted the right to abortion, which it had construed as a right of privacy under the Fourteenth
Amendment, as allowing very little regulation or constraint. In effect,
then, the *Roe* decision took abortion out of the realm of state politics and
set a single policy for the nation, at least regarding first-trimester abortion.
Was this a salutary course? Was this legal move necessary in order to ensure reproductive freedom for American women? Some doubt that Supreme Court action was the only recourse, since several states had moved
or were moving toward liberalization of abortion laws in the decade preceding *Roe*.[7] Yet supporters of *Roe* argue that only a constitutional decision could ensure equal freedom for all American women. This is surely
an important point, but in light of U.S. political history since 1973, we
have reason to wonder about the wisdom of leaving complex moral/politi-
cal issues such as abortion to the judiciary. The legal situation has left
prolife and prochoice advocates to struggle over the appointment of
judges; each side lobbies legislators and executives to choose judges on
the single criterion of how they intend (or can be surmised to intend) to
rule on abortion cases. Moreover, when state legislatures feel they have a
legitimate interest in regulating abortion procedures or in protecting late-
term fetuses, they enact laws to test the extent of *Roe*'s holding and to
provide opportunities for later courts to erode *Roe*. Rather than addressing
the factors that cause women to need or seek abortions in the first place,
some states get caught up in a protracted legal battle with the courts, which
only further distracts the nation from substantive moral discourse about
abortion.

As we have it today, the American political process is not structured in
such a way that a complex moral issue with political ramifications can be
addressed with due nuance. Both those who want to protect the life of fetuses and those who want to ensure women's rights to reproductive freedom feel locked out of the political system: prolifers because they feel the
law of the land has been settled by Supreme Court decisions that leave
no authority to local communities to enforce local values, and prochoicers
because they feel that the hard-won rights of women are gradually being
eroded through the same processes. I think both groups have reason to feel
alienated and disempowered in the political process as it exists. They want
to use their political agency to shape the common good, but they disagree

over what it will look like—what rights will be protected, where decisions will be made, and what goods society will promote.

I suggest that a common good perspective such as Maritain's offers useful principles for democratically working our way through the cultural conflicts that take place in our society. The centerpiece of this approach is renewing genuine and substantive public debate over these issues. It involves, in James Hunter's words, "facing up to the hard, tedious, perplexing, messy, and seemingly endless task of working through what kind of people we are and what kind of communities we will live in."[8] To seek the common good, our society cannot avoid the messy task of confronting our differences through substantive debate. Such debate involves addressing our political opponents as true neighbors and not as caricatures. Moreover, we must acknowledge the complexity of the moral and cultural issues inherent in abortion, as well as the fact that political approaches to these issues tend to support certain values at stake while imperfectly realizing others—hence, morally serious people can and will be found on many sides of the debate.

The challenge, as I see it, is to achieve the substance of the common good through democratic participation and not to set the two in opposition. When the personalist foundation of the common good is recognized, as in Maritain's work, then the tension is eased, for then the common good is seen to require both the participation of each person as a free and dignified subject and a return of its good to each person. The common good, in this view, embraces both procedural and substantive elements. The practical challenge is to reform and create institutions that will help us develop a growing consensus around the substance of the common good in our pluralist society.

COMMUNAL LIBERALISM'S RESOURCES FOR THE ABORTION DEBATE

Many U.S. churches approaching the abortion issue have found it difficult to articulate principled positions that transcend the narrow categories of the American political spectrum. The options, its seems, are to support either prochoice or prolife laws. Each option raises difficult questions about the attitudes churches display toward democracy. In the former case, why should churches support prochoice policies the rationales of which usually have little in common with religious values? In the latter case, why should churches, especially those that valorize American ideals of liberty, challenge laws that have been determined through a democratic process? Churches are often inconsistent in the way they answer these questions. However they resolve these questions, the underlying problem the churches face is whether to accept liberalism's terms for settling the abortion issue. Some have suggested that American churches have dissipated their resources for approaching abortion in a nuanced fashion. For instance, Elizabeth Mensch and Alan Freeman argue that, prior to the 1970s, abortion was a debatable moral topic in American society. Catholic natural law theory and Protestant neo-orthodox theology took nonabsolutist approaches to the problem; these major religious traditions served as resources for a nuanced academic and legal debate. Then two events changed the shape of the West's understanding of good and evil: Nazism and the civil rights movement. "We have, at least in retrospect, unequivocally named those two cultural images as perfect examples of villainy, on the one hand, and virtue on the other." Mensch and Freeman continue:

> Each, in its extremity, worked a convergence of law, theology, and politics, creating a sense of moral appropriateness that challenged all inconsistent premises and practices. In law, nothing short of an unprecedented and retroactively applied accountability for "crimes against humanity" was sufficient as a response to Nazism, despite overwhelming victory at war. Similarly, the moral force of the civil rights movement altered the American federal judiciary and, arguably, the structure of American federalism. Theologians, meanwhile, were haunted by the fear that their church's doctrine would not be able to counter the next cultural example of unambiguous evil. Civil rights then became the limiting case against inaction in the worldly sphere, challenging the doctrinal basis of all compelled otherworldliness.[9]

In the view of Mensch and Freeman, these concerns formed the crucible in which American churches struggled to respond to rapid political changes and growing cultural secularization from the 1950s through the 1970s.[10] Secularization influenced not only culture and politics, but religion as well. Many Christians felt anxious about their place in an ever more complex, pluralistic, and technology-driven world. Other Christians simply lost touch with their faith as a distinctive and authoritative force guiding their lives. Some denominations tried to provide a haven from the forces of secularization; others sought to revise the presentation of their faith so as to become more relevant to the concerns of contemporary Christians. Of course, this description presents two extremes: many, perhaps most, believers and churches worked through these issues gradually and in an ad hoc fashion, accommodating some cultural changes and resisting others. Yet Mensch and Freeman argue that a nuanced middle ground became more and more difficult to maintain in the new cultural situation. They hold that secularization had a twofold effect on religious activism: mainline denominations found their distinctive moral voice submerged in the wider culture (and often they willingly submerged it), while other denominations and traditions responded to the wider culture with suspicion and antipathy. The upshot was that

> abortion as a morally and theologically debatable subject in our culture was quickly replaced . . . by abortion as a question of medical expertise and personal choice. This move was supported with the language of scientific rationalism and secularized religion. All too quickly, religious opposition then became hostile, defensive, and absolutist, and a dialogue that might really have spoken to Americans within their own seriously considered religious traditions seemed to be lost.[11]

While I believe that their presentation draws an overly simple line of causation from some academics' celebration of religious secularization to the loss of the churches' moral voice,[12] Mensch and Freeman nonetheless rightly suggest that these swift cultural developments had deleterious effects on the interaction of religion and politics. If their reading of history is plausible, then the Supreme Court's ruling in *Roe v. Wade* was not the *cause* of the stark divisions between prolife and prochoice camps in American religion and society, but simply one further expression of the liberal attempt to transcend cultural conflict rather than confront it—and one further obstacle placed in the way of political debate and compromise.

We may well wonder whether religious traditions and institutions can still make a significant and distinctive contribution to the wider public discourse, which is characterized more often by debate than dialogue. I believe that they can and that Maritain's communal liberalism provides a useful framework for their efforts. Maritain's theory, while communitarian in significant respects, challenges the tendency of some communitarians to place the onus for our social problems on individualism and a profligacy of rights. A follower of Maritain would rather identify two other problems: frequent misunderstandings about the place of rights in the common good, and an inadequate institutional framework for connecting persons and communities in such a way that we can discuss and pursue the common good. Maritain has provided resources for reconceptualizing the place of rights and the role of institutions in a pluralist democracy. Common good theory tries to determine how social situations fall short of the common good. It asks, for instance, whether conditions for flourishing are being denied to some persons, whether some are locked out of participating, and whether some make inordinate sacrifices while others contribute too little. The theory then aims to develop ethical priorities and political strategies to remedy these deficiencies. It considers, for example, what personal and social goods could be bolstered by political initiatives, what institutions would be most effective in addressing social deficiencies, and how institutions at all levels can cooperate in the task.

I turn now to the resources for the political debate over abortion that can be found in communal liberalism, specifically in Maritain's substantive political philosophy. The three topics to be treated here are (1) how his conception of flourishing and rights helps us weigh the competing goods and values at stake in abortion, (2) the role that mediating institutions can play in promoting political cooperation that will address the systemic causes of abortion, and (3) the role of the law in addressing the issue.

Competing Goods and Values

Maritain, as I have shown, thought that common sense and natural law could guide citizens to a shared political conception of the basic components of human flourishing, which he described in terms of human rights. Human rights and the common good are mutually related: rights influence the common good, since they ensure that persons can participate in society; and the common good influences rights, for the content and enforcement of some rights may be limited by the legitimate demands of society. Undergirding human rights is the prepolitical, God-given dignity of persons—a status society does not confer but must recognize. It is important to remember that the common good aims at rights not as ends in themselves, but as means to the end of human flourishing considered both individually and corporately. Politics should be a process in which citizens discuss how basic personal and social goods can be promoted and what role governmental and other institutions should play in human development.

Though Maritain does not provide a method for weighing competing moral goods, the mutual relation he establishes between the common good and human rights helps frame the question. Recall, in particular, that Maritain's theological personalism, discussed in chapter 3, features an indirect subordination of the temporal common good to the supernatural common good. This subordination entails a particular relation between political values and the perfectionist moral values of Christian faith: Christians should not expect or advocate that their complete vision of the supernatural good be imported into political society. The temporal common good best serves the supernatural common good by respecting human rights and creating conditions for personal flourishing. Thus society should not give political preference to any single religious account of the content of human flourishing, but it should respect religious faith and the freedom of churches and religious organizations to articulate and to promote in the public realm their conceptions of flourishing. If people approach the abortion issue in light of this understanding of the common good, it might result in a deeper appreciation for the difficulty of promoting equally and in the same manner all goods and values that bear on human flourishing. As long as we live in a temporal society, we have to accept limitations upon our ability to realize the values of the supernatural common good and to share them with fellow citizens in a political order.

In considering how basic individual goods and social goods are impeded or promoted in the abortion issue, one must attend to the multiple goods at stake: the human life itself of a fetus; the quality of life a born child can expect; family stability and well-being; a pregnant woman's physical health and emotional well-being; reproductive freedom; the interests and participation of a father; and the social equality of women. All of these are important goods to society or can be reasonably defended as such. In an imperfect world, some pregnant women will experience conflicts among these goods. Society also experiences conflicts, for how it acts or refrains from acting will influence the decisions of particular women. How are we to approach these value conflicts in such a way that all goods are given their due and that no set of goods is consistently neglected? Do any of these goods trump others?

As a political theory, communal liberalism is not committed to a particular moral theory. It does, however, have to respect plural moral and religious perceptions and convictions, while at the same time allowing for adjudication of moral conflicts in the political realm. In pursuing this goal—admittedly a challenging one—communal liberalism is not morally neutral. Some moral approaches will facilitate this goal better than others. One general approach that fits with communal liberalism's aims is a relational view of goods. Lloyd Steffen advocates such a view and applies it to abortion. He argues that human goods have their value in connection with one another and cannot simply stand apart.

> A relational view of values holds open the possibility that in the complexity of existence, values that are inherently good and worthy of being promoted can come into conflict with one another. On the abortion issue, moral conflict arises when a pregnancy is determined to be undesirable and unwanted, and the good of life ingredient in pregnancy is challenged by other goods that cannot also be honored if one were to honor the good of life. The relational view of values . . . , by refusing to honor the good of life as an absolute good, opens the possibility that some pregnancies can be justifiably terminated and a developing form of life justifiably killed.[13]

A relational view of goods admits the possibility of moral dilemmas and requires an assessment of the total context of an action before it is morally judged. Any good has its value in relation to other goods; some goods are more fundamental and more important than others, but no good (except God, who is an Absolute Good) consistently trumps every other. Reproductive choice is instrumental to the goods of social equality and personal autonomy. These goods have their place in a network of human goods, others of which include concern for community and care for the vulnerable. The life of the fetus is good because the fetus is a genetically unique and irreplaceable human being and because it instantiates the power of humans to create new life—an act we engage in not merely as a biological imperative, but as the expression of loving commitment between a man and a woman. That, of course, is the ideal, yet sometimes pregnancies occur in painful and tragic circumstances. Even if a fetus's life is always a good in itself, it may not be experienced as a good by the pregnant woman. What to do when the good of the life of the fetus conflicts with other goods, or when it is experienced as a disvalue, is an exceedingly difficult moral choice for a woman or a couple, one that has to be made from an informed conscience. I do not want to delve into the personal moral issue here, except to make two general claims about abortion in light of a relational view of goods. First, the freedom to choose abortion is not an unmitigated good from a moral point of view—it matters what the circumstances are, what other goods are at stake, and how responsibly this freedom is exercised. Second, fetal life, as human life, is always a good, but it is not one that trumps every other good; competing goods may provide sufficiently serious reasons for choosing against the good of the human life of the fetus.[14]

These two claims are relevant to the social question at hand: What stance should social and political institutions take with respect to the practice of abortion? As a starting point, note that the common good is also a relational good: it neither consistently trumps, nor is it consistently trumped by, personal goods. For the sake of the common good, neither the right to life nor the right to reproductive choice can be absolutized. A relational view does not entail, however, that all goods have the same status. One good may be of such value that it gives rise to a prima facie obligation. Consider first the value of choice. As it is included in the right of reproductive freedom, abortion has been a factor in the civic and economic advancement of women. Even so, it is best understood as a last-resort resource: it has worked as a backup or alternative to other means such as birth control, paid family leave from work, and economic resources for families. Abortion is a last resort because many or most persons are reluctant to override the value of a fetal life except for serious reasons and also because it is not a particularly empowering choice for most women. That is, the mere right to abort does not address the deeper factors of gender inequality, economic injustice, and family insecurity that are among the underlying causes of most unwanted pregnancies. Though personal freedom, including reproductive freedom, is a high political value, abortion itself does not seem to carry the status of a prima facie moral value. To whatever extent it is good, it is so because of its instrumental value. Indeed, an overly narrow focus on abortion rights could well be disempowering to women if this focus distracts political and moral energies from the deeper issues just mentioned.

On the other hand, let us consider the moral value of human life. By ending the life of the fetus, abortion does frustrate the good of life. The good of life seems to have a certain priority in an account of the human good, for it is prerequisite to experiencing any other good. One has to be alive in order to flourish and to contribute to the common good. Each fetus, with a unique genetic constitution, will in the normal course of events be born as a singular and irreplaceable person, whose opportunities to flourish and to contribute to its family, society, and culture are likewise unique and unrepeatable. These claims provide a prima facie reason for starting with a *moral* presupposition in favor of preserving and protecting the human life of the fetus. The presupposition need not rest on a claim that the fetus is a "person." I would seek not to avoid that question but, rather, to include it within a broader set of questions about the character of a society: What are its hopes for the flourishing of its members (and potential members); what are the duties of its members to build up solidarity; and what can it hope to gain by seeking to include persons as broadly as possible in the task of the common good? Lisa Cahill focuses the issue well:

> If relatedness to and concern for others and for the sort of community in which we all associate is more important to us than "defending our own territory" (by defining the precise limits of our minimal obligations not to prevent other equal beings from promoting their own self-interested welfare), then it becomes less important to show whether or not the fetus is a human being with exactly the same right to consideration as our own. If we are able to foster a sense of duty to others and to our common society, a duty that precedes and grounds our own rights as individuals, then it also becomes possible to envision a moral obligation to support the cohesion in the human community of even its weakest members, those with the least forceful claim to consideration, whether they be the unborn, the sick, the poor, or the socially powerless.[15]

If we approach the issue in this way, Cahill thinks we may notice a common denominator in the current abortion debate:

> There is now more of a consensus in our culture than is usually recognized that a policy on abortion attributing to the fetus no value that can ever outweigh its mother's choice to terminate pregnancy is not consonant with its membership in the human community, disputed though the exact nature of that membership may be. Failing agreement on the precise status of the fetus, we may hope still for concurrence in a generally protective attitude toward the fetus, a bias in its favor, and an expectation that those seeking to kill it will

be able to claim reasonably that its continued existence imposes on others unjust and intolerable burdens.[16]

Like Cahill, I believe that the principle of promoting human flourishing supports a moral presupposition in favor of protecting fetal life. But, as I have also indicated, the value of this life must be considered in relation to a broad array of personal and social goods. As citizens consider and weigh these goods, institutional and policy questions inevitably arise. A society cannot avoid taking political and legal stances on moral questions; even to say that a particular matter should be left to private choice is to take a political position.

Identifying Institutional Responsibilities

Common good theory holds that a democratic society should pursue common values through public discourse. This pursuit embraces both the narrow realm of law and the broad realm of policy making and public deliberation. Looking at abortion, the theory urges that citizens cooperatively shape a society that respects both the life of fetuses and women's well-being, liberty, and equality. Institutions should provide the economic and medical support that would make childbearing a more attractive option for those who lack financial, medical, or familial resources. The provision of a more substantial safety net—including guaranteed health insurance, generous family leave policies, and affordable child care—will also have the positive effect of enabling some women, who would otherwise abort, to carry their pregnancies to term. Welfare policies should be reformed, not abolished, to encourage fathers to remain involved with the families they have helped create.[17] Women's lives and family stability must be protected through increased initiatives to prevent domestic abuse and to ensure that absent fathers pay child support. All these provisions benefit pregnant women, their future children, and society at large.

Two principles from Maritain's theory help to identify communal responsibilities in the sociopolitical realm. The first of these is *pluralism.* Maritain defends institutional, cultural, and religious pluralism, because these facilitate social participation, help us pursue diverse social goods, and protect against the centralization of power in the state or any one civic institution. Maritain's pluralism principle is undergirded by two principles linked in Catholic social thought: subsidiarity and solidarity. In applying the pluralism principle to political problems, we must ask subsidiarity-based questions like, "How will the proposed course of action support the autonomy of local communities and mediating institutions?" and "What kind of help can higher institutions offer to lower institutions?" We must also ask solidarity-based questions: "How will this decision help bring communities together in greater concert?" and "Where must the interests of lower communities give way to the needs of the greater common good?" Common good theory does not prefer one principle to the other, though it recognizes potential conflict between answers to the two sets of questions. In such cases, parties can adjudicate the conflict only by returning to discussion about personal and social goods, trying to achieve greater clarity about the relative priority of particular goods. In general, citizens and groups will find harmony between the two principles if they understand subsidiarity neither as a simple federalizing principle nor as a pure autonomy principle, but as a pluralism principle exercised for the sake of the common good.

Applying the pluralism principle to the abortion debate leads to the following considerations. First, public debate and discussion need to occur at a very local level. In recent years, examples of fruitful, voluntary discussion have come to light. *Common ground* discussions between prochoice and prolife activists, or just between people of different views, have helped these participants to hear the rationale of their opponents. The "other side" can be seen to consist of real people who are trying to protect values that are important, even if one disagrees with the political policies those people support. These discussions should take place away from television cameras—the point is not to score public relations points or even to convert the opponent, but to understand and perhaps to be understood better.[18]

A second implication of pluralism is that local institutions are more likely to be able to help women with crisis pregnancies compassionately and effectively. Hunter canvasses some examples of local efforts to reduce teen pregnancy and provide alternatives to abortion; he concludes:

> the people most receptive to the idea of talking and even working together are those who deal with women facing unplanned pregnancies on a day-to-day basis—either those who run abortion clinics or homes for pregnant women. Those who work in advocacy groups toward legal and political change seem to be the *least* receptive.[19]

Thus, a third implication of the pluralism principle should be a wariness to refine abortion policy further through the Supreme Court or national politics. The federal government can most help women and best build up the common good by making resources available to those institutions that work to prevent teenage pregnancy and by supporting economically distressed women and families. Policies that precipitously eliminate welfare and unravel the safety net are antithetical to the value that society should place on women, children, and the unborn.[20]

A second principle that shapes communal responsibilities is that all citizens must make *appropriate contributions and sacrifices*. As the common good must flow back over each person and contribute to each person's development, it also assumes that all members of society make appropriate contributions according to their particular gifts, resources, and interests.[21] The primary theme is not one of requirement, because a common good perspective assumes that we are by nature social and political beings: we want to and in fact do contribute to the common good in many ways, for instance, through our relationships, in raising and educating children, in our careers, through our churches and voluntary associations, and so on. Beyond what we already do, the common good holds us to voluntary standards, such as considering the ramifications of our speech and actions for the good of society and making contributions of time, money, and effort to volunteer enterprises. The common good also requires contributions that have legal backing, such as paying taxes and serving on juries. The common good may require stronger sacrifices when basic justice, basic equality, or public safety and order are threatened. Thus, the state as an agent of the common good may require citizens to fight in wars or may proscribe the exercise of certain rights for proportionally good reasons. In these cases, where the requirement is backed up with legal authority, the state may override the material interests of individuals for the sake of sustaining a community and its goods—goods that cannot be created or enjoyed privately. The justification for sacrifice is not "the greatest good of the greatest number," but "for the sake of sustaining communal goods that are also personal goods." And it scarcely needs repeating that society's exaction of contributions and sacrifices may never violate basic human dignity and basic rights.

In the cultural and ethical contest over abortion, citizens and institutions must make contributions and sacrifices for the sake of the common good. They must do so in order to promote a just and civil life together and to establish those conditions in which all citizens may have access to their fulfillment as human beings. I have already mentioned the support that government should provide; this in turn implies the need for citizens to share the tax burden for increased support for pregnant women, adoption services, and pregnancy prevention education. Churches should back up their teachings through concrete support for women with crisis pregnancies. Such programs exist, but they are not widespread enough. Parents and schools can enter into closer and more cooperative relationships for the education and oversight of children, building on creative models that are being tried throughout the country. Sex education is a complex matter that I cannot open here, but it is clear to me that it must deal with deeper issues (such as self-esteem and peer pressure) that influence teenage sexual activity. Couples must take responsibility before they are sexually active: this means much more than using birth control if they are unwilling to rear a child; it means deciding why they want to have a sexual relationship and if they are ready to deal with all of its consequences, including possible pregnancy.

Identifying the responsibilities of mediating institutions and avenues of cooperation with political institutions is crucial if society is to remedy the social deficits that make recourse to abortion seem necessary for so many. However, it is clear that improving and expanding support structures will not address every reason that women may have for seeking abortion. And so we must confront the question of abortion's legality. While I am convinced that, from a common good perspective, legal proscriptions are not the best way to make abortion less frequent and less necessary, the law does have to set parameters for the sake of both women and children. In the next section, I will briefly analyze the legal status of abortion and make a proposal for a legal approach that is consonant with communal liberalism's aims of linking rights and responsibilities and of creating space for religious contributions to political deliberation.

A Proposal Regarding the Legal Status of Abortion

The Supreme Court has followed a jagged path through abortion cases since the 1970s. While never overturning *Roe*, it has recently allowed greater state regulation of abortion. One line of cases has affirmed that the federal and state governments can refuse to pay public funds for abortion and that states can prohibit the use of government facilities or hospitals for abortions.[22] Until 1992, however, the Court struck down most laws that tried to regulate an adult woman's ability to procure an abortion.[23] In that year, a five-to-four majority handed down a decision in *Planned Parenthood of Southeastern Pennsylvania v. Casey*, which upheld the following regulations: (1) an informed consent requirement that a woman seeking abortion be given information on the nature of the procedure, the health risks of abortion and of childbirth, and the probable gestational age of the child; (2) a twenty-four-hour waiting period between counseling and the procedure; (3) parental consent for minors who seek an abortion; and (4) mandatory record-keeping and reporting requirements.[24] The one regulation struck down by the *Casey* court was that a woman notify her husband of her plan to abort, unless she had a fear of being abused or another excusing reason.[25]

The *Casey* majority saw the first four restrictions as compatible with the "central holding" of *Roe*—the right to procure previability abortions. Essentially, *Casey* discarded the trimester framework, keeping only viability as a relevant demarcation; and it modified its standard of review from a "strict scrutiny" analysis to an "undue burden" analysis. This latter change makes it simpler for restrictions to be placed on the abortion right: under strict scrutiny, almost any state regulation on a woman's freedom in the first trimester is deemed unconstitutional; in an undue burden analysis, only those regulations that have "the purpose or effect of placing a *substantial* obstacle in the path of a woman seeking an abortion of a nonviable fetus" are held unconstitutional.[26] It is legitimate for a state to express its "important and legitimate interest in potential life" throughout the course of pregnancy.[27] Early in pregnancy, this interest is not so compelling that it permits substantial hindrance of a woman's right to abort (for the fetus does not have the chance of living an independent life), but it is important enough that the state can in certain ways express its preference for childbirth over abortion. "What is at stake [before viability] is a woman's right to make the ultimate decision, not a right to be insulated from all others in doing so."[28] Under this new standard, the Court found that only the husband notification requirement of the provisions of the Pennsylvania law created an undue burden.

The challenging question for a common good perspective is: At what point(s) should the law draw line(s) in order to balance the goods of women's well-being, liberty, and equality with the good of the life of fetuses? In my view, common good principles do not in themselves commit our society to any particular balancing line. They do, however, require us to remain open to all the goods at stake—to respect and protect, as far as we can, each good. To my mind, this means that an abortion law responsive to the common good should do three things. First, respecting the value of human life, it should, at minimum, afford increasing protection to the fetus as it develops toward birth. Second, respecting the goods of women's well-being, liberty, and equality, it should, at minimum, retain the right to early abortion and allow exceptions throughout pregnancy for tragic situations—for pregnancies that threaten the mother's life or health and for those owing to rape or incest. Third, respecting the value of political deliberation, it should set in place a framework that will allow citizens to continue weighing and pursuing these goods and to continue confronting abortion as a moral problem. Such a legal framework would allow states some leeway in setting time lines in pregnancy after which their interest in the life of the fetus becomes compelling enough to proscribe the procedure. But the lines drawn could not reach so far back that women did not have some time in which freely to seek an abortion. States would have to allow a reasonable amount of time for women to exercise their privacy rights, for these rights are protective of basic human goods (well-being, liberty, and equality) and cannot be denied by the state without grave harm to human dignity.

The question then becomes: How are legislators and judges to decide how much time is "reasonable"? The answer will depend on two factors: (1) on a judgment about the effect of given time limits on women's well-being and liberty under current social conditions, and (2) on the consistency between the government's definition of human life at its beginning and at its end. The first criterion would tend to support a time limit no earlier (or not significantly earlier) than viability, for the reason that a precipitous encroachment upon the right to previability abortion would significantly shift the legal terrain for women. Yet it is not simply a matter of getting used to an earlier limit; there are good reasons why a time limit cannot be pushed too early. For instance, women who have striven to avoid pregnancy and conceive nonetheless may not discover this for several weeks. When these women are teenagers or otherwise inexperienced, it is possible for some not to realize they are pregnant until fetal movement starts (at about eighteen to twenty weeks).[29] The second criterion entails that our policies about the existence of human life have to be consistent. The possession of a heartbeat, the presence of brain waves, and the ability to live independent of life-support systems are all markers in fetal development that are also used (in different ways) in laws and decisions regarding the end of life. Any of these could potentially serve as a rational basis for identifying when the life of a fetus takes on a greater interest to the state. Brain activity is detectable at about seven to eight weeks—and this seems to me to be the absolute earliest time at which it would be just to begin regulating abortion.[30] A state, however, would not only have to show just a rational basis (the lowest standard of scrutiny) for a line drawn earlier than viability, but it would also have to demonstrate an *important* governmental interest (a standard higher than a rational basis, but not as high as a compelling interest) in protecting the fetus from that point. The discrepancy between these answers—the first justifying viability, the second countenancing earlier limits—serves to balance society's respect for the different goods at stake, to ensure a reasonable amount of time for women to exercise an abortion right while allowing states the option of setting the time line earlier than viability in the interest of protecting the developing fetus.

My proposed balance concurs with *Casey* in discarding the trimester framework and in acknowledging that communities have legitimate interests in the preservation of the human life of fetuses throughout pregnancy. I also agree with *Casey* in leaving intact a right to early abortion. In a complete treatment, it would be necessary to consider the other regulations *Casey* allowed: mandatory counseling, waiting periods, and parental notification for a minor. These regulations are difficult to assess because there are two ways to interpret them. On the one hand, they are means a political community can use to promote alternatives to abortion; on the other hand, they have the effect of restricting access to abortion for some women, hence the already vulnerable become further disenfranchised. In each case, various practical and factual matters have to be addressed. My provisional judgment is that any of these regulations *could* work for the common good if they emerged from a political process where common good principles were honored. But the various forms these regulations can take make the issues too complicated to go into here. My proposal, while probably troubling to prochoice advocates and less than satisfactory to prolife proponents, honors the vision of the common good wherein citizens discuss, compromise, and work out common solutions. Presently, some groups on each side of the political contest are looking for the slightest encroachment as a battle cry to rally their members to a thoroughly pro- or antiabortion policy. Most Americans, however, find themselves in the middle—which indicates, I think, that most people perceive the conflicting values at stake.[31] They are uneasy with any resolution that locks out one set of values or the other. Yet most of us are also uneasy with a middling policy, because it seems unsettled. Neither set of values trumps. But this is the way it must be, for the moral method I am advocating and its corresponding political policy do the greatest justice to all the values at stake.

Having considered abortion in light of the intellectual resources of common good theory, my main conclusion is that society needs to find ways to balance multiple and conflicting goods. Concern for the life of fetuses is a legitimate and important concern of a political community, a concern communities should express primarily through positive means. At the same time, women's well-being, liberty, and equality are important goods, so important that the rights to bodily autonomy and reproductive freedom are essential to human dignity and the common good, hence abortion must be preserved as a basic right. Some restrictions that states and citizens want to impose on this right are problematic and cannot be justified. Yet in the interest of the value of the human life of fetuses, the time within which women may regularly procure elective abortions may be limited as a matter of legislation. Because the common good requires localized deliberation and decision making wherever these are possible and justified, my policy would allow states, counties, and cities to set these time limits at varying points, depending on how citizens determine they can best affirm their interest in protecting human life and best ensure women's well-being. But because the common good also requires juridical protections that enable all members of society to participate fully and fairly in it, federal law should continue to ensure a right to early abortion, and judicial practice should continue to oversee state laws. Finally, regulations concerning counseling, waiting periods, and parental notification may also be adjusted though the democratic process. This policy aims to create "the necessary room in society so that abortion can be confronted as a moral problem, with society refusing on the one hand to play the role of moral absolutist while accepting on the other the practical and morally defensible position that some abortions are morally permissible and others are not."[32]

Beyond the legal regulations, the common good asks women and men to take responsibility for their reproductive decisions, so as reduce the incidence of unwanted pregnancy. It also asks persons to be open to the good that children bring into families and society, even if they are born with handicaps or serious diseases, and even if they add to an already large family. Finally, it asks women and couples faced with unwanted pregnancies seriously to consider continuing those pregnancies and offering the children for adoption.[33] Correspondingly, society must provide the resources and support structures that will enable persons to respond to these requests. These include, but are not limited to, providing funds and support to women with crisis pregnancies, supporting private and public-private ventures that meet the needs of such women and of single mothers, providing greater tax relief for families with children, increasing support for families with handicapped children, and finding ways to make adoption a more attractive option. Society must also continue to pursue economic and social justice for women in the workplace, in health care, and in personal security and safety. These conditions are necessary if the United States is to pursue the common good in the abortion debate.

THE CHURCHES' CONTRIBUTIONS TO
SOLIDARITY AND SOCIAL CHANGE

Communal liberalism aims to create room in society for substantive discussion about ethical issues and to guide cooperative political action for just and good solutions. In light of this theory, I have suggested that moral claims be weighed and discussed in a public conversation about abortion, but my approach leaves open the precise nature of any political resolution of the issue. The common good, as the temporal project of a pluralistic society, cannot be specified in detail apart from the actual form it takes in social cooperation. Yet common good theory can inquire into the possibilities and bases for such cooperation and offer principles that all participants must respect. I have also argued that the common good goes beyond legal compromise. The richer and more important work of the common good takes place in the political and cultural life of civil society. There citizens can do the concrete work of supporting families adequately, providing proper prenatal care for all, preparing youths to handle relationships maturely, and nurturing the self-esteem of young women and men so that when they come to be sexually active, they will do so as an expression of maturity, love, and commitment.

My approach to abortion in the previous section drew upon the intellectual resources of Maritain's common good theory. It did not indicate a specific role for churches and religious institutions in promoting the common good as it relates to abortion. And yet I have argued in earlier chapters that religion is an essential component of the common good for a pluralist society. So our consideration of abortion cannot be left where it is. Religious citizens can do much to advance *or* hinder the pursuit of the common good, depending on how responsibly they act in the political domain. Maritain's theory provides guidance to these persons and their churches on how to act responsibly for the common good. In this section, I present six maxims for the churches' contributions to building solidarity and cooperation for the common good in relation to abortion as a moral/political problem. These maxims find their ground partly in the intellectual resources that Catholic Christianity contributes to political life but more specifically in Catholicism's second and third contributions to the common good—its benefits for social harmony and its promotion of neglected goods.

Maxim 1: Churches are properly political, so they should engage in the abortion debate and concern themselves with policy questions. Yet they must remember that politics is more than policy. Churches must be political because they are called by their divine mandate to build up the common good. In the Catholic view, among other religious views, churches have a duty to shape the culture and society in which they live, a duty implicit in their witness.[34] At the community level, witnessing consists primarily in ordering the community's life around the vision of life to which believers are called. It involves faith (that the call is genuine and is true to our deepest longings), obedience (in honoring a good greater than oneself), and sacrifice (a willingness to cede certain individual preferences and priorities for the good of the community and the integrity of its witness). When a religious community lives in faithful obedience to its call, it cannot help but manifest to the wider society, to anyone who cares to notice, the goods and virtues that are made possible by such living. Thus, an "inward" focus on faithful, obedient living is a political act—it makes a statement about the values the community prizes and their social consequences.

Witnessing does not end with manifesting a way of life; it requires social, cultural, and political engagement with the wider society. The reason is not only defensive (to protect the space within which religious communities can freely live out their vision of the good), but also responsive (to help those in need, to contribute to intellectual and social solidarity, and to create conditions for the pursuit of the common good). Churches are properly political if they know they must care for all persons. Certainly all major religious traditions, at their best, call their adherents to this inclusive caring.

Therefore, churches have a duty to enlighten and guide their members about the political implications of their faith and to present their moral views to the larger society. To be effective, both forms of teaching rely upon the participation of the lay members of the church, for lay members both pass on a church's teachings to other members (through education of their children and various forms of lay leadership) and serve, for better or worse, as representatives of their religion in the eyes of other people. Churches may also appropriately analyze and commend particular political policies to their members and to others, activities that are straightforwardly implied by their right and duty to teach. Here, again, the lay, nonordained members of the church play an important role in mediating the moral views of their tradition into the sociopolitical arena.

When we come to direct political action, though, some limits appear. Even though church and state should cooperate, Maritain's pluralism principle and his distinction of the temporal and supernatural common good keep the church's role in politics indirect. It is best for the common good when churches refrain from endorsing candidates and indicating how their members ought to vote on candidates and parties. However, nothing in common good theory rules out such actions in principle; rather, my statement rests on the empirical warrant that, in the United States at least, such direct endorsements by churches tend to undermine their religious mission and incline many citizens to argue that religion has overstepped its bounds and should be pushed out of the political sphere. An appropriate way for churches to engage in political action in consonance with their ethical teachings is to support para-church organizations that work for political change.

Churches should orient all their political speech and activity toward creating conditions for civil conversation and constructive action. If they think through common good principles in relation to abortion, churches can discern ways to protect and promote goods such as the life of fetuses, women's well-being, and social justice. They would make their first priority manifesting a faithful way of life to others, by respecting these goods in their own common lives. They might then seek policies that give them the freedom to choose morally good lives, rather than having the state try to ensure this for them, as in the following proposal by Kathy Rudy:

> Because . . . morality is constructed by competing ideological discourses, it ought to be the task of each tradition to regulate abortion, reproduction, and sexuality inside its own boundaries. Rather than expending time and money to alter and influence legislation, I believe that each tradition should spend more time and money instead on making its world more plausible, internally coherent, and attractive. For example, if . . . Christians see the world as a place where children ought to be welcomed, believers should work to make adoption services more humane and available; they should strive to make single mothers with unwanted pregnancies feel accepted and honored; they should live and act in ways that would allow pregnant women to feel positively about surrendering their babies to a Christian community. In doing so,

Christians would allow people to participate in their entire community-based worldview, rather than forcing their opinions on others with different ideologies.[35]

Rudy makes similar recommendations regarding feminists—that they "ought to be striving against the things that make childrearing the exclusive burden of women and working toward ways in which raising children receives the support of the wider community." The upshot is that "it behooves all competing ideologies to focus their energy and attention on advancing their entire worldviews rather than on lobbying for pro-choice or pro-life legislation."[36]

Maxim 2: Churches should bring their teachings on abortion and their promotion of alternatives under a comprehensive ethic of care for children and families. One should not gloss over the very real differences among various churches in their approaches to abortion as a specific moral issue. I would argue, though, that churches are called to respect life and thus to confront honestly the moral challenge to respect the lives of both women and fetuses. As I have indicated, genuine conflicts between these values persist. In trying to respond sensitively to such conflicts, churches will devise different moral, pastoral, and political approaches to the issue. This maxim pushes churches to seek consistency between their teachings on abortion and other moral problems. Let me demonstrate, by reference to Catholicism, how churches might seek consistency in their moral approaches to abortion.

The U.S. Catholic Church took a much-needed step toward consistency in the early 1980s, when Cardinal Joseph Bernardin of Chicago articulated a "consistent ethic of life." The consistent ethic seeks to subsume all of the Church's moral denunciations of killing—whether through abortion, war, murder, or capital punishment—under a theological vision of human life's sacredness. Bernardin applied the consistent ethic to multiple threats on life, while acknowledging the differences among these threats. The urgency for making such linkages is to prevent an erosion in society's respect for life: "When human life is considered 'cheap' or easily expendable in one area, eventually nothing is held sacred and all lives are in jeopardy. Ultimately it is society's attitude about life—whether of respect or nonrespect—that determines its policies and practices."[37] In its political context, Bernardin's consistent ethic had a double purpose, according to Todd David Whitmore: it was "at once an attempt to make the Catholic abortion argument plausible to a hesitant if not skeptical public and an effort to convince pro-life advocates that their range of concern needs to extend beyond the problem of taking the life of the fetus."[38]

To be sure, the consistent ethic does not go so far as to acknowledge genuine conflicts in moral values, and in this way, it remains limited as a model for a communal liberal approach to abortion. Whitmore argues that the consistent ethic of life was only partially successful in overcoming a moral imbalance between the Church's traditional teaching on abortion and its ethic of care for children. The consistent ethic "remains fragile because the methodological split between sexual and social ethics in official documents continues."[39] Whitmore contends that, of the moral methods available to the Catholic Church, "subsuming abortion under the issue of care for children within the context of a responsibility approach is the most stable."[40] The U.S. Bishops undertook this approach in their 1991 document "Putting Children and Families First."[41] As exemplified there, the approach has several pastoral advantages, including the potential for promoting discussion and cooperative action among disputants in the abortion debate.

> This is because the responsibility approach focuses on the reasons why women have abortions. It therefore highlights what is required of a pastoral response: the care of children. Such care can serve as a point of contact between persons who disagree in many cases on the morality of taking the life of the fetus, but who, through consensus and cooperation in the care of children, can lower the incidence of abortion.[42]

If churches bring their pastoral responses to abortion under a responsibility approach, Whitmore concludes, they will heighten their credibility when they speak about abortion in the public forum, and thus will need to hold themselves to the same high standards to which they call women who face crisis pregnancies.[43] A responsibility approach directed to the care of children conduces to the common good in the abortion debate, for it points to what Margaret Farley calls a "beyond abortion" position, a position that "must argue for values and structures that will liberate women, and men, and that will conduce to mutuality in child-rearing. Only through such a position can human life finally be valued, from its beginning to its end, wherever it is to be found."[44]

Maxim 3: The churches should draw attention to the interlocking responsibilities of communities. A clear corollary of the responsibility approach is that churches must critique social structures that place unjust burdens on women. Many abortions that are criticized as "abortions of convenience" occur because women find that too much of the burden of child rearing and supporting a family falls on them. Remedying this situation means, for one, challenging fathers to meet their child-rearing and support obligations and helping them to do so. Churches are well situated to provide both moral and practical guidance in this regard. The unequal burdens require, secondly, that society should place equal responsibilities on, and provide equal benefits for, mothers and fathers. How many working women have been told by their superiors, in subtle or overt terms, that having a child would hinder their career or even threaten their employment? How many men have been told the same thing? On an anecdotal basis, we know that the disparity between the answers must be massive. Churches should be vigorous critics of practices that rely upon individualist and patriarchal assumptions.

As part of its duty to critique unjust social structures, churches must call attention to such unequal treatment, as well as to the many social deficits that leave women (and couples) isolated in their child-rearing duties. The churches appropriately commend policies to overcome these deficits. Respecting the dual principles of subsidiarity and solidarity, their recommendations should be neither statist nor privatistic:

> The undeniable fact is that our children's future is shaped by both the values of their parents and the policies of our nation. . . . It is time to move beyond rigid ideologies and political posturing to focus on the real needs of families. We believe parental responsibility, changed behavior and changed policies are complementary requirements to help families.[45]

Maxim 4: *Churches should strive to bring their actions in line with their teachings and their teachings in line with one another.* Writing shortly after the *Roe v. Wade* decision, Farley suggested that the impasse in the abortion debate owes its continued existence to the failure of the disputants to consider seriously the experience of their opponents "as a genuine experience of moral obligation." The breaking of the impasse would require "that each group take serious account of the opponent's charge against it of 'bad faith.' " Bad faith is the "self-deception, pretentiousness, hypocrisy" in which "one fails to understand and to disclose one's own position."[46] Farley interestingly locates examples of bad faith arguments by strong pro- and antiabortionists under the same general areas—in arguments regarding the nature of the fetus, in the consideration given to the needs of pregnant women, and in making valuations of human life and assigning moral terms to abortion.[47] In each of these areas, we can identify examples where each group holds so strongly to their own experience of moral obligation that they disregard other important values and refuse to acknowledge inconsistencies or nuances in their positions.

Increasingly, I think, people have been taking to heart the challenge Farley articulates. Recently, several authors have seriously investigated the experience of moral obligation felt by multiple sides in the abortion debate, and they have turned critical eyes on the potential bad faith of the communities with which they identify.[48] Similar moves can be found not only among academic theologians and ethicists, but also in the official statements of various denominations. For example, the consistent ethic of life and the care-of-children approach are plausibly seen as attempts by the U.S. Bishops to address some instances of bad faith within the Catholic tradition. The Evangelical Lutheran Church in America and the Presbyterian Church USA have tried to bring their prochoice and prolife members together in drafting documents that downplay legal judgments, avoid absolutism, acknowledge bad faith in their own traditions, and hold themselves accountable for creating alternatives to abortion.[49] Churches should continue to turn a critical eye on their own traditions, particularly to ensure that the same moral method is applied to abortion as to other issues[50] and that women are held to the same standards as men in comparable situations.

The move to address one's own bad faith arguments and to take seriously the moral experience of others must be applauded wherever it occurs. In general, churches do act consistently with their teachings; yet they have to be on guard against instances where their actions might slide back from their ideals. Examples of such "slippage" are buying into simplistic solutions, focusing on single-issue politics, and forming overly comfortable alliances with a single political party. Such actions compromise a church's integrity. Churches also slip back from their ideals through omission, for example, by failing to provide adequate support structures for women and families or by failing to make such programs the centerpiece of their moral witness on abortion.

Maxim 5: Churches ought to promote ecumenical conversation about complex moral problems such as abortion. Different denominations and religions can strive to be examples to members of other faiths. Adherents of various faiths should establish dialogue to see if they can develop consensus either on principles or, if that proves too difficult, on practical priorities to reduce the need for abortion and to provide alternatives. Some religious leaders, like many politicians, would rather avoid the issue. For instance, an important interfaith statement on the common good, released in 1993 by the general secretaries of three national religious bodies, sidestepped abortion for the sake of unity and focus.[51] While such avoidance may be understandable, and while not every ecclesial social statement need address abortion, ecumenical and interfaith discussions about the common good should not neglect abortion entirely. If the abortion debate is a source of political contention, and if some abortions undermine human and social goods, then abortion is a problem for the common good, and interreligious dialogue ought to address it. A method of avoidance demonstrates a lack of courage to the wider society; in a way, it validates the bracketing of controversial moral views that a political-liberal culture tends to encourage.

The public debate benefits when persons of different faiths speak collectively and thoughtfully about their shared moral commitments regarding abortion, even if these statements reflect uniformly prolife or prochoice positions.[52] It would be even more beneficial if those groups could reach out and dialogue *across* the prolife/prochoice divide. If the "common ground" discussions I mentioned earlier in this chapter were tried out in explicitly interreligious contexts—among religious leaders and theological writers—they could well set a highly positive example for political debates and other public conversations.

Maxim 6: Churches should cooperate with other institutions to create the conditions that promote human and community development. The last maxim holds that churches need to take cooperative, institutional approaches to achieve the many goals mentioned under the previous maxims. Their task is a public one—but, as Hunter reminds us, *public* refers to the regional and local levels as much as to the national.[53] The most effective way for churches to engender respect for life in the context of common good principles is to participate in developing local networks of support and social change. Hunter cites an example:

> In Bridgeport, Connecticut, a city and state that are both highly prochoice, the Catholic diocese has initiated a program to help women of all faiths work through their feelings over having had an abortion. Church officials there do not in any way deny the sinfulness of abortion, but the emphasis is not on theological judgment, nor is it on church politics or social activism. Rather, Project Rachel, as it is called, offers group therapy and one-on-one spiritual counseling to women who "feel like shit," who have "got pain and guilt and depression coming out of every pore in [their] body," who never had "a chance to grieve" over or because of their abortion. Monsignor Martin Ryan, who oversees the diocese and started the local chapter, insists that the church set an example of generosity, believing this to be a precondition of the larger society paying attention: "In a Catholic state we want to show we love the sinner and hate the sin."
>
> What is interesting in all of this is that in Bridgeport, much of the church's work is accomplished in conjunction with the Bridgeport Adolescent Pregnancy Prevention Program, a coalition that includes (besides the Catholic church) city social service agencies and even Planned Parenthood. The coalition is tenuously held together, to be sure, working in large part because of the existence of separate tracks for different kinds of clients, yet there still is cross-fertilization among the groups; discussions are held, information is shared, and so on.[54]

In this context, Hunter makes the observation I cited earlier—that "the people most receptive to the idea of talking and even working together are those who deal with women facing unplanned pregnancies on a day-to-day basis."[55]

If this is so, then talking and working with women—those facing crisis pregnancies, those hoping to avoid them, and those wanting to improve the quality of life for themselves and their neighborhoods—is a precondition of pursuing the common good. Through such involvement, the churches not only assist concrete individuals; they place themselves in a position where it makes practical sense to talk and collaborate with other institutions and for those institutions to reciprocate. Institutions and their members ought to practice the virtues that enhance the common good, but they do not develop these by mere good intention. Only by joining in the work of the common good—even for narrow and self-referential reasons—do persons and institutions have the opportunity to engage in the practices that develop these virtues.

Participation in such initiatives reflects the primary and truest sense in which churches should be political with respect to abortion or any other issue. The churches' political task is to foster the common good through meeting social needs, proclaiming the value of all human life, and engaging in dialogue and cooperative work with other churches and institutions. Only by way of derivation from these tasks does their witness also include speaking to legal questions and supporting particular policies. If churches fail to participate in the first level of politics, their engagement in the second becomes an instance of bad faith, detrimental to the common good. But if churches abide by common good principles, they contribute things to political life that liberalism alone cannot provide: concern for all human life, special focus on the needs of the vulnerable and marginalized, a willingness to press questions of value and meaning into political debates, and the ability to help persons feel their connections and obligations to others both far and near. Most important, churches have a great potential for modeling the common good in their own lives, by joining diverse persons together in peace and friendship to experience a good greater than themselves—and one in which they find their fulfillment.

NOTES

1. *Roe v. Wade*, 410 U.S. 113 (1973); see also the companion case *Doe v. Bolton*, 410 U.S. 179 (1973).
2. See John Rawls, *Political Liberalism* (New York: Columbia University Press, 1993), 243 n. 32.
3. *Roe v. Wade*, 164–65.
4. *Roe v. Wade*, 164–65.
5. *Planned Parenthood of Southeastern Pennsylvania v. Casey*, 505 U.S. 833 (1992).
6. *Roe v. Wade*, 159.
7. "In the five years preceding *Roe*, sixteen liberalized abortion laws had been enacted in states with 41 percent of the national population. . . . [By 1973], 'about

70% of the nation's population lived within 100 miles—an easy two hour's drive—of a state with a legalized abortion law' " (Elizabeth Mensch and Alan Freeman, *The Politics of Virtue: Is Abortion Debatable?* [Durham, N.C.: Duke University Press, 1993], 126, quoting Michael Barone, *Our Country: The Shaping of America from Roosevelt to Reagan* [New York: Free Press, 1990], 756 n. 14).

8. James Davison Hunter, *Before the Shooting Begins: Searching for Democracy in America's Culture War* (New York: Free Press, 1994), 12–13.

9. Mensch and Freeman, *Politics of Virtue*, 9.

10. Cf. Mensch and Freeman, *Politics of Virtue*, chap. 7: "Schism."

11. Mensch and Freeman, *Politics of Virtue*, 109.

12. Mensch and Freeman hold out Christian ethicist Joseph Fletcher for specific criticism: "Fletcher represented something other than just an antidote to religious absolutism. To the extent that he sought to fuse Christian 'love' with rationalist utilitarianism, he was trying to have it both ways, to seize on the rhetorical power of the Christian tradition without having to make concessions to its ethical content. That peculiar relationship to tradition would soon characterize mainline religion in its relation to moral issues such as abortion" (*Politics of Virtue*, 108). While this criticism of Fletcher's situation ethics may be plausible, its straightforward connection to the moral and political stance of "mainline religion" is overdrawn.

13. Lloyd Steffen, *Life/Choice: The Theory of Just Abortion* (Cleveland, Ohio: Pilgrim Press, 1994), 26–27.

14. Proportionalism is a moral methodology falling under a relational approach by which these two claims could be further defended. Variations of proportionalism are important to many ethicists both within the Roman Catholic tradition and outside it. For an overview of the method and an application to abortion, see Vincent J. Genovesi, S.J., *In Pursuit of Love: Catholic Morality and Human Sexuality*, 2nd ed. (Collegeville, Minn.: Michael Glazier/Liturgical Press, 1996), 100–105 and 362–96. For various perspectives on the principle of proportionality, see Charles E. Curran and Richard A. McCormick, eds., *Moral Norms and Catholic Tradition*, Readings in Moral Theology, no. 1 (New York: Paulist Press, 1979).

15. Lisa Sowle Cahill, "Abortion, Autonomy, and Community," in *Abortion and Catholicism: The American Debate*, ed. Patricia Beattie Jung and Thomas A. Shannon (New York: Crossroad, 1988), 85–97, quote at 94. Broadening the question from the status of the fetus (though that is always important) to include consideration of "the kind of society we want to be" seems to be characteristic of "prolife feminism." Cf. Sidney Callahan, "Abortion and the Sexual Agenda: A Case for Prolife Feminism," in *Abortion and Catholicism*, ed. Jung and Shannon, 128–40.

16. Cahill, "Abortion," 94.

17. For a pilot program that honors common good principles, see Jonathan Rabinovitz, "A Hartford Program to Put Fathers Back in the Family," *New York Times*, 16 June 1996, sec. 1, p. 1. "The Hartford program seems to solve the debate over welfare reform by agreeing with both sides. It subscribes to the liberal idea that people fall into poverty because of larger forces over which they have no control, forces the government can improve. It also accepts the conservative notion that individuals must take responsibility for their actions and that welfare has perpetuated dependency" (p. 28).

18. *Common ground* can refer either to the general style of open-ended, non-judgmental conversation or to formal dialogues sponsored by organizations that popularized the style in the early 1990s—specifically the Common Ground Network for Life and Choice, based in Washington, D.C. For various examples, see Faye D. Ginsburg, *Contested Lives: The Abortion Debate in an American Community* (Berkeley: University of California Press, 1989); Cythnia Gorney, *Articles of Faith: A Frontline History of the Abortion Wars* (New York: Simon & Schuster, 1998); and Hunter, *Before the Shooting Begins*, chap. 9. Representative newspaper and magazine articles are Sandy Banisky, "Ceasing Fire in the Abortion War," *Baltimore Sun*, 15 November 1992, p. 1A; Virginia Culver, "Abortion Foes Find Common Ground," *Denver Post*, 13 January 1995, p. B1; Dolores Kong, Peter S. Canellos, and Anne Kornblut, "Twenty-five Years Later, Passions Fading on Abortion," *Boston Globe*, 18 January 1998, Third edition, p. A1; Julie Polter, "Women and Children First," *Sojourners,* May–June 1995, 16–20; Martha Shirk, "Tears Melt Hostility at Abortion Meeting," *St. Louis Post-Dispatch*, 3 June 1996, p. 1A; and Paul Tough, et al., "Should the Clinics Come to Davenport?" *Harper's,* August 1996, 39–49. The last item is a transcript of a discussion among Common Ground members in Davenport, Iowa.

19. Hunter, *Before the Shooting Begins*, 233–34; emphasis removed from the first sentence.

20. The U.S. Catholic Bishops represented the only prominent prolife voice arguing this view in the welfare-reform debates of 1995. See Robert Pear, "Catholic Bishops Challenge Pieces of Welfare Bill," *New York Times*, 19 March 1995, sec. 1, p. 1; and the Administrative Board of the United States Catholic Conference, *Moral Principles and Policy Priorities for Welfare Reform* (Washington, D.C.: United States Catholic Conference, 1995).

21. I am indebted to Richard O. Randolph for his suggestion that *sacrifice* is a principle for pursuing the common good. He identifies this as one of the social conditions (alongside *access* and *opportunity*) that guarantee everyone's participation in the common good. Randolph presented these ideas in a paper, "Renewing the Common Good Tradition: Some Implications for U.S. Capitalism," delivered to the American Academy of Religion annual meeting, Ethics section, Chicago, Ill., 21 November 1994.

22. *Beal v. Doe*, 432 U.S. 432 (1977); *Maher v. Roe*, 432 U.S. 464 (1977); and *Harris v. McRae*, 448 U.S. 297 (1980), upheld regulations denying Medicaid funds for nontherapeutic abortions. *Webster v. Reproductive Health Services*, 492 U.S. 490 (1989), upheld a Missouri state ban on the use of public facilities for abortions.

23. Beginning with *H.L. v. Matheson*, 450 U.S. 398 (1981), the Court began upholding parental notification laws, as long as they included a judicial bypass provision. Other cases allowed relatively minor regulation of the abortion procedure: *Planned Parenthood v. Ashcroft*, 462 U.S. 476 (1983), upheld laws requiring a pathology report after an abortion and the presence of a second physician in a postviability abortion; and *Simopoulos v. Virginia*, 462 U.S. 506 (1983), upheld a law requiring abortions after twelve weeks to be performed in a hospital or an outpatient clinic.

24. *Planned Parenthood v. Casey*, 879–901.

25. *Planned Parenthood v. Casey*, 887–98.

26. *Planned Parenthood v. Casey*, 877, emphasis added.

27. *Planned Parenthood v. Casey*, 871, citing *Roe v. Wade*, 63.

28. *Planned Parenthood v. Casey*, 877.

29. As Ruth Colker notes, adolescent females constitute the age group that has the highest abortion rate and that is most likely to have second-trimester abortions. "There appears to be an inverse, geometric relationship between age and second-trimester abortions for women under the age of 20. Thus, when adolescent females do face unintended pregnancies and do decide to have an abortion, they disproportionally face the high health risks of second-trimester abortions. Our silence about contraception and abortion, plus parental consent laws, may cause them to risk their lives and health in order to incur an abortion" (*Abortion and Dialogue: Pro–Life, Pro-Choice, and American Law* [Bloomington: Indiana University Press, 1992], 71).

30. Mensch and Freeman write: "It seems probable that real compromise will mean, as it does in many Western European countries, a public policy that allows abortion while regulating it to some degree and seeking ways to discourage it. Compromise may mean retreating back from the line of viability with respect to presumptively legal abortions. Lines could be drawn, for example, at sixteen weeks, twelve, or ten—perhaps as consistent with the start of brain waves, which, in its scientific objectivity and consistency with the determination of death, should hold some appeal for natural law theorists" (*Politics of Virtue*, 149).

31. See the public opinion data and analysis in Hunter, *Before the Shooting Begins*, chap. 4.

32. Steffen, *Life/Choice*, 129. This is how Steffen articulates the aim of his theory of just abortion, which I consider quite similar to my own position. However, I do not claim that Steffen would fully endorse my approach, nor do I endorse every feature of his.

33. I am well aware that there are many difficulties in such a proposal, in part because it can be very insensitive to ask women to undergo nine months of pregnancy and then to part with the baby, as if no emotional bond would develop through the process of carrying to term. Here, again, I do not think government can require women to continue pregnancies for the sake of enabling adoptions, but it can do much more than it is to facilitate adoption and to make the option attractive. See Colker, *Abortion and Dialogue*, 72–75.

34. Conversation with David Clough shaped and sharpened my thoughts on the meaning of religious witness.

35. Kathy Rudy, *Beyond Pro-Life and Pro-Choice: Moral Diversity in the Abortion Debate* (Boston: Beacon Press, 1996), 142–43.

36. Rudy, *Beyond Pro-Life*, 143. Rudy then draws a political corollary that has, I believe, less plausibility. She argues for the repeal of all abortion laws—the law should simply not address abortion, which would then leave voluntary communities free to focus their energies on demonstrating their forms of life to the wider society. The problems are both practical (while the Supreme Court could conceivably repeal *Roe*, it is implausible that all fifty states would leave abortion a neutral matter) and philosophical (while Rudy considers this a communitarian proposal,

she overlooks the fact that local political communities [states and towns] have political traditions and forms of life that they want to manifest and that these lead them to "regulate abortion, reproduction, and sexuality inside [their] own boundaries"). I do not believe there is any pure neutrality in the law on this issue.

37. Cardinal Joseph Bernardin, "The Consistent Ethic: What Sort of Framework?" in *Abortion and Catholicism*, ed. Jung and Shannon, 260–67, quote at 262. The U.S. Bishops explicitly adopted Bernardin's consistent ethic in a 1985 document: National Conference of Catholic Bishops, *Pastoral Plan for Pro-Life Activities: A Reaffirmation* (Washington, D.C.: United States Catholic Conference, 1985).

38. Todd David Whitmore, "Moral Methodology and Pastoral Responsiveness: The Case of Abortion and the Care of Children," *Theological Studies* 54, no. 2 (June 1993): 316–38, quote at 320–21.

39. Whitmore, "Moral Methodology," 338.

40. Whitmore, "Moral Methodology," 338.

41. National Conference of Catholic Bishops, "Putting Children and Families First: A Challenge for Our Church, Nation, and World," *Origins* 21, no. 25 (28 November 1991): 393–404.

42. Whitmore, "Moral Methodology," 338.

43. Whitmore, "Moral Methodology," 338.

44. Margaret A. Farley, "Liberation, Abortion, and Responsibility," in *On Moral Medicine*, 2nd ed., ed. Stephen E. Lammers and Allen Verhey (Grand Rapids, Mich.: Eerdmans, 1998), 633–38, at 637. This article originally appeared in *Reflection* 71 (May 1974): 9–13.

45. National Conference of Catholic Bishops, "Putting Children and Families First," 398–99.

46. Farley, "Liberation," 635.

47. Farley, "Liberation," 635–36.

48. Several authors already cited are good examples: Hunter, *Before the Shooting Begins*; Steffen, *Life/Choice*; Mensch and Freeman, *Politics of Virtue*; and Rudy, *Beyond Pro-Life*. Noteworthy from the feminist perspective are Colker, *Abortion and Dialogue*; and Naomi Wolf, "Our Bodies, Our Souls," *New Republic* (16 October 1995): 26–35.

49. See the account in Hunter, *Before the Shooting Begins,* 236–38.

50. For example, Christine Gudorf criticizes the divergence between the Catholic Church's use of "proportional consequentialism in public-realm issues," such as warfare, and a "deontological natural law approach in private-realm issues," such as abortion. See "To Make a Seamless Garment, Use a Single Piece of Cloth," in *Abortion and Catholicism*, ed. Jung and Shannon, 279–96, quote at 283.

51. United States Catholic Conference, National Council of Churches, and Synagogue Council of America, "The Common Good: Old Idea, New Urgency," *Origins* 23, no. 6 (24 June 1993): 82–86. Some conservative Catholics criticized the statement for not addressing other issues that the Catholic Church has thought important to the common good, particularly abortion. On that matter, Rev. Joan Brown Campbell, general secretary of the National Council of Churches, said, "We had to agree to disagree." Rabbi Henry Michelman, general secretary of the

Synagogue Council, added, "We put aside that which divides us. . . . There are just things we can't touch" (p. 83).

52. In two declarations from a clearly prolife direction, signatories have articulated their concern for women and their interest in dialogue, while affirming the continued importance of protecting the unborn through the law. Among the signatories were Catholics, mainline Protestants, Evangelicals, and Jews prominent in academia, prolife activities, and (generally) conservative politics. See "A New American Compact: Caring About Women, Caring for the Unborn" *First Things*, no. 27 (November 1992): 43–46; and "The America We Seek: A Statement of Pro-Life Principle and Concern," *First Things*, no. 63 (May 1996): 40–44. I am not aware of a similar statement articulating a pro-choice position. However, the Religious Coalition for Reproductive Choice has compiled over thirty official statements on reproductive choice from its member groups and denominations, which represent various Protestant, Jewish, and other faith groups. The pamphlet is titled "We Affirm," available from the Religious Coalition for Reproductive Choice, 1025 Vermont Ave., NW, #1130, Washington, D.C., 20005.

53. Hunter, *Before the Shooting Begins,* 231.

54. Hunter, *Before the Shooting Begins,* 233. The quotes are from Alissa Rubin, "Project Rachel: Regretting Abortions," *Alicia Patterson Foundation Reporter* 15, no. 2 (1992): 40–47, a document that describes the initiative. Hunter notes that Project Rachel can be found in eighty other dioceses in forty states.

55. Hunter, *Before the Shooting Begins,* 233–34, emphasis removed.

Conclusion

This study has explored the meaning of the common good and the prospects for pursuing it in a liberal society. Three aims, ranging in scope from general to specific, have characterized the investigation. The study's most general and ambitious aim has been to outline a theoretical synthesis of liberalism and communitarianism. Its second, more focused aim was to present Jacques Maritain's common good theory as one successful example of such a synthesis and so, through an interpretation of his theory, to suggest the main components and principles of communal liberalism. The third aim focused the argument even further: it was to show that religion can make substantial contributions to the common good for a liberal society. A successful argument on this last point would show that a liberal society can benefit from the political and social contributions that citizens make as members of particular communities, speaking and acting from the wealth of their distinctive worldviews. Let me conclude by surveying how these aims were met in the course of the argument.

The need for a synthesis of liberalism and communitarianism arises from the inadequacies of both theories as they try to describe how citizens in a pluralistic society can achieve a sense of common purpose. Both liberals and communitarians articulate visions of the common good, but they interpret its meaning and scope differently. Significantly, each doubt that a pluralistic society can pursue a substantive common good. I have argued that this doubt is unwarranted and, moreover, that liberal and communitarian perspectives contribute in their own ways to an adequate understanding of the common good. I argued, therefore, that liberal and communitarian principles can be mediated and synthesized into a theory of communal liberalism. I began by considering the resources for a mediation in the thought of John Locke and Moses Mendelssohn. We saw that these classical liberals advance substantive conceptions of the common good: they build their arguments for rights, tolerance, and pluralism on foundations informed by the communal values of their religious worldviews.

178 *Conclusion*

Our world today clearly differs from the worlds of the seventeenth and eighteenth centuries, both in the kinds of questions we ask and in the nature of the challenges we face. Thus my investigation needed to turn to contemporary debates and problems. For a variety of reasons, to which I could only allude, liberalism as a philosophical theory lost touch with its communitarian foundations. John Rawls's political theory—both in its early philosophical-liberal form and its recent political-liberal form— leaves little space in the political process for substantive conceptions of the common good to inform policies and to shape institutions. A concrete instance of this shortcoming is the constrictions Rawls places on religious argument concerning fundamental political questions. Michael Sandel's communitarianism calls into question these constrictions and, more broadly, the liberal understanding of justice as prior to and independent of views of the good. Sandel points toward a mediation of the two theories but leaves unresolved important questions about the shape of communitarian politics.

One of the reasons Sandel is unclear here is that he does not rely on any particular narrative traditions, other than some general appeals to civic republicanism in the early United States. His communitarianism—more of the discourse than the narrative variety—seems unable to offer particular models for engaging in politics and structuring political life. For this reason, I turned to another conversation partner, the modern Catholic social tradition, whose understanding of the common good arises from its particular narratives but is also proffered to the wider public as an intelligible account of the social order.

My second aim in this study was to present Maritain's theory of the common good as a successful mediation of liberal and communitarian principles. This aim was achieved in two stages: first, by demonstrating how his methodology links a natural law approach and a theological approach to the common good; and second, by showing how he synthesizes liberal and communitarian understandings of self-identity, human goods, voluntary communities, and political society. In Maritain's theory, the human person has rights as an expression of his or her precommunal dignity, yet these rights are given a strongly communal interpretation at the practical level. Persons need social and political interaction in order to achieve their fulfillment, but the source of their dignity and worth lies outside of society. Normatively, then, persons require avenues of communication, interaction, and cooperation with others, and they also require the freedom and space to resist being completely defined by their communities if such is their wish. In other words, persons can and must have a common good, but the common good should serve them and facilitate their flourishing.

The third goal of this study was to specify the relationship of persons to the common good by resolving a question about religion's role in a liberal society: Does religion substantially contribute to the common good? I addressed this question in order to bring out the tensions between liberal and communitarian construals of the political status of particular communities. Members of communities that are based on shared narratives and practices often stand at a point of conflict in a liberal society. They may experience conflicts between their responsibilities to the community and the demands society places on them; between the thick bonds established in the community and the requirements of social justice; between fidelity to a particular moral way of life and the limitations of social morality and of the state's role in promoting it. Communal liberalism sees these as points of creative tension and seeks not to settle such conflicts in one direction or the other, but to do justice to the competing values at stake. We have seen several ways the theory attempts to do this. For instance, the theory notes how subcommunities significantly shape the identities and self-understandings of their members, yet it normatively holds that persons must be left enough social space and personal autonomy to modify or change their communal roles and affiliations. Also, the theory acknowledges that citizens of a pluralist society will never come to a consensus on *all* the values and virtues that are implicit in the common good; yet it considers it possible to speak of pursuing a substantive and not only a procedural common good. In order to establish a public consensus, citizens need to be able to articulate their particular moral and religious values in the public forum, so as to strengthen their motivation to a good broader than those of their particular subcommunities. Though public consensus on matters of justice and the good is a hard-won and fragile achievement, the common good is more surely secured by encouraging citizens to speak publicly and politically in the particular language and ideas of their religious and moral communities.

The conceptual and practical success of Maritain's mediation was evinced in how he presents Christianity's role in promoting the common good. The presentation suggests that religion can make three important contributions to the common good: intellectual resources for the public debate, conditions for social harmony, and attention to neglected goods. I believe these contributions suggest ways that other religious and particular communities are shaping and promoting the common good or how they might do better in this regard. The contributions also give liberal polities reasons to revise and enlarge the part they encourage religious groups to play in public life. Both ways of following out the argument lie beyond the scope of this study. However, I did begin to explore the practical import of these contributions through an application to the abortion debate. Maritain's theory, I argued, is relevant to divisive political issues such as this one: it provides a way of understanding the conflicting goods at stake; it suggests avenues of cooperation among political institutions and voluntary communities; and it looks for religious communities to point a way toward the common good through their discourse and actions. Through both conceptual and practical arguments, then, I have answered the question— whether religion can contribute to the common good of a liberal society—in the affirmative.

As with any study so broad in its scope, one encounters limitations and the need for further investigations. I have not been able to undertake a sweeping review of liberalism and communitarianism but only of representative figures. Likewise, many conceptual issues in the liberal-communitarian debate have been left aside or treated briefly. The present study could be usefully extended in two directions, then: first, its thesis should be explored in conjunction with a number of contemporary liberals and communitarians, with the eventual aim of developing a comprehensive theory of communal liberalism; and second, my focus on Catholicism and on one interpretation of modern Catholic social thought should be complemented by other substantive theological investigations of the common good and by other religious and interreligious investigations. I have presented one religious view of the common good and tried to indicate how it is open to different religious articulations and contributions; this view must be supplemented and critically tested by those voices.

The theory of communal liberalism is also limited by social realities, by "the real world." The common good, in a communal liberal view, is not a panacea: persons will remain divided in their comprehensive views of the good, and these divisions will be reflected in conflicts over moral, religious, and political issues. No theory can eliminate such conflicts. But the theory of communal liberalism, I maintain, is better at addressing these conflicts than either the liberalism of Rawls and his fellow travelers or the communitarianism of his most influential critics. I have only begun to defend this proposition by seeing what fruits my thesis bears in the political and moral debate over abortion. It remains for future investigations to test the adequacy of my thesis by pursuing other concrete comparisons of the ways that liberalism, communitarianism, and communal liberalism can handle divisive public issues. Further work needs to be done as well to specify the institutional arrangements that would be required and justified by communal liberalism. In this study, I have suggested several practical ramifications—from reconsidering the meaning of rights to restructuring public debate—but have not been able to treat any one of these in depth.

Despite the work that is yet to be done, communal liberalism presents a promising vision of the possibilities for building community in modern societies. Liberal societies can and should understand their overarching purpose as the ongoing pursuit of the common good. They should be open in principle and in practice to the contributions that religions make to this pursuit. Religious believers and groups, for their part, should draw forth from their rich traditions visions of the common good to share in the public realm, doing their best to make these intelligible to their fellow citizens. Communal liberalism articulates both sets of responsibilities: it enables a liberal society to understand what stake it has in the contributions of the particular subcommunities it embraces, and it helps these subcommunities appreciate the importance of striving for a common good greater than their own. I commend this theory, as well as the work of further explicating it, to political theorists, religious ethicists, and, indeed, to all those who are concerned to deepen our understanding and advance our pursuit of the common good.

Bibliography

Administrative Board of the United States Catholic Conference. *Moral Principles and Policy Priorities for Welfare Reform.* Washington, D.C.: United States Catholic Conference, 1995.

Alinsky, Saul. *Reveille for Radicals.* Chicago: University of Chicago Press, 1946.

———. *Rules for Radicals.* New York: Vintage Books, 1972.

Altmann, Alexander. *Moses Mendelssohn: A Biographical Study.* University, Ala.: University of Alabama Press, 1973; reprint, Portland, Oreg.: Littman Library of Jewish Civilization, 1998.

"The America We Seek: A Statement of Pro-Life Principle and Concern." *First Things*, no. 63 (May 1996): 40–44.

Aquinas, St. Thomas. *De Regimine Principum (On Princely Government).* In *Aquinas: Selected Political Writings*, edited by A. P. D'Entreves, translated by J. G. Dawson. Oxford: Blackwell, 1954.

———. *Summa Contra Gentiles.* In *Introduction to St. Thomas Aquinas.* Edited by Anton C. Pegis. The Modern Library. New York: Random House, 1945.

———. *Summa Theologiae*, edited by Thomas Gilby, O.P. 61 vols. London: Blackfriars, 1964–76.

Ashcraft, Richard. *Locke's Two Treatises of Government.* London: Allen & Unwin, 1987.

———. *Revolutionary Politics and Locke's "Two Treatises of Government."* Princeton, N.J.: Princeton University Press, 1986.

Audi, Robert, and Nicholas Wolterstorff. *Religion in the Public Square: The Place of Religious Convictions in Political Debate.* Lanham, Md.: Rowman & Littlefield, 1997.

Baier, Annette C. "Claims, Rights, and Responsibilities." In *Prospects for a Common Morality*, edited by Gene Outka and John P. Reeder, Jr., 149–69. Princeton, N.J.: Princeton University Press, 1993.

Barnes, Michael H. "Community, Clannishness, and the Common Good." In *Religion, Ethics, and the Common Good.* Annual publication of the College Theology Society, vol. 41, edited by James Donohue and M. Theresa Moser, 27–52. Mystic, Conn.: Twenty-Third Publications and the College Theology Society, 1996.

Baynes, Kenneth. "The Liberal/Communitarian Controversy and Communicative

Ethics." In *Universalism vs. Communitarianism: Contemporary Debates in Ethics*, edited by David Rasmussen, 61–81. Cambridge, Mass.: MIT Press, 1990.

Bell, Daniel. *Communitarianism and Its Critics*. Oxford: Clarendon, 1993.

Bellah, Robert N., Richard Madsen, William M. Sullivan, Ann Swidler, and Steven M. Tipton. *The Good Society*. New York: Alfred A. Knopf, 1991.

———. *Habits of the Heart: Individualism and Commitment in American Life*. Berkeley: University of California Press, 1985; rev. ed., 1996.

Berger, Peter, and Richard Neuhaus. *To Empower People: The Role of Mediating Structures in Public Policy*. Washington, D.C.: American Enterprise Institute, 1977.

Bernardin, Cardinal Joseph. "The Consistent Ethic: What Sort of Framework?" In *Abortion and Catholicism: The American Debate*, edited by Patricia Beattie Jung and Thomas A. Shannon, 260–67. New York: Crossroad, 1988.

Cahill, Lisa Sowle. "Abortion, Autonomy, and Community." In *Abortion and Catholicism: The American Debate*, edited by Patricia Beattie Jung and Thomas A. Shannon, 85–97. New York: Crossroad, 1988.

Callahan, Joan C. "The Fetus and Fundamental Rights." In *Abortion and Catholicism: The American Debate*, edited by Patricia Beattie Jung and Thomas A. Shannon, 217–30. New York: Crossroad Publishing Co., 1988.

Callahan, Sidney. "Abortion and the Sexual Agenda: A Case for Prolife Feminism." In *Abortion and Catholicism: The American Debate*, edited by Patricia Beattie Jung and Thomas A. Shannon, 128–40. New York: Crossroad, 1988.

Calvin, John. *Institutes of the Christian Religion*. Edited by John T. McNeill, translated by Ford Lewis Battles. 2 vols. Library of Christian Classics, vol. 21. Philadelphia: Westminster Press, 1960.

Carter, Stephen L. *The Culture of Disbelief*. New York: Basic Books, 1993.

Colker, Ruth. *Abortion and Dialogue: Pro-Life, Pro-Choice, and American Law*. Bloomington: Indiana University Press, 1992.

Curran, Charles E., and Richard A. McCormick, eds. *Moral Norms and Catholic Tradition*. Readings in Moral Theology, no. 1. New York: Paulist Press, 1979.

De Koninck, Charles. *De la primauté du bien commun, contre les personnalistes*. Quebec: Éditions de l'Université Laval, 1943.

———. "In Defense of Saint Thomas: A Reply to Father Eschmann's Attack on the Primacy of the Common Good." *Laval théologique et philosophique* 1, no. 2 (1945): 9–109.

Dennehy, Raymond. "Maritain's 'Intellectual Existentialism': An Introduction to His Metaphysics and Epistemology." In *Understanding Maritain: Philosopher and Friend*, edited by Deal W. Hudson and Matthew J. Mancini, 201–33. Macon, Ga.: Mercer University Press, 1987.

Doering, Bernard, ed. *The Philosopher and the Provocateur: The Correspondence of Jacques Maritain and Saul Alinsky*. Notre Dame, Ind.: University of Notre Dame Press, 1994.

Doppelt, Gerald. "Beyond Liberalism and Communitarianism: Towards a Critical Theory of Social Justice." In *Universalism vs. Communitarianism: Contemporary Debates in Ethics*, edited by David Rasmussen, 39–60. Cambridge, Mass.: MIT Press, 1990.

Dorr, Donald. *Option for the Poor: A Hundred Years of Vatican Social Teaching.* Maryknoll, N.Y.: Orbis Books, 1983.

Douglass, R. Bruce, Gerald M. Mara, and Henry S. Richardson, eds. *Liberalism and the Good.* New York: Routledge, 1990.

Dunn, John. *Locke.* Past Masters series. Oxford: Oxford University Press, 1984.

———. *The Political Thought of John Locke: An Historical Account of the Argument of the "Two Treatises of Government."* Cambridge: Cambridge University Press, 1969.

Eschmann, I. Th. "In Defense of Jacques Maritain." *Modern Schoolman* 22 (May 1945): 183–203.

Evans, Joseph W. "A Maritain Bibliography." *New Scholasticism* 46 (1972): 118–28.

———, ed. *Jacques Maritain: The Man and His Achievement.* New York: Sheed & Ward, 1963.

Farley, Margaret A. "Liberation, Abortion and Responsibility." In *On Moral Medicine*, 2nd ed., edited by Stephen E. Lammers and Allen Verhey, 633–38. Grand Rapids, Mich.: Eerdmans, 1987.

Fern, Richard L. "Religious Belief in a Rawlsian Society." *Journal of Religious Ethics* 15, no. 1 (spring 1987): 33–58.

Finnis, John. *Natural Law and Natural Rights.* Oxford: Clarendon, 1980.

———, and Martha Nussbaum. "Is Homosexual Conduct Wrong? A Philosophical Exchange." *New Republic,* 15 November 1993, 12–13.

Gallagher, Donald and Idella Gallagher. *The Achievement of Jacques and Raïssa Maritain: A Bibliography 1906–1961.* Garden City, N.Y.: Doubleday, 1962.

Genovesi, Vincent J., S.J. *In Pursuit of Love: Catholic Morality and Human Sexuality.* 2nd ed. Collegeville, Minn.: Michael Glazier/Liturgical Press, 1996.

George, Robert P., ed. *Natural Law Theory: Contemporary Essays.* Oxford: Clarendon, 1992.

Ginsburg, Faye D. *Contested Lives: The Abortion Debate in an American Community.* Berkeley: University of California Press, 1989.

Gorney, Cythnia. *Articles of Faith: A Frontline History of the Abortion Wars.* New York: Simon & Schuster, 1998.

Gudorf, Christine. "To Make a Seamless Garment, Use a Single Piece of Cloth." In *Abortion and Catholicism: The American Debate*, edited by Patricia Beattie Jung and Thomas A. Shannon, 279–96. New York: Crossroad, 1988.

Gutmann, Amy. "Communitarian Critics of Liberalism," *Philosophy and Public Affairs* 14 (summer 1985): 308–22.

Hargrove, Barbara. *The Sociology of Religion: Classical and Contemporary Approaches.* 2nd ed. Arlington Heights, Ill.: Harlan Davidson, 1989.

Hellman, John. "The Humanism of Jacques Maritain." In *Understanding Maritain: Philosopher and Friend*, edited by Deal W. Hudson and Matthew J. Mancini, 117–31. Macon, Ga.: Mercer University Press, 1987.

Herberg, Will, ed. *Four Existentialist Theologians.* Garden City, N.Y.: Doubleday Anchor, 1958.

Hollenbach, David. "Afterword: A Community of Freedom." In *Catholicism and Liberalism: Contributions to American Public Philosophy*, edited by R. Bruce

Douglass and David Hollenbach, 323–43. Cambridge: Cambridge University Press, 1994.

———. "Civil Society: Beyond the Public-Private Dichotomy." *Responsive Community* 5, no. 1 (winter 1994–95): 15–23.

———. *Claims in Conflict: Retrieving and Renewing the Catholic Human Rights Tradition*. New York: Paulist Press, 1979.

———. "The Common Good in the Postmodern Epoch: What Role for Theology?" In *Religion, Ethics, and the Common Good*. Annual publication of the College Theology Society, vol. 41, edited by James Donohue and M. Theresa Moser, 3–22. Mystic, Conn.: Twenty-Third Publications and the College Theology Society, 1996.

———. "The Common Good Revisited." *Theological Studies* 50, no. 1 (March 1989): 70–94.

———. "A Communitarian Reconstruction of Human Rights." In *Catholicism and Liberalism: Contributions to American Public Philosophy*, edited by R. Bruce Douglass and David Hollenbach, 127–50. Cambridge: Cambridge University Press, 1994.

———. "Contexts of the Political Role of Religion: Civil Society and Culture." *San Diego Law Review* 30 (1994): 879–901.

———. *Justice, Peace, and Human Rights: American Catholic Social Ethics in a Pluralistic Context*. New York: Crossroad, 1988.

———. "Politically Active Churches: Some Empirical Prolegomena to a Normative Approach." In *Religion and Contemporary Liberalism*, edited by Paul J. Weithman, 291–306. Notre Dame, Ind.: University of Notre Dame Press, 1997.

———. "Public Reason/Private Reason? A Response to Paul J. Weithman." *Journal of Religious Ethics* 22, no. 1 (spring 1994): 39–46.

———. "Virtue, the Common Good, and Democracy." In *New Communitarian Thinking: Persons, Virtues, Institutions, and Communities*, edited by Amitai Etzioni, 143–53. Charlottesville: University of Virginia Press, 1994.

Hudson, Deal W., and Matthew J. Mancini, eds. *Understanding Maritain: Philosopher and Friend*. Macon, Ga.: Mercer University Press, 1987.

Hunter, James Davison. *Before the Shooting Begins: Searching for Democracy in America's Culture War*. New York: Free Press, 1994.

———. *Culture Wars: The Struggle to Define America*. New York: Basic Books, 1991.

John XXIII, Pope. *Mater et Magistra: Christianity and Social Progress* (15 May 1961). In *Catholic Social Thought: The Documentary Heritage*, edited by David J. O'Brien and Thomas A. Shannon. Maryknoll, N.Y.: Orbis Books, 1992.

Jospe, Alfred. "Introduction: Prelude to Jewish Modernity." In *Moses Mendelssohn: Selections from His Writings*, edited by Eva Jospe, 3–46. New York: Viking Press, 1975.

Kernan, Julie. *Our Friend, Jacques Maritain: A Personal Memoir*. Garden City, N.Y.: Doubleday, 1975.

Keys, Mary M. "Personal Dignity and the Common Good: A Twentieth-Century Thomistic Dialogue." In *Catholicism, Liberalism, and Communitarianism: The Catholic Intellectual Tradition and the Moral Foundations of Democracy*, edited by Kenneth L. Grasso, Gerard V. Bradley, and Robert P. Hunt, 173–95. Lanham, Md.: Rowman & Littlefield, 1995.

Kymlicka, Will. *Liberalism, Community, and Culture*. Oxford: Clarendon, 1989.

Locke, John. *A Letter Concerning Toleration*. Edited by James H. Tully. Indianapolis, Ind.: Hackett, 1983.

———. *Locke on Money*. Edited by Patrick Hyde Kelly. New York: Oxford University Press, 1991.

———. *The Reasonableness of Christianity: As Delivered in the Scriptures*. Washington, D.C.: Regnery Gateway, 1965.

———. *Second Treatise of Government*. Edited by C. B. Macpherson. Indianapolis, Ind.: Hackett, 1980.

———. *The Works of John Locke*. 9th ed. 9 vols. London: Printed for T. Longman, et al., 1794.

MacIntyre, Alasdair. *After Virtue*. 2nd ed. Notre Dame, Ind.: University of Notre Dame Press, 1984.

Macpherson, C. B. *The Political Theory of Possessive Individualism: Hobbes to Locke*. Oxford: Oxford University Press, 1962.

Mancini, Matthew J. "Maritain's Democratic Vision: 'You Have No Bourgeois.'" In *Understanding Maritain: Philosopher and Friend*, edited by Deal W. Hudson and Matthew J. Mancini, 133–51. Macon, Ga.: Mercer University Press, 1987.

Maritain, Jacques. *Antimoderne*. Paris: Revue des Jeunes, 1922.

———. *Christianity and Democracy*. Bound with *The Rights of Man and Natural Law*. Translated by Doris C. Anson. New York: Scribner, 1944; reprint, San Francisco: Ignatius Press, 1986.

———. *Existence and the Existent*. Translated by Lewis Galantière and Gerald B. Phelan. New York: Doubleday, 1947.

———. *Freedom: Its Meaning*. Edited by Ruth Nanda Anshen. London: Allen & Unwin, 1940.

———. *Integral Humanism*. Translated by Joseph W. Evans. New York: Scribner, 1968.

———. *Man and the State*. Chicago: University of Chicago Press, 1951.

———. *The Peasant of the Garonne: An Old Layman Questions Himself About the Present Time*. Translated by Michael Cuddihy and Elizabeth Hughes. New York: Holt, Rinehart & Winston, 1968.

———. *The Person and the Common Good*. Translated by John J. Fitzgerald. New York: Scribner, 1947; reprint, Notre Dame, Ind.: University of Notre Dame Press, 1966.

———. *La personne et le bien commun*. In *Oeuvres complétes Jacques et Raïssa Maritain*, vol. 9, 167–237. Fribourg, Switzerland: Éditions Universitaires, 1982–95.

———. *Principes d'une politique humaniste*. New York: Éditions de la Maison Française, 1944.

———. *The Range of Reason*. New York: Scribner, 1952.

———. *Ransoming the Time*. Translated by Harry Lorin Binsse. New York: Scribner, 1941.

———. *The Rights of Man and Natural Law*. Bound with *Christianity and Democ-

racy. Translated by Doris C. Anson. New York: Scribner, 1943; reprint, San Francisco: Ignatius, 1986.

———. *Scholasticism and Politics*. Edited and translated by Mortimer J. Adler. New York: Macmillan, 1940.

———. *The Social and Political Philosophy of Jacques Maritain: Selected Readings*. Edited by Joseph W. Evans and Leo R. Ward. New York: Scribner, 1955.

———. *Three Reformers: Luther, Descartes, Rousseau*. Translated by Frank Sheed. New York: Sheed & Ward, 1933.

———. *Truth and Human Fellowship*. Princeton, N.J.: Princeton University Press, 1957.

Maritain, Raïssa. *Adventures in Grace*. Vol. 2 of *The Memoirs of Raïssa Maritain*. Translated by Julie Kernan. Garden City, N.Y.: Image Books, 1961.

———. *We Have Been Friends Together*. Vol. 1 of *The Memoirs of Raïssa Maritain*. Translated by Julie Kernan. Garden City, N.Y.: Image Books, 1961.

The Maritain Volume of the Thomist. Published as volume 5. New York: Sheed & Ward, 1943.

McInerny, Ralph. *Art and Prudence: Studies in the Thought of Jacques Maritain*. Notre Dame, Ind.: University of Notre Dame Press, 1988.

———. "Maritain in and on America." In *Reinhold Neibuhr Today*, edited by Richard John Neuhaus, 33–45. Grand Rapids, Mich.: Eerdmans, 1989.

Mendelssohn, Moses. *Jerusalem: Or, On Religious Power and Judaism*. Translated by Allan Arkush. Introduction and commentary by Alexander Altmann. Hanover, N.H.: University Press of New England for Brandeis University Press, 1983.

Mensch, Elizabeth, and Alan Freeman. *The Politics of Virtue: Is Abortion Debatable?* Durham, N.C.: Duke University Press, 1993.

Morgan, Michael L. "Liberalism in Mendelssohn's *Jerusalem*." *History of Political Thought* 10, no. 2 (1989): 281–94.

Mulhall, Stephen, and Adam Swift. *Liberals and Communitarians*. Oxford: Blackwell Publishers, 1992.

National Conference of Catholic Bishops. *Economic Justice for All: Pastoral Letter on Catholic Social Teaching and the U.S. Economy* (18 November 1986). In *Catholic Social Thought: The Documentary Heritage*, edited by David J. O'Brien and Thomas A. Shannon. Maryknoll, N.Y.: Orbis Books, 1992.

———. *Pastoral Plan for Pro-Life Activities: A Reaffirmation*. Washington, D.C.: United States Catholic Conference, 1985.

———. "Putting Children and Families First: A Challenge for Our Church, Nation, and World." *Origins* 21, no. 25 (28 November 1991): 393–404.

"A New American Compact: Caring About Women, Caring for the Unborn." *First Things*, no. 27 (November 1992): 43–46.

Novak, David. *Jewish Social Ethics*. New York: Oxford University Press, 1992.

Novak, Michael. *Free Persons and the Common Good*. Lanham, Md.: Madison Books, 1989.

———, ed. *Democracy and Mediating Structures: A Theological Inquiry*. Washington, D.C.: American Enterprise Institute, 1980.

Nussbaum, Martha. "Aristotelian Social Democracy." In *Liberalism and the*

Good, edited by R. Bruce Douglass, Gerald M. Mara, and Henry S. Richardson, 203–52. New York: Routledge, 1990.

Outka, Gene. *Agape: An Ethical Analysis*. New Haven, Conn.: Yale University Press, 1972.

Outka, Gene, and John P. Reeder, Jr., eds. *Prospects for a Common Morality*. Princeton, N.J.: Princeton University Press, 1993.

Pius XI, Pope. *Quadragesimo Anno: On Reconstructing the Social Order* (15 May 1931). In *Catholic Social Thought: The Documentary Heritage*, edited by David J. O'Brien and Thomas A. Shannon. Maryknoll, N.Y.: Orbis Books, 1992.

Polter, Julie. "Women and Children First." *Sojourners*, May–June 1995, 16–20.

Pope, Stephen J. "Knowability of the Natural Law: A Foundation for Ethics of the Common Good." In *Religion, Ethics, and the Common Good*. Annual publication of the College Theology Society, vol. 41, edited by James Donohue and M. Theresa Moser, 53–63. Mystic, Conn.: Twenty-Third Publications and the College Theology Society, 1996.

Rahner, Karl. *Foundations of Christian Faith: An Introduction to the Idea of Christianity*. Translated by William V. Dych. New York: Seabury Press, 1978.

Ramsey, Paul. *Nine Modern Moralists*. Englewood Cliffs, N.J.: Prentice-Hall, 1962.

Rawls, John. "The Idea of an Overlapping Consensus." *Oxford Journal of Legal Studies* 7 (February 1987): 1–25.

———. "Justice as Fairness: Political Not Metaphysical." *Philosophy and Public Affairs* 14 (summer 1985): 223–52.

———. "Kantian Constructivism in Moral Theory." *Journal of Philosophy* 77, no. 9 (September 1980): 515–72.

———. *Political Liberalism*. New York: Columbia University Press, 1993.

———. "The Priority of Right and Ideas of the Good." *Philosophy and Public Affairs* 17 (summer 1988): 251–76.

———. *A Theory of Justice*. Cambridge, Mass.: Harvard University Press, 1971.

Raz, Joseph. *The Morality of Freedom*. Oxford: Clarendon, 1986.

Redpath, Peter A., ed. *From Twilight to Dawn: The Cultural Vision of Jacques Maritain*. Notre Dame, Ind.: University of Notre Dame Press for the American Maritain Association, 1990.

Rossner, William L., S.J., "Love in the Thought of Jacques Maritain." In *Jacques Maritain: The Man and His Achievement*, edited by Joseph W. Evans, 237–58. New York: Sheed & Ward, 1963.

Rudy, Kathy. *Beyond Pro-Life and Pro-Choice: Moral Diversity in the Abortion Debate*. Boston: Beacon Press, 1996.

Sandel, Michael J. *Democracy's Discontent: America in Search of a Public Philosophy*. Cambridge, Mass.: Harvard University Press, 1996.

———. *Liberalism and the Limits of Justice*. Cambridge: Cambridge University Press, 1982.

———. "Moral Argument and Liberal Toleration: Abortion and Homosexuality." *California Law Review* 77, no. 3 (May 1989): 521–38.

———. "Morality and the Liberal Ideal." *New Republic,* 7 May 1984, 15–17.

———. "The Political Theory of the Procedural Republic." In *Reinhold Neibuhr*

Today, edited by Richard John Neuhaus, 19–32. Grand Rapids, Mich.: Eerdmans, 1989.

———. "The Procedural Republic and the Unencumbered Self." *Political Theory* 12 (1984): 81–96.

———. Review of *Political Liberalism*, by John Rawls. *Harvard Law Review* 107, no. 7 (May 1994): 1765–94.

———, ed. *Liberalism and Its Critics*. New York: New York University Press, 1984.

Schall, James V. *Jacques Maritain: The Philosopher in Society*. Twentieth-Century Political Thinkers series. Lanham, Md.: Rowman & Littlefield, 1998.

Second Vatican Council. *Gaudium et Spes: Pastoral Constitution on the Church in the Modern World* (7 December 1965). In *Catholic Social Thought: The Documentary Heritage*, edited by David J. O'Brien and Thomas A. Shannon. Maryknoll, N.Y.: Orbis Books, 1992.

Steffen, Lloyd. *Life/Choice: The Theory of Just Abortion*. Cleveland, Oh.: Pilgrim Press, 1994.

Stiltner, Brian. "Who Can Understand Abraham? The Relation of God and Morality in Kierkegaard and Aquinas." *Journal of Religious Ethics* 21, no. 2 (fall 1993): 221–45.

Stiltner, Jeffrey W. "Rethinking the Wall of Separation: *Zobrest v. Catalina Foothills School District*—Is This the End of *Lemon?*" *Capital University Law Review* 23, no. 3 (1994): 823–61.

Tough, Paul, et al. "Should the Clinics Come to Davenport?" *Harper's,* August 1996, 39–49.

United States Catholic Conference, National Council of Churches, and Synagogue Council of America. "The Common Good: Old Idea, New Urgency." *Origins* 23, no. 6 (24 June 1993): 82–86.

Verba, Sidney, Kay Lehman Schlozman, and Henry Brady. *Voice and Equality: Civic Voluntarism in American Politics*. Cambridge, Mass.: Harvard University Press, 1995.

Walzer, Michael. *The Revolution of the Saints: A Study in the Origins of Radical Politics*. Cambridge, Mass.: Harvard University Press, 1965.

———. *Spheres of Justice: A Defense of Pluralism and Equality*. New York: Basic Books, 1983.

Watkins, Michelle, and Ralph McInerny. "Jacques Maritain and the Rapprochement of Liberalism and Communitarianism." In *Catholicism, Liberalism, and Communitarianism: The Catholic Intellectual Tradition and the Moral Foundations of Democracy*, edited by Kenneth L. Grasso, Gerard V. Bradley, and Robert P. Hunt, 151–72. Lanham, Md.: Rowman & Littlefield, 1995.

Weithman, Paul. "Rawlsian Liberalism and the Privatization of Religion: Three Theological Objections Considered." *Journal of Religious Ethics* 22, no. 1 (spring 1994): 3–28.

Whitmore, Todd David. "Moral Methodology and Pastoral Responsiveness: The Case of Abortion and the Care of Children." *Theological Studies* 54, no. 2 (June 1993): 316–38.

Willumsen, Kristopher Louis. "The Relationship of the Mystical and the Political

Dimensions of the Christian Faith in the Writings of Jacques Maritain." Ph.D. diss., Catholic University of America, 1992.

Wilson, John F., Barbara Hargrove, and Julian N. Hartt. Reviews of *Habits of the Heart*, by Robert N. Bellah, et al. *Religious Studies Review* 14, no. 4 (October 1988): 304–10.

Wolf, Naomi. "Our Bodies, Our Souls." *New Republic*, 16 October 1995, 26–35.

Index

abolition, 2, 3, 61–66

abortion: alternatives to, 157, 161, 163, 170, 174n33; debate and dialogue about, 144–45, 149–52, 155–56, 157, 163–64, 167, 168–70, 175n51, 176n52, 179–80; as a legal issue, 73–74, 146–48, 157, 159–63, 171n7, 173n22, 173n23, 174n36; Maritain's relevance to, 144–45, 151–52, 156–57; as a moral issue, 144, 148, 150–51, 152–56, 157–59, 162–71; as a political and social issue, 63–64, 144–49, 156–59, 164–65, 169, 174n30; prochoice and prolife advocates, 46, 144, 146, 148, 151, 157, 162, 168–70; Rawls's political liberalism and, 63–64, 146; religion and, 60, 64, 147, 149–52, 163–71, 172n12; state regulation of, 147, 160–61; terminology, 145. *See also* equality, of women; fetus; freedom, reproductive; pregnancy; Supreme Court

adoption, 158, 163, 165, 174n33. *See also* pregnancy

African Americans, 2, 62, 126

Alinsky, Saul, 125–26, 140n55, 140n58

anthropology (moral, philosophical, or theological): Aquinas's, 93–94; Catholicism's, 14, 114; Locke's, 26; Maritain's, 94, 110n35, 114–15,

121, 136; Mendelssohn's, 30–31, 38; Rawls's, 50, 67–69, 81n72, 129. *See also* person

antiperfectionism, 56, 131. *See also* neutrality; perfectionism

anti-Semitism, 85

Aquinas, St. Thomas, 9, 84–85; Anthropology of, 93–94; compared to Locke, 21, 41n20; on natural law, 89–90; on person and community, 93, 109n31; on political authority, 21, 41n21

Aristotle, 4, 9, 137n2

Ashcraft, Richard, 41n28

atheists, 25, 33, 37, 99

autonomy: of groups, 25, 36; of persons, 74–75, 115, 117, 119, 132, 134, 136, 154, 156, 157, 162, 179. *See also* rights

Baier, Annette, 53

Bellah, Robert, 17

Bernardin, Cardinal Joseph, 166

Bishops, U.S. Catholic, 127, 167, 169, 173n20. *See also* Catholic Church; United States Catholic Conference

Blackmun, Harry, 147

Bowers v. Hardwick, 74

Calvin, John, 21, 40n18, 41n19

Campbell, Rev. Joan Brown, 175n51

Carter, Stephen, 3–4, 48, 54

Catholic Church, 13, 73, 85, 124, 133, 144, 167, 175; abortion and, 73–74, 144–45, 166–67, 170, 175n50, 175n51; Maritain and, 85, 108n10, 113, 124, 133. *See also* Bishops, U.S. Catholic; church

Catholicism (Catholic social thought): contributions to the common good, 12–14, 114, 127, 137n1, 164; historical relationship to liberalism, 9; Locke and, 24–25, 40n14; on mediating institutions, 119; as resources for communal liberalism, 5, 10, 113, 178, 180; on rights, 116–19

Catholics: as Maritain's audience, 84–85, 100–101, 121; views of abortion, 145, 175n51, 175n52

Charles II (king of England), 40n14

Christianity and Democracy (Maritain), 85, 99

Christians, 25, 62, 121, 127, 130, 150; abortion and, 165–66; common good and, 1, 98, 114, 122, 124–25, 152; cooperation and dialogue with Jews and other believers, 55, 88, 100–101; Mendelssohn and, 18, 34, 36. *See also* Catholics; Jews

church (Christian or generic): contributions to the common good, 35–36, 114, 125, 133, 163–71; in Maritain, 125, 130–31; in Mendelssohn, 29, 31–35, 42n53, 43n57, 43n63; state and, 46, 132, 165. *See also* Catholic Church; religion

citizenship, 11, 55, 59, 70–72, 102, 129

civic republicanism, 72, 178. *See also* Sandel, Michael

civil rights movement, 2, 62, 66, 126, 150

Colker, Ruth, 174n29

common good, 17, 49, 83, 143–44, 158; abortion and, 149, 157–59, 160, 162–63, 164–65, 167, 170, 175n51; in American public life, 1–4; in Aquinas, 21, 41n21; in Catholic and Christian thought, 9–10, 15, 85, 97, 100, 108n13, 114, 144, 171; communal liberalism and, 9, 99, 177–81; defined by author, 4, 10; defined by Catholic tradition, 10, 108n13; defined by liberals and communitarians, 5–8; defined by Maritain, 86–88, 109n14; human flourishing and, 86, 105, 114, 152; in liberalism, 13, 45–46, 57, 62, 65, 67, 69, 81n71, 177, 180; in Locke, 18, 23, 25–26; in Mendelssohn, 18, 28–39; natural law approach to, 13, 14, 83, 88–93, 99, 103, 105, 106, 121, 143, 178; primacy of, 84, 95; procedural and/or substantive, 5, 7, 10, 143, 149, 179; public conversation and, 101, 123–24, 169; relation to political society or the state, 10, 39, 87, 95, 120, 130, 132–34; religion's role in, 10–15, 25, 36, 76, 100, 102, 113, 126–28, 169, 132–34; religious liberty and, 25, 97; rights and, 86, 116, 118, 136, 152; sacrifices for, 158; theological approach to, 84–85, 93–99, 103, 105, 143, 178; theological distinctions of, 87, 94–97, 122, 152, 165; toleration and, 35, 69, 76; types of goods involved in, 87, 154–55, 178. *See also* communal liberalism; politics, of the common good; religion; society

"common ground" conversations, 157, 173n18. *See also* abortion; public conversation

communal liberalism, 14–19; abortion and, 145, 151–53, 163, 166–67; definition of, 9, 143; in Maritain, 86, 106, 114, 134–36, 143, 151–52; in Mendelssohn, 26, 33, 34, 36–39, 76; moral theory and, 153; political liberalism and, 54–55, 101–2; summarized and assessed, 177–81. *See also* communitarianism; liberalism; political liberalism

communism, 70, 85–86

communitarianism, 14, 113, 180; common good and, 13, 83, 177; debate with liberalism, 7–9, 56, 69–73, 102–6, 128–34, 142n81; definition of, 6–7; discourse communitarianism, 7, 178; egalitarian, 7; Maritain and, 88–89, 134–36, 151; moral objectivism/subjectivism and, 104; narrative, 7, 135; neutrality and, 56, 131; synthesized with liberalism, 18, 37, 76–77, 88, 99, 102, 106, 143, 177. *See also* communal liberalism; liberalism; political liberalism; Sandel, Michael
community: abortion and, 155, 156–59, 161–68, 174n36; as constitutive of identity, 67–71, 76, 128–31, 178; development of, 72–73, 122–28; person and, 93–94, 99, 151; political, 4, 7–9, 26, 54, 93, 117, 120, 128, 131, 143; rankings of, 130–31; religious, 9, 11–12, 15, 18, 27, 75, 77, 122–24, 164, 179–81; rights and, 91, 116–18, 135; voluntary, 7–9, 13, 36, 69–73, 87, 105, 120, 130–31, 133, 136, 143, 148, 177–81. *See also* mediating institutions; society
comprehensive doctrines, 50–51, 52, 54, 57, 60–65, 83; bracketing of, 73–76; consensus on, 100; definition of, 50. *See also* political liberalism; Rawls, John
conservatism, 6, 72
consistent ethic of life, 166–67
Constitution, U.S., 62, 64, 132. *See also* Supreme Court
constitutional government/order, 4, 6, 17–18, 23, 26–27, 37, 48, 51, 53, 54, 57, 80n60, 147
constitutional law, 59, 73–74, 79n44, 79n45, 146–48, 159–62
constitutional values, 59, 60–62, 64–65
Culture of Disbelief, The (Carter), 3

De Koninck, Charles, 84–85, 109n31
Democracy's Discontent (Sandel), 70, 72

democratic society. *See* society
dignity, human, 84, 116, 117, 124, 142n80, 152
Dunn, John, 21, 41n28

education, public and private, 59, 61
Enlightenment, the, 4, 5–6, 17, 36, 45
equality, 19, 50, 117; in liberalism and communitarianism, 6, 7; in Locke, 19, 23, 25–26, 41n28; of women, 63, 146, 153, 156, 160, 162
Eschmann, I. Thomas, 84
Establishment Clause, 3, 79n44
Evangelical Lutheran Church in America, 169
excommunication, 35, 37, 43n66

family, 130–31
Farley, Margaret, 167, 168
fascism, 70, 85
feminism, 166, 172n15; Fern, Richard, 48
fetus, 54, 153–56, 165; use of term, 145; viability of, 73, 146–48, 159, 160–61, 174n30. *See also* abortion; pregnancy
Finnis, John, 137n2
First Amendment, 3, 79n44
Fletcher, Joseph, 172n12
Fourteenth Amendment, 148
freedom (liberty): in American public life, 1–3, 17, 46; communal liberalism and, 9, 134–35; in liberalism and communitarianism, 5–6, 8, 47, 70; of the person, 26, 53, 65, 84–85, 87–88, 95, 99, 127, 131; religious, 2, 12, 18, 24–26, 33–36, 60, 76, 85, 123, 132; reproductive, 148, 153–54, 159–62, 165; rights to, 97, 118, 138n12; of society, 30, 52, 85, 115, 121, 124
Freedom: Its Meaning (Maritain), 85
Free Exercise Clause, 3
free market, 6, 9, 23, 72, 136n1
Freeman, Alan. *See* Mensch, Elizabeth and Alan Freeman
friendship, civic, 1, 5, 87, 88, 122, 171

God, 84, 85, 126, 132; as absolute
good, 87, 153; common good and,
93–96, 121; grace of, 98–99,
140n54; in Locke, 21, 25; in
Mendelssohn, 29–33, 35, 37, 42n53;
the person's fulfillment in, 100–101,
127, 135
good, the, 7, 75–76, 101, 142n81, 178;
definition of, 55; in Rawlsian liberalism, 47, 48, 56, 66; relational view
of, 153–54. *See also* right, the
Gospel, 85, 98, 122, 124
governance, definition of, 2
Greenawalt, Kent, 54
Gudorf, Christine, 175n50
Gutmann, Amy, 69–70, 71–72

Hollenbach, David, 116, 123–24,
137n1
homosexuality, toleration of, 73–75,
137n2
human flourishing: common good and,
39, 75, 96, 121, 152, 178; the fetus
and, 156; Maritain's account of, 14,
114–16, 127; natural law and, 89,
92, 105; use of term, 137n2
human rights. *See* rights
Hunter, James Davison, 46, 149, 157,
170

individualism, 17, 39, 84, 86, 129, 136,
151
institutions. *See* mediating institutions
intelligibility, standard of, 55, 65
intolerance. *See* toleration

James II (king of England), 24, 40n14
Jerusalem (Mendelssohn), 27, 32, 34,
38
Jesus, 14, 114, 122
Jews (Judaism), 1, 25, 55, 60, 176n52;
Mendelssohn and, 34, 36, 45, 100,
103
John XXIII (Pope), 108n13
justice, 4, 6, 14, 73, 75, 88, 98, 99, 158;
the church's actions for, 114, 122,
125–27; cross-cultural application

of, 102–5; debates about, 53–55,
128; economic/social, 72, 163, 165,
179; political conception of, in
Rawls, 48, 51, 53, 56, 59, 60, 64, 67,
74, 141n64, 178; principles of, in
Rawls, 47, 49, 50, 52, 53, 55–56, 57,
67, 77n14, 102; public reason and,
58–65; Rawls's theory of justice as
fairness, 47–50, 56–57, 66

Kant, Immanuel, 66, 77n11
Keys, Mary, 109n31
King, Rev. Martin Luther, Jr., 62, 126
Kingdom of God, 14, 26, 97, 103, 125

Lemon v. Kurtzman, 79n44
Letter Concerning Toleration, A
(Locke), 23
liberalism: abortion and, 146–50, 171;
in American public life, 3–4; anthropology of, 67–68, 69; classical, 6;
common good and, 13, 45, 76, 83,
177; communitarian foundations of,
178; community and, 70, 119; definition of, 5–6; deontological, 80n63;
Kantian, 66–68; Locke's view of,
17–19, 26; Maritain and, 88–89,
102, 134–36; Mendelssohn and,
37–39; moral objectivism/subjectiv-
ism and, 104; moral vision of, 47,
69–70, 81n76; philosophical, 6, 76;
Rawlsian, 48, 55, 65, 66; religion
and, 12–15, 46–47, 88, 180; religious argument and, 54, 73–76; welfare liberalism, 6, 72, 75. *See also*
communal liberalism, communitarianism; political liberalism
Liberalism and the Limits of Justice
(Sandel), 66
libertarianism, 6, 72
liberty. *See* freedom
Locke, John, 6, 13, 86, 177; on Catholicism, 24–25, 40n14; on Christianity's social role, 45, 100; on civil society, 19–23; on the common good,
18, 23, 25–26; compared to Aquinas, 21, 41n20; compared to Mari-

tain, 99, 102–3; compared to Mendelssohn, 28, 37, 45, 46; on equality, 19, 23, 25, 26, 41n28; historical context of his political thought, 19, 21, 24–25, 40n14; influence of, 17–19; on limited government, 22; on property rights, 21–23; on a religious calling, 25; on revelation, 25; on the right to life, 22; on the right to rebellion, 20, 40n14; on the social contract, 19–20; on the state of nature, 19–21; on toleration, 18, 23–25, 26, 38; on trust, 21, 26

love, 84, 88, 94, 95, 103, 135, 140n54, 163; as *agape* or *caritas*, 125; as benevolence in Mendelssohn, 30–31, 32, 34–35; definition of, 125; social impact of, 14, 114, 122, 125–27

McInerny, Ralph. *See* Watkins, Michelle and Ralph McInerny
MacIntyre, Alasdair, 104–5, 141n78
Man and the State (Maritain), 85, 89–90, 99, 120
Maritain, Jacques, 10, 14–15, 77, 83, 107n8, 141n65; anthropology of, 94, 110n35, 114–15, 121, 136, 178; assessment of his linked approaches to the common good, 98–102; on atheism, 98–99; on Christianity's promotion of human goods, 124–27; on church and state, 132–34, 165; as a communal liberal, 86, 106, 134–36, 143, 177–79; compared to Locke and Mendelssohn, 99, 102–3; compared to Rawls and Sandel, 101–2, 129, 143; on conditions for social harmony, 122–24; conservative interpretations of, versus the author's, 86, 108n12; on constitutive community, 129–31; debate with De Koninck, 84, 109n31; defense of pluralism, 119–22; definition of the common good, 86–88, 104n14, 108n13; on freedom, 84–85; friendship with Alinsky, 125–26, 140n55, 140n58; on grace, 98–99, 103; on

human flourishing, 14, 114–16, 127, 137n2; liberal-communitarian debate and, 102–6, 128–34; on love, 84, 88, 94, 95, 103, 125–26; on mediating institutions, 119–21; as a moral objectivist, 105, 132; on neutrality and perfectionism, 132–34; as a political and religious philosopher, 84–85, 107n10; on public conversation, 100, 104; on rights, 116–19, 135–36, 138n12, 138n18; on society and the state, 119–22; universalism of, 103. *See also* abortion; Catholic Church; Catholics; Christians; church; common good; communal liberalism; communitarianism; liberalism; natural law; personalism, theological; religion
Maritain, Raïssa, 141n65
mediating institutions, 12, 114, 130, 136, 143, 152, 156, 159; definition of, 119
Mendelssohn, Moses, 6, 14, 18, 113, 177; anthropology of, 30–31, 38; on benevolence, 30–31, 32, 34–35; biography, 27; on church, society, and state, 27–35, 42n53, 43n57, 43n63; on the common good, 18, 28–39; communal liberalism and, 26, 33, 34, 36–39, 76; compared to Locke, 23, 37, 45, 46; compared to Maritain, 99, 102–3; on excommunication, 35, 37, 43n66; on Jews' support for political society, 36; reason for writing *Jerusalem*, 27; on toleration, 14, 30, 33–35, 37, 38, 45. *See also* communal liberalism; Jews
Mensch, Elizabeth and Alan Freeman, 150–51, 172n12, 174n30
Michelman, Rabbi Henry, 175n51
moral objectivism/subjectivism, 104, 132
Morgan, Michael, 38–39
Mulhall, Stephen and Adam Swift, 57, 60, 79n60, 104
Muslims, 25, 60

National Conference of Catholics Bishops (NCCB). *See* Bishops, U.S. Catholic; United States Catholic Conference

National Council of Churches, 1, 175n51

natural law, 85, 175n50; abortion and, 150, 174n30; acknowledgment of, 122, 133; conscience and, 90; content and knowledge of, 89–91; foundation in God, 98; human flourishing and, 92, 114–15, 137n2, 152; in Locke, 23–24; practical reason and, 59, 92, 103, 115; rights and, 65, 89, 92, 97, 116–17. *See also* common good, natural law approach to; Maritain, Jacques

needs, 21, 26, 29, 56, 58, 127, 133; basic human, 23, 53, 91, 116–17, 138n12; of families, 163, 168; natural law and, 89, 91; religion and, 113; rights and, 116–18, 138n12; of society, 87, 157, 171

neutrality, 7–8, 14, 25, 56–57, 73–75, 131–32, 142n81, 175. *See also* antiperfectionism; perfectionism

Novak, David, 55

Novak, Michael, 108n12

Nussbaum, Martha, 137n2

option for the poor, 14, 114, 126–27

original position. *See* Rawls, John, on the original position

overlapping consensus. *See* Rawls, John, on an overlapping consensus; political liberalism

Penn, William, 2

perfectionism, 39, 104, 132–34. *See also* antiperfectionism; neutrality

person (self): the common good and, 96–98; as personality in Maritain, 93–94, 110n35; as socially situated, 68–71, 128–31. *See also* anthropology

Person and the Common Good, The (Maritain), 85, 99

personalism, theological, 93–99, 106, 114, 136. *See also* common good, theological approach to; Maritain, Jacques

Planned Parenthood, 170

Planned Parenthood v. Casey, 147, 159, 161

Plato, 4

pluralism, 9, 13, 53, 71, 102, 120, 177; abortion and, 156–57, 165; a challenge for society, 1–2, 50, 60, 134; common good and, 26, 36, 85; communal liberalism and, 143; of comprehensive doctrines, 51; in Mendelssohn, 34, 36–38; religious, 2, 18, 24, 51, 122; secularization and, 46–47

pluralist society. *See* society

political debate, 2, 8, 13, 15, 80, 85, 101, 146, 151; appeals to religion in, 51, 63–65, 73–76. *See also* public conversation

political liberalism, 6, 14, 39, 80n64, 81n71, 83, 141, 146; common good and, 57–58; communal liberalism and, 54, 101, 143–44; cross-cultural application of, 79n60, 102; definition of, 51; effects on public discussion, 58–65, 75–76; ideas of the good in, 56–57, 66, 78n35; neutrality and, 39, 56; the priority of right and, 55–57; religion and, 49, 52. *See also* liberalism; Rawls, John

Political Liberalism (Rawls), 51, 56, 63, 79n60

political society. *See* society

politics: abortion and, 63–64, 144–49, 156–59, 164–65, 169; of the common good, 14, 58, 69–72, 75–76, 101, 143; communitarian, 68–73, 75–76, 178; definition of, 2; human flourishing and, 134; liberal, 6, 14, 38, 46, 56, 75; toleration and, 39, 69–70; voluntary communities and, 131. *See also* church, state and; religion, politics and pregnancy: crisis and teenage, 153–54, 156–59, 160–61, 163, 165, 167, 170–71, 174n29; legal issues, 63, 146–47, 160–61; prevention of, 73, 158–59, 170–71, 174n29; trimester framework of, 146–47, 159, 161

Presbyterian Church USA, 169

Principes d'une politique humanist (Maritain), 85

priority of right over the good. *See* right, the

prochoice and prolife advocates. *See* abortion, prochoice and prolife advocates

Project Rachel, 170, 176n54

proportionalism, 172n14, 175n50

public conversation (public dialogue, discourse, or discussion): abortion debate and, 15, 146, 157, 163, 169–71, 173n18; common good theory and, 100–102, 122, 149, 156, 163, 179–80; intellectual solidarity and, 123; intelligibility and, 65, 100; liberal and communitarian views of, 7, 8, 53–55, 75–76; public reason and, 48–49, 52, 61–62, 65; religion and, 11, 51, 88, 104, 123–24, 169–71. *See also* political debate

public life: attempts to exclude religion from, 48, 66, 75; character of, in America, 1–3, 8, 46, 146; definition of, 2; mediating institutions and, 71, 119. *See also* politics; religion, politics and

public reason, 47–48, 52, 58–65, 101, 123, 132, 146; background culture and, 59, 64–65; comprehensive doctrines and, 58, 60–61; definition of, 58; exclusive and inclusive, 61; flaws of, 62–65, 66, 76; as ideal and duty, 48; nonpublic reason and, 61–63, 65–66; religious discourse and, 49, 61–63, 65, 123–24; scope and application of, 59, 64, 79n45, 79n60; stability and, 59. *See also* political liberalism; Rawls, John

Rahner, Karl, 110n50

Ramsey, Paul, 90

Range of Reason, The (Maritain), 85

Ransoming the Time (Maritain), 85

Rawls, John, 6, 14, 76–77, 77n11, 79n60, 141n64, 178; on abortion, 63, 146; anthropology of, 50, 67–69, 81n72129; communal liberalism and, 39, 54–55, 101–2; compared to Maritain, 101–2, 129, 143; concern for stability, 49, 62; definition of society, 49; ideas of the good in his theory, 56–57, 66, 78n35; on legitimacy, 51, 53, 60; as a moral objectivist, 104, 132; move from philosophical to political liberalism, 50–51; on neutrality, 56; on oppression, 52, 60; on the original position, 50, 56, 67–68, 80n71; on an overlapping consensus, 52–55, 58, 61, 62, 101; on political construction, 59; on religion as potentially dangerous, 51–53; on society as well-ordered, 14, 47–50, 52, 57, 60, 68; on the standard of reasonableness, 55, 59, 62; on the veil of ignorance, 50, 56. *See also* comprehensive doctrines; justice; liberalism; political liberalism; public reason; Sandel, Michael, responses to Rawls

reasonableness, standard of, 55, 59, 62

Reformation, religious strife during the, 52–53

religion: civil, 122; concerns about divisiveness of, 11–13, 51–53, 106; constitutive community and, 76, 129–31; contributions to the common good and public life, 3, 9–15, 18, 23–25, 31, 36, 46, 52, 65–66, 72, 83, 88, 98, 101, 113, 122–24, 128, 137n1, 143, 164, 177–81; definition of, 11–12, 15n6; in jurisprudence, 59, 79n44, 147; liberalism and, 12–15, 46–47, 88, 180; politics and, 2–4, 8, 11, 97, 132–34, 144, 150–51, 163–71; positive and negative effects of, 12; privatization of, 46–49, 65, 150–51, 172n12. *See also* freedom, religious; liberalism; pluralism, religious; toleration

religious liberty. *See* freedom, religious

right, the, 66, 116; definition of, 55; priority of, over the good, 52–55, 58, 66–67. *See also* good, the; political liberalism

rights, 69, 75, 102, 114, 135–36, 138n12, 138n18, 141n78, 142n80; communal orientation of, 118; distinctions of, 116–17; natural law and, 91; negative and positive, 117–118; to participation, 116, 128; to privacy, 74; to property, 21–23. *See also* autonomy

Rights of Man and Natural Law, The (Maritain), 85, 99, 116

Roe v. Wade, 73, 146–48, 151, 159, 168, 174n36

Roman Catholic Church. *See* Catholic Church

Rudy, Kathy, 165, 174n36

Sandel, Michael, 14, 49; anthropological assumptions of, 67; compared to Maritain, 101–2, 129, 143; on constitutive community, 68–71; as a discourse communitarian, 178; on moral and religious argument, 73–76; on moral objectivism, 104; on politics of the common good, 70–73, 75; responses to Rawls, 66–69, 73–75, 80n64, 80n71, 104; on toleration of homosexuality, 74–75; status of religion in his theory, 76; suggestions for developing communal liberalism, 76–77, 178. *See also* communitarianism

Scholasticism and Politics (Maritain), 85

Scripture, 101, 103, 111n57, 121

Second Treatise of Government (Locke), 19–20, 40n14

Second Vatican Council (Vatican II), 15, 86, 108n10, 108n13

secularization. *See* society, secularization of

self. *See* person

Shaftesbury, first Earl of, 19, 40n14

slavery. *See* abolition

social contract, 19–20, 35, 40, 42n53, 50, 67

society: Catholic thought on, 85, 88, 120, 122–24; common good and, 3–5, 8, 10, 25–26, 37, 78, 85–87, 92–93, 115, 149, 155, 164, 177–81; communal liberalism and, 9, 143–44, 163; communitarianism and, 7, 68–69, 73–76, 131; cooperation in, 11, 53, 115, 132, 149; democracy and, 8, 17; ethical character of, 127, 132–34, 155, 162, 163, 188; liberalism and, 4, 6, 8, 99–100, 104; mediating institutions or particular communities and, 2, 5, 7, 91, 119–21, 136; the person and, 95–97, 115–16, 129, 131, 158; pluralism and, 9, 10, 71, 121, 132–33, 144; religion and, 2, 11–12, 26, 37, 65, 88, 100–101, 122–24, 127, 132–33, 137n1, 144, 152, 164; rights and, 117–19, 136, 138n6, 152, 158; secularization of, 46–49, 65, 150–51, 172n12. *See also* community, political; Maritain, Jacques; Rawls, John; state, the

solidarity, principle of, 156–57

soul, 24, 31, 94–95, 110n35

state, the, 6, 10, 71, 165; coercion and, 31–32; its enforcement of common good provisions, 10, 97, 158, 179; in Locke, 23, 26; mediating institutions and, 38, 119; in Mendelssohn, 28, 29, 31–33, 35, 37; neutrality toward religion and morality, 7–8, 14, 25, 56–57, 73–75, 131–32; perfectionism of, 39, 132–34; promotion of moral values, 133; society and, in Maritain, 93, 120, 122, 130–31, 135–36, 156. *See also* church, state and; society

Steffen, Lloyd, 153, 174n32

subsidiarity, principle of, 119, 130, 139n27, 156–57

Supreme Court, 79n49; abortion jurisprudence, 73–74, 146–48, 151, 157, 159, 160, 173n22, 173n23, 174n36; awareness/use of religious arguments, 73–75, 147; employing public reason, 59. *See also* Constitution, U.S.; constitutional law

Swift, Adam. *See* Mulhall, Stephen and Adam Swift

Synagogue Council of America, 1, 175n51

Theory of Justice, A (Rawls), 49–51, 56

Thomistic philosophy, 84, 89, 93–95, 137n2

toleration (tolerance), 2, 9, 39, 47, 52, 57, 102, 177; of homosexuality, 73–75, 137n2; intolerance, 24, 33, 69; in Locke, 18, 23–25, 26, 38; in Mendelssohn, 14, 30, 33–35, 37, 38, 45; negative and positive, 34

totalitarianism, 86

Trinity, 93, 95–96. *See also* God

Two Treatises of Government (Locke). *See Second Treatise of Government*

United Nations, 92

United Nations Educational, Scientific, and Cultural Organization (UNESCO), 107n8, 109n29

United States Catholic Conference, 1, 175n51. *See also* Bishops, U.S. Catholic; Catholic Church

Vatican II. *See* Second Vatican Council

veil of ignorance. *See* Rawls, John, on the veil of ignorance

viability, fetal. *See* fetus, viability of

Watkins, Michelle and Ralph McInerny, 134–36, 142n80, 142n81

Weithman, Paul, 48, 136n1

welfare liberalism, 6, 72, 75

welfare reform, 156, 172n17, 173n20

welfare state, 46, 69, 71–72

Whitmore, Todd David, 166

witness, religious, 164, 171

About the Author

Brian Stiltner is assistant professor of religious studies at Sacred Heart University in Fairfield, Connecticut, and directs its Hersher Institute for Applied Ethics. He studied at John Carroll University, Yale Divinity School, and Yale University, from which he received the doctorate in 1997. He has taught at the College of the Holy Cross, Mount Holyoke College, and Worcester Polytechnic Institute. In his current research, he is developing the notion of public conversation as a means for pursuing the common good.